How Christianity Came to China

How Christianity Came to China

A Brief History

Kathleen L. Lodwick

Fortress Press
Minneapolis

HOW CHRISTIANITY CAME TO CHINA

A Brief History

Copyright © 2016 Fortress Press. All rights reserved. Except for brief quotations in critical articles or reviews, no part of this book may be reproduced in any manner without prior written permission from the publisher. Visit http://www.augsburgfortress.org/copyrights/ or write to Permissions, Augsburg Fortress, Box 1209, Minneapolis, MN 55440.

Cover image: Missionary on an evangelical propaganda tour across China. Ca. 1920/Snark / Art Resource, NY

Cover design: Laurie Ingram

Library of Congress Cataloging-in-Publication Data

Print ISBN: 978-1-4514-7230-1

eBook ISBN: 978-1-5064-1028-9

This book was produced using Pressbooks.com, and PDF rendering was done by PrinceXML.

Contents

	Acknowledgments	vii
	Chronology of China's Major Dynasties and Twentieth-Century Events	ix
	Note on Romanization	xi
	Introduction	xiii
1.	Chronology	1
2.	Denominationalism	63
3.	Sociopolitical	117
4.	Geographic	149
5.	Missionary and Chinese Christian Biographies	173
6.	Four Theological Issues in the China Missions	203
	Conclusion	231
	Bibliography	233
	Index	241

Acknowledgments

No scholar writes a monograph without the help of numerous others. In this case, my "thank yous" are to some newly made friends and colleagues whom I have not yet met, and to longtime friends and colleagues. In the former category, I wish to thank Dyron Daughrity, Pepperdine University, editor of this series on Christianity in different parts of the world. He asked me to write this work and also answered my many questions cheerfully. I also want to thank the people at Fortress Press. Thanks also to Daryl Ireland, Boston University, who sent me his article on John Song, at the speed of the Internet. In the latter category are those with whom I have shared research interests over the years. Xi Lian, Duke University Divinity School, answered innumerable questions, particularly about the indigenous Chinese churches today, a topic on which he is extremely well versed and has written about extensively. He also read the manuscript, making valuable contributions. We first met at an American Historical Association session on China missions, almost twenty years ago. Our families have enjoyed many times together in the years since. And thanks to Temur, who teaches in the Department of History, University of Nanjing, who also read the manuscript and offered valuable comments, particularly about the Mongols and their attitudes toward religion, one of his research interests. I term ours a twenty-first-century friendship, as we met in 2001 via the Internet because of our common interest in the Reverend James Gilmour and his travels in Mongolia. Temur and I met in Nanjing in 2002 and in the years since, his family and mine have traveled together in China, Mongolia, Siberia, and the United States.

Both Xi and Temur most graciously have corrected my various mistakes in pinyin: I learned Chinese with an earlier system!

Fr. Robert Carbonneau, C.P., answered my questions about Roman Catholic missions in China and, in particular, about the murders of the three Passionist priests in China in 1929. We met at an Association for Asian Studies meeting more than twenty years ago, also as a result of our interest in the China missions.

Thanks also to my longtime friend, Christine Kulikowski, for her ever-patient ears and encouragement. Also to my colleague of many years, Barbara Cantalupo, Professor of English, Pennsylvania State University, for her always-encouraging words. And to Liu Yanyve for help with the map.

And to my daughter, Kathryn Elizabeth, about to graduate from Pennsylvania State and begin her graduate work, who after a lifetime accustomed to "Mom writing a book," has become my first-class research assistant.

Without the help of all these people, this book would not have been written. All mistakes are mine.

Kathleen L. Lodwick
Professor Emerita of History
Pennsylvania State University

Chronology of China's Major Dynasties and Twentieth-Century Events

Chronology of China's Major Dynasties

Qin	221–207 BCE
Han	206 BCE–220 CE
Sui	581–617
Tang	618–960
Song	960–1279
Northern Song	960–1127
Southern Song	1127–1279
Yuan	1279–1368
Ming	1368–1644
Qing	1644–1911

Twentieth-Century Events

1911   Revolution, ended the Qing
1927   Northern Expedition
1937   Japan invades China, starting World War II
1941–42   Missionaries evacuate China after Pearl Harbor
1949   Chinese Communists win Civil War and establish government
1966–76   Cultural Revolution

Map

Map of China in the Republican Era, modified from The Christian Occupation of China, 1922, by Liu Yanyve.

Note on Romanization

Various romanizations have been used by foreigners to transliterate Chinese into the Latin alphabet. The nineteenth- and twentieth-century versions were all done by foreigners who each heard Chinese sounds differently, based on their native languages, and some even tried to denote tones, although users soon forgot what the tone symbols were! Those who created these systems were both missionaries and diplomats living in China. The Chinese Postal Service had its own romanization system, which complicated the issue.

The newest system, done by native Chinese speakers who were linguists, most closely approximates Mandarin, the official language of China, in the Latin alphabet.

To the reader familiar with older systems which produced Chiang Kai-shek, Mao Tse-tung, Canton, etc., pinyin (which renders these Jiang Jishi, Mao Zedong, and Guangdong) may take a bit of getting used to. Today Western scholars use pinyin almost exclusively.

Introduction

> "I have seen a Chinese graduate of a Western university, dressed in proper Western clothes, in his dress-suit, with an opera hat crushed under his arm, beseech the goddess of mercy in her temple with many rich gifts, to give him a male child."
>
> Attributed to Reverend C. Scott,
probably Charles Scott, Bishop of North China,
Church [of England] Missionary Society (CMS).

> "[The Chinese woman] confided one day that there seemed little inducement to repent and be saved if going to heaven would entail associating with foreigners for all eternity."[1]

Writing a short monograph on such a large and complicated topic as the history of Christianity in China is a daunting task, even though the author has studied the topic for more than forty years. Undertaking this work reminds the author of a story a Chinese friend told her when the author was beginning graduate work in this field. A foreigner visited Beijing in the 1930s, and with his friends set off to see the Great Wall, built during the Ming dynasty (1368–1644), which stretches for hundreds of miles across north China. On the way, bandits

---

1. Mildred Cable, *The Fulfillment of a Dream of Pastor Hsi and the story of the work in Hwochow* (London: Morgan & Scott, China Inland Mission, 1917), sections XX and XXI. This work, like many from the CIM, was never copyrighted, and there are many editions with different pagination—hence, the author lists the sections.

robbed them taking the man's eyeglasses, among other things. The group continued on to the Wall and reaching it, climbed up. The man then bent down, picked up a clod of rammed earth, of which the Wall is built, held it close to his eyes, and exclaimed, "Ah, this is what the Great Wall looks like."

One is also reminded of the story that John King Fairbank, longtime dean of the American China scholars, relates in his autobiography, *Chinabound*. John Keswick, a twenty-year resident of China and brother of the taipan of Jardine, Matheson Company (the great China trading house that got its start by smuggling opium in the early nineteenth century, and today is a Fortune 500 company), published a book entitled *What I Know About China*. The book, which he gave away, was beautifully bound, and went through several editions, but contained only blank pages! Fairbank observes that he wished he had thought to publish it; and that over the years he had sent Keswick additional pages to be included as appendices and illustrative material. Fairbank adds that he never included the book on any bibliography he compiled, although he seldom neglected to tell his students about it.[2]

In addition, there is that old description of a "China expert," namely, a person who has been in China less than two weeks or more than twenty years. The author falls into neither category; but will forge on.

At present, some scholars estimate that there are sixty-seven million Christians in China.[3] If that is accurate, we can guess that there may have been at least 150 to 200 million Christians in the entire history of Christianity in China. There

---

2. John King Fairbank, *Chinabound: A Fifty-year Memoir* (New York: Harper and Row, 1982), 121–22.
3. Global Christianity: A Report on the Size and Distribution of the World's Christian Population, Pew Research Center, http://www.pewresearch.org/2011/12/19/global-christian-exec/.

were perhaps fifty thousand foreigners engaged in missionary work in China between 1809 and 1949.[4] Some scholars speculate that today there are more missionaries in China than there ever were before 1949, even though the Chinese government does not officially recognize them as such. Anyone seeking to generalize about groups of such sizes does so at his or her peril.

China's vast population, estimated to have been fifty-nine million during the Han dynasty interregnum (the beginning of the Christian era in the West), is today about one and one-third billion. According to the Pew Research Center, China's Christian population today is 5 percent of the population, which places it among the top ten Christian countries in the world, with only the United States, Brazil, Mexico, Russia, the Philippines, and Nigeria having greater numbers. Each of those countries has between fifty and 95 percent of their populations identified as Christians.[5]

At the time of the victory of the Chinese Communist Party in 1949 it was estimated that there were one million Protestants and three million Roman Catholics in China. In 1976, at the time of the death of Mao Zedong, it is thought that the number of Protestants was about three million and that the Roman Catholic population remained at about three million. How the number of Christians increased to the current estimate of sixty-seven million in such a short time puzzles many people, especially since there has been a decrease in the rural population as the Chinese moved to cities in recent years, and previously most Christians lived in the countryside.

---

4. The fifty thousand number is the author's guess, which is based on the work Kathleen L. Lodwick, *The Chinese Recorder Index: A Guide to Christian Missions in Asia, 1867-1942*. 2 vols. (Wilmington, DE: Scholarly Resources, 1986). (See chapter 4 for more on guesses about mission and Christian statistics.)
5. Global Christianity.

To further complicate the question of how many Christians there are in China today, the Chinese government puts the number around twenty-three million, which Western scholars think is too low. Evangelical groups, who like to point to the growth of Christianity despite the Communist government, put the number at one hundred million, which most scholars think is too high.

In an article by Tom Phillips, "China on Course to Become the World's Most Christian Nation Within Fifteen Years," in the 19 April 2014 issue of the British periodical *The Telegraph*,[6] Yang Fenggang, a sociologist and director of the Center on Religion and Chinese Society, Purdue University, Indiana, predicts that, given the seven to ten percent growth in the number of Chinese Christians, by 2030 they will number two hundred forty-seven million, surpassing the current two hundred forty-three million in the United States, which Yang thinks will remain fairly constant. The Chinese government refuted Yang's prediction, but again it was only a prediction; no one really knows what the numbers are. Figuring out how many Christians there are in China today is akin to figuring out how many missionaries went to China between 1809 and 1949. Anyone's guess in regard to either group should be considered just that—a guess.

Writing about missionaries presents the scholar with the difficulties of working in archives. Early Christians who arrived in China did not leave written records for historians to find in later centuries. Even from the nineteenth and early twentieth centuries, the height of the evangelistic crusade to convert China to Christianity, contemporary sources are often few and

---

6. Tom Phillips, "China on Course to Become the World's Most Christian Within Fifteen Years," *The Telegraph*, United Kingdom (19 April 2014). See also Fenggang Yang, *Religion in China: Survival and Revival Under Communist Rule* (New York: Oxford University Press, 2012).

difficult to find. Some church archives are extremely difficult to use, either through their limited operating hours (some are open as few as ten hours a week) or policy restrictions on what historians may research. Yet, other church archives are extremely accommodating to researchers, with the result that their churches are the ones most studied. Some mission agencies have turned their records over to universities, making them accessible to all. One archivist, at a large university's mission archives, told the author that even though there were more missionaries in China than anywhere else, they have fewer papers about China than most other places.

There are several reasons for this, but the primary one is that missionaries fled China on four separate occasions: at the time of the Boxer Uprising (1900); at the time of the Northern Expedition (1927); during the early years of World War II (1937–41); and at the time of the Communist victory in the civil war (1949). During World War II those missionaries who had not left by December 1941 were imprisoned by the Japanese, although two groups were repatriated in 1942 and 1943.

When fleeing for one's life one does not think to carry along the records of the mission, although there were exceptions such as Margaret Moninger, who in 1927 carried home a box of correspondence about the American Presbyterian Mission (APM) on Hainan Island, only to have the mission board in New York write her that they did not want it.[7] They quickly changed their minds, thus preserving the history of one of their stations from the 1880s on.

This author has visited more than twenty mission archives in the United States and Great Britain. Those that have been used most extensively are at the Presbyterian Historical

---

7. Mary Margaret Moninger, *Papers*. Record Group 39. Presbyterian Historical Society, Philadelphia.

Society, Philadelphia; at Yale Divinity School, New Haven; at the Widener Library, Harvard University, Cambridge; and at the University of London, School of Oriental and African Studies Archives, London.

The story of the foreign missionaries who served in China between 1809 and 1949 is one of fervent religious commitment and of the loss of faith, of determined perseverance and of angry frustration, of accepting people as they are and of cultural superiority, of brave adventurers and of those who shrank from the reality of China, of skilled linguists and of those who never got beyond pidgin, of human kindness and of narrow prejudice, of altruism and of hoaxes, of the pious and of the charlatans; of peacemakers and of dictators, of kindly physicians and of dogmatic medical practitioners, of those who loved China and of those who refused to acknowledge the society in which they lived, of those who spent their entire adult lives in China and of those who fled home at the first opportunity, and of those who admired China and of those who were driven insane by living in China. In short, it is a story of ordinary people with all their good qualities and all their shortcomings.

Besides teaching Christianity, the missionaries' contributions to China were: the introduction of Western education with subjects like chemistry, physics, world geography, history of Western countries, and physical education; modern schools for women; education for the blind and the deaf; Western medicine; nationalism; Western philosophy; humane treatment and hospitalization for the mentally ill; control of dangerous drugs, namely opium; and equal treatment for men and women. Each of these attacked the fundamental basis of Chinese society, which, when it collapsed, it was replaced by Communism.

INTRODUCTION

Among the missionaries' contributions to their home countries were: a scholarly knowledge of China and the Chinese classics, along with descriptions of China's culture, government, politics, geography, agriculture, etc.; scholarly knowledge of the east Asian religions of Buddhism and Daoism, as well as the philosophy of Confucianism or Ruism, and two ideas that would transform Christianity in the West in the late twentieth century: Protestant ecumenism and the feminization of Christianity, which some see as a movement equal in importance to that of the Reformation. The missionaries helped transform both China and their home countries in ways they never imagined or intended.

In short, the great missionary endeavor to convert the Chinese to Christianity is an enormous example of the law of unintended consequences. The missionaries who went to China in the years between 1809 and 1949 were the largest group in the history of the world that voluntarily left their home countries to live in a foreign country for the express purpose of fundamentally changing the host country. Seen as a massive human experiment, it defies generalization. Every missionary went to China to change it, but as social awareness of cultural differences emerged in the twentieth century, some, more progressive missionaries, would say they were going to teach in China. Yet, none ever said they were going to China to learn. Jonathan Spence's *To Change China: Western Advisers in China 1620-1960* details the long history of Westerners' many failed attempts to achieve the goal of change.[8] Perhaps the Westerners failed because few, if any, ever asked the Chinese if they wanted to change or to be changed.

---

8. Jonathan Spence, *To Change China: Western Advisers in China, 1630-1960* (Boston: Little, Brown, 1969).

The two quotes that precede this Introduction are from the writings of A. Mildred Cable, CIM, who with her colleagues, Evangeline and Francesca French, trekked across Central Asia at their own expense, spreading the gospel to the Muslim population in the 1920s and 1930s. The subsequent book they published about their journey won for Cable the position of first female member of the Royal Geographic Society. Together the quotes sum up much of the history of Christianity in China, namely, that foreigners thought a Western university education and Western clothing would naturally transform the cultural and religious beliefs of the Chinese; that is they could change their beliefs as easily as they could change their clothes. At the same time, the Chinese woman contemplating eternity in the company of foreigners clearly did not want such a future, but how many foreign missionaries understood her feelings? Western missionaries had been working to convert the Chinese to Christianity for more than a century when these two statements were written, which indicates how complicated and entangled the story of Christianity in China is.

China's emergence on the world scene as a leader in the late twentieth and early twenty-first centuries cannot be denied, but as China becomes more and more like Western countries on the surface, it remains, at its core, China, with its own culture, quite different from the West. What will become of Christianity in China in the future is anyone's guess. The author's guess is that Chinese Christianity will likely continue to appeal to a minority of the Chinese and will retain its fundamentalist ethos. The fundamentalism of the Chinese church today is largely the result of the influences of the indigenous churches, and the widespread influence of the CIM in the days of the missionaries. Today, most churches in China resemble the Western church of the nineteenth century, and some American groups working with Chinese Christians still hope that they will always be like Western Christians. In many of the Protestant churches in China today, one can hear English hymns, translated into Chinese, being sung; and the order of service follows that of Western churches. Many churches have Sunday school preceding the service. Yet, today there are many Chinese hymns, written by Chinese Christians, that are used in Chinese churches, and occasionally sung in translation at churches in the West. Perhaps the future will produce an entirely Chinese version of Christianity, incorporating more of Chinese culture than it has so far. Perhaps China will produce a version of Christianity as have the Koreans and the Filipinos, to which Westerners have varying responses. Entrenched as it is in China, Christianity will likely continue there in some form in the future, but in all likelihood it will never attract a majority of the population.

During the missionary period and at present, China has also produced pseudo-Christian sects, which are a mixture of indigenous folk beliefs and Christian teachings, as was the Taiping Rebellion in the nineteenth century. Some of the current groups are the Shouters, the Weepers, the Lightning Out of the East, the Three Grades of Servants, and the Narrow Gate of the Wilderness. Many Chinese Christians are reluctant to denounce such groups, but the government's Three-Self Patriotic Movement (TSPM) denounced the Shouters as an "evil religion" in the 1980s. Some of these groups have ties to the early twentieth-century Chinese indigenous churches while others have ties with foreign Christians wanting to influence the church in China. David Aikman, a journalist, in his work *Jesus in Beijing*, has detailed some of these groups.[9]

---

9. David Aikman, *Jesus in Beijing: How Christianity Is Transforming China and Changing the Global Balance of Power* (Washington, DC: Regnery, 2003), 236.

Some scholars have viewed China's rural churches, both Protestant and Roman Catholic, as offshoots of folk religion. Daniel Bays's *A New History of Christianity in China* covers some details of these groups and the reaction of the Chinese government and the TSPM to them.[10]

China also has what are called "cultural Christians." They are those who, having carefully studied Christianity, have adopted the good works of the religion, but have rejected most of its theological aspects. They generally are not church attenders, but live lives guided by the teachings of Jesus.

Acknowledging that history is not what happened, but rather what got remembered, written down, and left in a place where a historian could find it and that no one can read all the sources, the author nonetheless forges on with this fascinating story!

---

10. Daniel Bays, *A New History of Christianity in China* (West Sussex, UK: Wiley-Blackwell, 2012), 194–96.

1

Chronology

No one will ever know when the first knowledge of Christianity reached China. Today, some historians like to push the entry of Christianity to China back to the days of Thomas, claiming that after establishing the church in southern India, he went on to China. Evidence for this is unclear, but it is probably safe to assume that some form of Christianity made its way across the great Eurasian landmass in the early centuries of the Christian era, with the nomadic tribes who roamed along the Silk Route, stopping at the oasis towns to trade. For the historian it is unfortunate that these tribes were illiterate leaving no records for the historian to find, detailing how they became knowledgeable about Christianity.

Some scholars of Central Asia, like Jack Weatherford, who writes in *Secret History of the Mongol Queens: How the Daughters of Genghis Khan Rescued His Empire* that some of these tribes likely came into contact with Nestorian Christians or Manicheans.[1]

We do know that the Nestorian Monument, with the date 781 inscribed on it, was found near Xian, Shaanxi, in 1623 or 1625, giving proof that at least Nestorian Christianity had made its way that far into China during the Tang dynasty (618–960). The Monument is inscribed in both the Syriac script and Chinese characters.

Farmers digging in a field uncovered the Monument, which is not an unusual occurrence in China, particularly in the Xian region which has been inhabited for thousands of years. In the same area in 1974, farmers digging a well uncovered pottery that led archaeologists to the tomb of Qin Shi Huang-ti (First Emperor of the Qin dynasty) and his army of terra cotta warriors and horses, gold horses with a gold chariot, and other treasures.

When the Nestorian Monument was found, Chinese alerted the Jesuits working in China, who were then engaged, with their detractors, in the Chinese Rites Controversy. Immediately, a controversy erupted over the authenticity of the Monument, with the Jesuits taking the view that it was authentic while their detractors, in other Roman Catholic orders working in China, insisted it was not. The Nestorian Monument is now on display in a museum in Xian, and most scholars consider it authentic.

The Han Chinese did not have control of Central Asia on anything like a permanent basis by the eighth century, so it is impossible to tell if the practitioners of Nestorianism were ethnically Han, or if they were members of the various nomadic groups of the region. Interestingly, the first reports

1. Jack Weatherford, *The Secret History of the Mongol Queens: How the Daughters of Genghis Khan Rescued His Empire* (New York: Crown Publishers, 2010). Nestorianism is a heresy of the eastern branch of Christianity that survived by moving eastward. Manicheanism, long thought to be an offshoot of Christianity, is now acknowledged as a separate religion.

of Judaism and Islam reaching China also date from about the same time, but again, it is unclear whether the followers of either faith were ethnically Han or sojourners who came overland, in the case of the Jews who settled in Kaifeng, Henan, and by sea, in the case of the Muslims, who had a mosque at the southern city of Guangzhou, Guangdong.

Certainly Christianity was tolerated, if not widely practiced, in the Mongol empires of Chinggis Khan, his daughters, and his grandson, Kubilai, all of whom were known not to interfere with the religious beliefs of those they conquered. It is also likely that at least some of Chinggis's daughters were Christians, and some scholars think Kubilai's mother, Sulqartani, was a Nestorian Christian.

Several priests, sent out by religious orders in Europe, journeyed to China during the Song dynasty (960–1279), making this yet another of China's encounters with Christianity. John of Plano Carpini, traveling in 1245–47, visited the center of Mongol rule. William of Rubrick made the trip in 1253–56. Then in 1289 John of Monte Corvino made the trip under the sponsorship of the Vatican, apparently at the request of Rabban Sauma, a Nestorian bishop, who had made the trip westward from Asia to Europe.[2] None of these Western visitors and a dozen or so others made little, if any, impact on China. It is likely that at least some of these travelers were in search of the lost Christian community led by Prester John, a tale widespread in medieval Europe, and known to Christopher Columbus. Alternatively, it is also possible that one or more of these travelers was the source of the Prester John story. Likely, we will never know.

---

2. Morris Rossabi, *Voyager to Xanadu: Rabban Sauma and the First Journey from China to the West* (Berkeley: University of California Press, 2010).

Orthodox Christianity in China

In the early modern era, the Orthodox form of Christianity arrived overland in China from the north, at about the same time the Roman Catholic form arrived by sea from the south. In the sixteenth and seventeenth centuries as the Russians were pushing eastward to the Pacific to lay claim to Siberia, on occasion they came into contact with the Manchus, who were consolidating their power in the southern Siberian and northern Manchurian regions prior to their sweep into China, when they established the Qing dynasty (1644–1911). The Russian explorers were largely military men, many of them Kazaks, but they had with them some Orthodox priests.

After the battle at Albazin in 1685, which led to the signing of the Treaty of Nerchinsk in 1689, some of the Russians decided to side with the Manchus and moved to Beijing. Their descendants were still there, and still practicing their religion, in the nineteenth century when Russia, along with other Western countries, sought to "open" China to the West.

Some groups of Orthodox Christians remain in China today, although their church is not officially recognized by the government. The Orthodox church in China split with its patriarch in Moscow in the 1950s. At a 2001 conference on Christianity in China held in Moscow which the author attended, the Orthodox patriarch stated, at that time, clergy from Russia were allowed to visit China to conduct services on Christian holidays. Obviously, in the twenty-first century there are both advantages and disadvantages to being officially recognized as a Christian church in China or operating on an ad hoc basis, but with the government's knowledge.

It is also noteworthy that on the steppes of Siberia, the Treaty of Nerchinsk (1689), the first between China and a

Western country, Russia, was negotiated in part by Orthodox priests and Jesuits, who communicated in Latin!

St. Francis Xavier in Asia

While the Russians were penetrating northeastern Asia, the Reformation was in full bloom in Europe, producing the Protestants and, in time, the resurgence of Catholicism in the Catholic Reformation that gave birth to the Society of Jesus (Jesuits or SJ). The Society was organized for the express purpose of reconverting Protestants to Catholicism, but when the Jesuits found that few Protestants were interested in rejoining the Church of Rome, they turned their efforts to education and to the conversion of the non-Christian world to Catholicism. For the Jesuits, Asia loomed as the place most in need of conversion. Accordingly, the Jesuits sent one of the founding members of the order, Francis Xavier (1506–52), to carry the gospel to the Dutch East Indies (today Indonesia) and later to Japan.

The Protestant Dutch were in control of much of the Dutch East Indies, but Xavier worked in the Moluccas and Amboina for about a year. He then traveled to Japan where he arrived in the midst of warfare that ultimately resulted in the establishment of the Tokugawa shogunate in 1600.

Various daimyo in Japan were vying for power, with episodes of warfare that involved great armies of monks from the Buddhist monasteries, many located in the mountains around Kyoto, the imperial capital. Unaware of the political turmoil into which he had wandered, Xavier quickly found favor among some daimyo, who hoped to use the foreigner and his religion to counteract the Buddhist armies. It was not long before the Japanese, who had been aware of the arrival of Europeans on the China coast and in Southeast Asia, began to fear that Xavier was the forerunner of a military invasion by his countrymen, particularly as the Japanese knew this had happened in the Philippines.

Although Xavier made some converts, eventually the Japanese leaders asked him the one question he could not answer, namely, if his religion were the one true religion for all people for all time, why had the Chinese never heard of it? It was a question only a Japanese would ask, as they had borrowed much of their culture from China, via Korea, and it seemed to the Japanese that Xavier's religion could not be too important if the Chinese did not know of it.

Without an answer, and losing favor with his supporters, Xavier decided to leave Japan and go to China to convert the people there. It was on the island of Shangchuan, within sight of the Chinese mainland, that Xavier died in 1552.

Xavier's body traveled almost as far in death as he had in life. He was buried first on Shangchuan, then the body was moved to Malacca, a Portuguese colony after 1511. After the Protestant Dutch seized Malacca in 1641 Xavier's body was taken to Goa, where it rests today. (His former grave in Malacca became a tourist attraction!) Periodically, the Goanese Catholics take his body on a great religious procession through the city. This is supposed to happen every ten years, in years ending in nine, but the date of the parade is quite flexible. The remains of Xavier's right hand, which was severed at the time the body was moved to Goa, is in the Vatican Museum in Rome. The relic of his left arm was on display for many years in a church in the former Portuguese enclave of Macau, on the south coast of China, across from Hong Kong.

Macau reverted to China in 1997, but its Christian past remains in the façade of the Roman Catholic church the missionaries founded and in the Protestant cemetery, where many nineteenth-century missionaries, along with traders, globetrotters, assorted sailors and other foreigners who died on the China coast, are buried. Both the façade and the cemetery are tourist attractions today, but do not attract as many visitors as do the casinos!

Xavier became a saint in 1622 at the same time as Ignatius Loyola, founder of the Jesuit order, and Xavier is remembered in popular Catholicism as an important missionary to China. Several years ago a retired colleague of the author's traveled to France and brought her a postcard of the altarpiece from a village church he had visited. It showed a beautiful mosaic of Xavier standing under a Burmese Buddhist monk's umbrella, baptizing Chinese who were in the dress of the Tang dynasty, with the caption "St. Francis Xavier baptizing Chinese." Upon glancing at the postcard the author immediately began laughing, and her colleague, a devout Catholic, looked distressed until the author explained to him what was wrong with the altarpiece. Somehow, these French villagers and the artist who had created the altarpiece had come to believe, as many Catholics do, that Xavier was a missionary to China, a country whose mainland he had never reached. Later, when the author related this story on H-Asia, a history networking site, one Asian specialist admitted that he too had not realized immediately what was so funny about the altarpiece's portrayal of Xavier.

Christianity Challenges Chinese Society

It was not until 1582 that the Jesuits could actually establish themselves in China. The first prominent member of the Society to have a place in China's history was Matteo Ricci

(1552–1610).³ For the first time in the history of Christianity in China, Christians wrote letters home about their experiences that were preserved for historians to find and write about the missionary endeavor from the viewpoint of those who participated in it. This was perhaps the fourth or fifth time that Christianity had reached China, but this time there was to be a lasting, if not always tranquil, presence.

These early Jesuits who embarked for China went to convert a society about which they knew very little. Traditional Chinese society was patriarchal, patrilineal, and patrilocal, and each person knew his or her place based on the traditional hierarchy of emperor to subject, father to son, elder brother to younger brother, husband to wife, and friend to friend, termed the Confucian relationships by Western historians. Only the last relationship was based on equality, not bloodlines or marriage. Under this system, women were clearly subservient.

For Christianity, with its teaching of the equality of all in the sight of God, to succeed in China, it had not only to challenge the traditional hierarchy, it had to destroy it. The acceptance of Christianity's idea of equality was further complicated by such teachings as "render unto Caesar that which is Caesar's" and "honor thy father and thy mother," which educated Chinese would have seen as ideals they were already practicing, albeit in their own ways.

Indeed, Ricci tried to tie Christianity to traditional Chinese beliefs and practices by pointing out the similarities between them. Liam Brockey in his *Journey to the East* noted that the Jesuits introduced rosaries and other religious tokens without much explanation to the Chinese as to what they were. As similar items are used by Buddhists, Brockey concluded the

---

3. The best biography of Ricci is Jonathan Spence, *The Memory Palace of Matteo Ricci* (New York: Viking Penguin, 1984).

Chinese understood these to be the Christian versions of Buddhist amulets. He also notes that the Jesuits told the Chinese that holy water and the sign of the cross were spiritual means of protection, but it was reported that on one occasion two Christians saw their children devoured by wild wolves despite the parents making the sign of the cross repeatedly. The priests explained this by condemning the parents for not carefully observing the Ten Commandments, which had caused their actions to be ineffective![4]

Sorting out and understanding Christian teachings was difficult for the Chinese who became inquirers, a status that missionaries imposed before they accepted Chinese for baptism and lives as Christians. Certainly, many inquirers realized that if they became Christians they would change the dynamics of their families' lives, as well as many aspects of the wider society, where one's extended lineage group was very important. One can only imagine that this made many an inquirer pause before taking the step. Most missionaries, who understood or appreciated little of China's culture, were likely unaware that they were attacking the very foundations of Chinese society with their conversion efforts. And it was that attack on the foundations of the Chinese belief system and society that contributed to the crumbling of the traditional society in the twentieth century and its replacement by Communism, which offered a better life here and now rather than the reward Christians were promised, after death, in Heaven.

Another big problem for the Chinese was the exclusivity that Christianity demanded. All five of the world's great religious traditions originated in Asia, but only the southern Asian ones,

---

4. Liam Brockey, *Journey to the East: The Jesuit Mission to China, 1579-1724* (Cambridge, MA: Harvard University Press, 2007), 96–97.

Hinduism and Buddhism, did not require exclusivity. Those religions coming from extreme Western Asia and from Arabia—Judaism, Christianity, and Islam—demand exclusivity of their adherents. For the Chinese it was common to practice whatever indigenous folk religion was common in their region, along with Buddhism and Daoism, an indigenous Chinese belief. Few Chinese could understand why Christian beliefs could not simply be grafted on to the beliefs they had practiced for generations. (The author once witnessed a funeral procession in San Francisco's Chinatown that closely resembled those she had seen in Taiwan. Traditionally, Chinese musical instruments are played loudly to scare off evil spirits, but in this procession a Western-style marching band with trombones and a bass drum repeatedly played "Onward Christian Soldiers." The author was unable to determine if it were a Christian funeral.)

Some historians think it was monotheism that the Chinese could not accept, which was a stumbling block the missionaries could not alter or adapt. These same issues were to plague the Protestant missionaries who arrived in China in the nineteenth century.

It was during these early years of the Roman Catholic mission that the Three Pillars of the Faith—Xu Guangxi, Li Zhizao, and Yang Tengyun—were all baptized. D. E. Mungello notes that the origin of the term is uncertain even though Ricci had referred to Xu, who was the Jesuits' first convert and who took the name Paul, as a "great pillar" of the church.

The Jesuits' Influence in China

The Jesuits also struggled with how to refer to God in Chinese. This was a problem because, as in most mission fields, the

Jesuits wanted a special term to refer to the Christian god. In China this was an extremely difficult problem as the concept of "heaven" meant the realm of the supernatural, and the emperor was referred to as the "Son of Heaven," and he ruled by the "Mandate of Heaven." Annually, the emperor performed ceremonies to heaven for good crops and plentiful rain. Calling the Christian god the Heavenly Father confused the question further, as it seemed to suggest that Jesus and the Chinese emperor were somehow brothers or at least from the same family, and all Chinese knew different dynasties were controlled by different families. The same issue plagued the Protestants in future centuries. The Jesuits' policy of accommodating Chinese beliefs and customs to their teachings aroused opposition from other Roman Catholic missionaries, and eventually gave rise to the infamous Chinese Rites Controversy that raged at the Holy See for more than a century (seventeenth to eighteenth), involved eight popes, and saw the Church's official opinion change several times. (See chapter 6 for more on the Chinese Rites Controversy.)

As the Jesuits had become influential at the Catholic royal courts in Europe, they hoped to repeat that pattern in China, as they believed the best way to convert the Chinese was from the top down: if they could convert the emperor, they thought, the entire country would follow. This, of course, indicates that the Jesuits understood nothing of the emperor's ceremonial role of making annual sacrifices to heaven. The Jesuits' methods attracted criticism from other Catholic religious orders, specifically, the Dominicans and Franciscans, as well as the French Foreign Mission Society (Société des Missions Étrangères de Paris, also called Missions Étrangères) and secular priests. Members of these orders thought China should be converted from the ground up, and they were adamantly opposed to Ricci's accommodation policies.

Largely due to the Chinese Rites Controversy, but also because of the opposition to Christianity by powerful bureaucrats at the Qing Court, in 1707 a struggle broke out between a papal legate and the Kangxi emperor over what the missionaries could teach. Of course, the emperor was the final arbitrator of disputes in his kingdom, so he dismissed the papal legate and ordered all the missionaries to obtain a ticket from the government if they wanted to continue their work. To get the ticket the missionaries had to agree to Ricci's accommodation policy, which the legate had indicated was forbidden by the pope, on pain of excommunication. Only those Jesuits working at the court were exempt.

Christianity was proscribed by the Qianlong emperor (1736–1796), the Kangxi emperor's grandson, in 1736, and all missionaries were expelled to Guangzhou, the only place they were allowed to work. Of course, this did not mean that Catholicism disappeared from China. Mungello has written several excellent works about the church in the years after the proscription. *The Forgotten Christians of Hangchow*[5] is an account of the long-established Christian community in that city, whom the Kangxi emperor visited on one of his Southern Tours. Mungello's *The Flesh and the Spirit in Shandong* is an account of the sexual issues that plagued the European clergy and both their male and female converts, and has a startlingly contemporary ring.[6] Brockey estimates that there were two hundred thousand Chinese Christians practicing their faith in the year 1700.[7]

---

5. D. E. Mungello, *The Forgotten Christians of Hangchow* (Honolulu: University of Hawaii Press, 1994).
6. D. E. Mungello, *The Spirit and the Flesh in Shandong, 1650-1785* (Lanham, MD: Rowman and Littlefield, 2001).

Robert Entenmann's article, "Christian Virgins in Eighteenth Century Sichuan" in Daniel Bays's *Christianity in China*,[8] is an excellent account of the Institute of Christian Virgins, an order of nuns, who lacking a convent lived with their natal families. The women sometimes had trouble with local officials who did not understand the women's lifestyle and thought they should conform to the broad cultural norms that required women to marry and have children so they would have someone to support them in their old age.

So it was that communities of Catholics survived in China despite the proscription. Heterodoxy was never tolerated in China, and those who clung to the foreign religion were considered outside the mainstream of Chinese cultural norms.

The Protestants Arrive in China, 1809

The evangelical Protestant missionary movement, which introduced its form of Christianity to China in the early nineteenth century, was destined to last one hundred forty years and involved many thousands of foreign individuals. It is impossible to ever make an accurate count of the number of people who served in the Protestant endeavor in China, because mission agencies' records do not contain such information. The vast majority of the missionaries associated with this endeavor were Anglo-Americans, but they also included Australians, Canadians, Danes, Dutch, French, Germans, New Zealanders, Norwegians, Swedes, Swiss, and many others. They stayed in China for periods ranging from a few months (in the case of Aimee Semple, later McPherson)

---

7. Brockey, *Journey to the East*, 4.
8. Robert Entenmann, "Christian Virgins in Eighteenth Century Sichuan," in *Christianity in China from the Eighteenth Century to the Present*, ed. Daniel H. Bays (Stanford: Stanford University Press, 1996), 183.

to thirty, forty, or fifty years. Some families served two generations in China, and a few spent three generations there.

In the early years of the Westerners' trading venture in China, that is, the end of the eighteenth and the beginning of the nineteenth centuries, the Qing government confined the traders to the port of Guangzhou and the first missionaries had to abide by the same regulations as the businessmen. This isolation of the foreigners was understood by many missionaries and traders, and some historians, to be traditional Chinese xenophobia, which they thought had long dominated the culture. However, Joanna Waley-Cohen demonstrates in her monograph, *Sextants of Beijing: Global Currents in Chinese History*, that the Chinese always had foreigners living in their country and they had welcomed their presence.[9] Indeed, one of the many sayings of the Chinese is: When friends come from afar, my heart is glad!

Missionaries and Their Diplomats

After the Opium War (1839–41) the Chinese were forced to accept a series of unequal treaties with the West. Missionaries helped the Chinese with these negotiations by translating some Western works on diplomatic relations, so that the Chinese officials might have some idea about the principles on which the Westerners based their demands. With these treaties, most of which were signed between 1842 and 1860, all foreigners in China gained extraterritoriality, which meant they were not subject to Chinese laws. This provision, when coupled with the most-favored nation clause, which every country sought to include in all its treaties, meant that

---

9. Joanna Waley-Cohen, *The Sextants of Beijing: Global Currents in Chinese History* (New York: Norton, 1999).

whenever a foreigner committed a crime in China that person was tried in his own country's courts, under his country's laws.

Someone once said that extraterritoriality was as difficult to say as it was for the Chinese to live with it. Sometimes it was shortened to extrality, but this did not make the concept any easier to tolerate. The idea probably was first used in treaties between Western nations and those in the Middle East in the early nineteenth century, because the Westerners did not believe that the laws of those countries measured up to the laws of the Western countries. In China, extraterritoriality became a crucial part of Chinese-Western relations, and a huge problem for the missionaries.[10]

Thus whenever missionaries had legal disputes with Chinese they called on their diplomats to resolve the issue. Many of these disputes resulted from local folks and local officials being unaware of the extraterritorial rights the foreigners possessed. Many, if not most, of the disputes were decided in favor of the missionaries, not unreasonably angering the Chinese who were involved. Some Protestant, and all Roman Catholic, missionaries tried to extend the right of extraterritoriality to their converts, which also caused resentment on the part of non-Christian Chinese.

Indeed, some Chinese who were involved in clan or other legal disputes joined Christian churches to gain the help of the foreigners in resolving their problems. When the missionaries realized that this was happening, some required that Chinese prove they had no legal or clan disputes before they were accepted as inquirers, or even as servants working for the

---

10. Similar provisions were included in early treaties between Western countries and Japan, but, as part of the modernization of Japan in the period between 1867 and 1900, they implemented legal reforms, based on the Code Napoleon, to bring their laws more in line with those of Western countries, and then got all the extraterritorial provisions of their treaties eliminated by the early twentieth century.

mission or individual missionaries. The French government styled itself the protector of all the Roman Catholic missionaries in China, and generally, the Vatican deferred to the French when diplomatic disputes arose. In the early 1940s extraterritoriality was abolished by all the foreign countries.

The China Inland Mission (CIM) was the first to give up the right to call in diplomats, and usually gunboats, to settle disputes, as its founder James Hudson Taylor (1832–1905) felt that his mission, as a faith mission, needed to rely on God, not secular authorities. At the same time, the British diplomats despaired over the CIM missionaries who were wont to wander hither and yon throughout the Chinese countryside without informing the diplomats of their plans, causing great difficulties whenever there were troubles.

Over the years many nationalistic Chinese came to see Christianity and extraterritoriality as two sides of the same coin, and they disliked both. By the unequal treaties, the missionaries also gained the right to own property in China's interior. Even as the Chinese officials were forced to sign these treaties, they knew the agreements were going to bring many problems because it was impossible to know how Chinese in the interior would respond to foreign demands. (Despite a central government, headed by the emperor, China for centuries had been only lightly governed from the core. Pamela Kyle Crossley's *The Wobbling Pivot* is an excellent explanation of how this situation prevailed for centuries and continues to do so, with only the years of the Cultural Revolution as an exception.)[11]

---

11. Pamela Kyle Crossley, *The Wobbling Pivot: China since 1800: An Interpretative History* (New York: Wiley-Blackwell, 2010).

Misunderstanding Christianity and Violent Opposition

The failure of the missionaries to accurately convey the nature of Christianity to the Chinese helped produce serious episodes of warfare, the Taiping Rebellion in the 1850s and 1860s, the local Tianjin Incident in 1870, and the Boxer Uprising at the end of the nineteenth century, as well as the curse of opium addiction.

The Taiping Detour

The early Protestant missionaries, with the assistance of Chinese scholars, translated parts of the Bible into Classical Chinese, the written language of the literati. Hoping to convert the elite scholar-official-gentry class, some missionaries either went themselves, or hired Chinese helpers to go, to the examination grounds and hand out Christian pamphlets to scholars as they headed home after completing the government examinations. Liang A-fa (1789–1855), one of the first Protestant converts to Christianity, handed out one of these pamphlets, *Good News to Exalt the Age,* in the examination area of Guangzhou. (See chapter 5 for a short biography of Liang.) Among those accepting a pamphlet, sometime in the 1840s, was Hong Xiuquan (1814–1864), a Hakka (literally, guest), one of the five major ethnic groups living in China. The Hakka had migrated out of north China and into Fujian, northeastern Guangdong, and surrounding areas when the Song dynasty (960–1279) split into the Northern (960–1127) and Southern Song (1127–1279). Even though the Hakka are Chinese, the Han power elites and the Manchu rulers of the Qing discriminated against the Hakka in many areas of life, including the official examinations, where quotas were set to limit the number of Hakka who could pass.

Some Hakka had been converted to Christianity by German-speaking missionaries of the Basel Mission Society (BMS). For an excellent account of these early converts see Jessie G. Lutz and Rolland Ray Lutz, *Hakka Chinese Confront Protestant Christianity, 1850-1900: With the Autobiographies of Eight Hakka Christians and Commentary.*[12]

Hong took the first level of the Chinese government examinations, those at the provincial level, several times, repeatedly failing. After one such occasion, he fell quite ill and was delirious for several days. Later, he reported he had had strange dreams in his delirium, but he did not understand them until he read a Christian pamphlet that had lain unread among his books. Upon reading this new story, Hong understood his dreams and realized he was the Younger Brother of Jesus Christ, called by his Heavenly Father to free China from the rule of the foreign Manchus of the Qing. (Of course, in Confucian society one never would have presumed to be anyone's elder brother!) Hong had had some contact with the Guangzhou missionaries, but he had been refused baptism on the grounds that he did not understand enough of the religion. The best account of Hong and his rebellion is Jonathan Spence's *God's Chinese Son.*[13]

Massive economic changes affected southeastern China in the aftermath of the signing of the treaties following the Opium War, as five treaty ports were opened along the coast,[14] ending the confinement of foreign trade to Guangzhou. Consequently, porters who had for years been transporting tea, silk, and porcelain overland to Guangzhou for sale to the

---

12. Jessie G. Lutz and Rolland Ray Lutz, *Hakka Chinese Confront Protestant Christianity, 1850-1900: With the Autobiographies of Eight Hakka Christians and Commentary* (Armonk, NY: EastBridge, 1998).
13. Jonathan Spence, *God's Chinese Son: The Taiping Heavenly Kingdom of Hong Xiuquan* (New York: W. W. Norton, 1996).
14. The five original treaty ports were Guangzhou, Fuzhou, Xiamen, Ningpo, and Shanghai.

foreigners found themselves out of jobs, as goods could be transported much more cheaply by water to Shanghai. That city soon came to be called "the foreigners' capital of China."

In this economic turmoil that beset many regions in Guangdong and Fujian, Hong was able to gather some of his disaffected clan brothers, and others unhappy with their situations, to attack Qing officials. The central government responded to his Rebellion, as they did all rebellions, with force, but they were unable to crush it, and the Rebellion spread, first among the Hakka and then among the Han.

Hong eventually created his Heavenly Kingdom of Great Peace (*Taiping Tianguo*) from among the rebels. He used his interpretation of the Christian pamphlet he had read to organize his government. Accordingly, among his followers men and women were equal, everyone had to work, foot binding was forbidden, everyone had to attend Sunday school and read the Bible, and opium use was strictly forbidden. In short, the government Hong had created was distinctly anti-Confucian. Every successful rebellion in China's history had seen its fortunes change for the good once China's scholar-official-gentry class threw its support to the rebels. Yet, in the case of the Taiping its leader espoused ideas that were too radically different from the traditional order and government for the scholars to support it. They simply could see no place for themselves in the Taiping Kingdom.

In the meantime, Hong was becoming mentally unbalanced. He claimed he had gone to Heaven and spoken to his Heavenly Father, who communicated with Hong through trances. With God telling Hong how to rule, he appointed himself king of the center, while various relatives became kings of each of the cardinal points.

The missionaries on the coast were elated to learn that a

Christian leader had formed his own government in opposition to the Qing; they had never imagined Christianity would be so successful in China so rapidly. From the Taiping capital at Nanjing, bits and pieces of the new government's beliefs and practices filtered to the missionaries living in the coastal cities. The reforms Hong instituted greatly encouraged the missionaries that a New Day had arrived in China, and the country was becoming Christian.

Then several missionaries journeyed up the Yangzi to Nanjing to observe this Christian nation. Appalled and greatly disappointed by what they saw, they returned to the coast to report to their brethren that the Taiping was not a Christian revolution, and to convince their countries' diplomats not to support it.

The Taiping Kingdom disintegrated from internal decay, with Hong growing more and more deranged, and eventually the Rebellion crumbled, helped out by battles with the Qing army and the Ever Victorious Army funded by the foreigners. Commanded by the British officer, Charles George "Chinese" Gordon (1833–85), the Ever Victorious Army was China's first modern, Western-style force.

Estimates of how many people died as a result of the Taiping violence vary widely. However, one of the most recent scholarly accounts, that of Cao Shuji, puts the death toll at about seventy-three million in the seven provinces that saw most of the fighting: Jiangsu, Zhejiang, Anhui, Fujian, Jiangxi, Hubei, and Hunan.[15] (As a point of comparison, the American Civil War, which occurred at about the same time, is now estimated to have killed seven hundred fifty thousand people.) Before it ended, the Taiping rebels controlled fifteen of the

---

15. Cao Shuji, "Qing Dynasty," vol. 5, in *History of China's Population (Zhongguo Renkou Shi)*, ed. Ge Jian-Xiong, 6 vols. (Shanghai: Fudan University Press, 2001).

eighteen provinces of China below the Great Wall. The pseudo-Christian uprising was the biggest rebellion in the history of the world that did not topple a government. One can also term it the largest misunderstanding of Christianity ever.

While the Taiping Rebellion ravaged the countryside, the Qing government also had to deal with more warfare, on the coast, with the Western countries. These hostilities resulted in the Treaties of Beijing of 1860, which expanded the Westerners' rights in China. Again, some Protestant missionaries served as intermediaries, trying to breach the language barrier.

Largely because of this missionary involvement, the Treaties contained provisions giving the missionaries the right to legally work in China, to own property, and to travel beyond the treaty ports, whereas previously they could not remain outside the treaty ports at night, greatly limiting their mobility.

The provision allowing the ownership of property was of great concern to the Roman Catholics, who immediately sought out the sites where their churches had been in previous centuries, so that they might purchase those pieces of property. Of course, the Protestants also wanted to own property where they could establish mission stations with homes, churches, schools, and hospitals. Although they were forced to sign the treaties, Chinese officials were concerned that if foreigners were to be permitted to travel in the interior and to remain outside the treaty ports overnight, it was going to be extremely difficult to protect them.

The Tianjin Stumble, 1870

Roman Catholic nuns arrived in China in the nineteenth

century to run schools and orphanages. Most of the nuns lived entirely inside their nunneries and had almost no contact with Chinese society. The French Sisters of Charity, who ran an orphanage in Tianjin, managed in 1870 to set off an anti-Christian riot that caused many deaths. (Tianjin is the port for nearby Beijing.)

Because of their church's teachings, Roman Catholic missionaries in China were particularly concerned that anyone near death needed baptism, and it was the practice of this teaching that resulted in the outbreak of anti-Christian violence. Like other foreign establishments, the nuns' compound was walled, leaving the local people to imagine what went on inside.

Because the Sisters were concerned that abandoned children might die without the benefit of Christian baptism, they took into their orphanage children *in extremis* and baptized them. Many of the children died quickly after baptism and were given Christian burials. This alone might have resulted in violence, but the Sisters made the matter worse when they began offering a small sum of money for delivery of homeless children to the orphanage door.

In a time of widespread famine and starvation which were ravaging the countryside around Tianjin, many unscrupulous people needed the funds the nuns provided and began delivering babies to the orphanage door without determining if the children were indeed orphans. Of course, the Sisters could not make such determinations. A rumor began to circulate among the Chinese in the surrounding community, due in part to the traditional suspicions the uneducated held about foreigners, that the babies were being killed to use their body parts to make Western medicine! (This story was widespread among the uneducated in China, throughout the

1809–1949 period when missionaries were active.) The Chinese saw that babies entered the mission compound, and more and more tiny graves appeared nearby, so the rumor that death followed Christian baptism gained credence.

Rumors gave way to violence on 21 June 1870. The French minister, who resided in the city, went to the local yamen to discuss the problem, but panicked when a crowd gathered. The Frenchman fired his pistol, missing the magistrate but killing one of his attendants. Chinese then stormed the nearby Roman Catholic compound and killed twenty foreigners. How many Chinese died in the chaos is not known.

The missionaries called the clash the Tianjin Massacre and it produced a diplomatic incident. Warfare was averted only when the Chinese agreed to send a mission of apology to France, but the incident left a lasting antipathy toward foreigners, especially missionaries.

The Boxer Interlude

The Boxer Uprising was long thought to have been an anti-Christian movement, because many missionaries died during the violence. However, recent research clearly indicates that the violence that wracked north China at the end of the nineteenth century and culminated in the siege of the foreign legations in Beijing in the summer of 1900, causing an international army to invade China to lift the siege, was the result of floods and the following famines pushing more and more people onto marginal uplands. One of the best studies of the Uprising is Joseph Esherick's *Origins of the Boxer Uprising*.[16] The Boxers were not initially anti-Qing or anti-foreign, but

---

16. Joseph Esherick, *Origins of the Boxer Uprising* (Berkeley: University of California Press, 1987).

they became both as the occasion demanded. Boxer violence was confined to the northern provinces, because the governors in the southern provinces refused to support the movement. Most of the Westerners living in China were missionaries, and they became the victims of violence because they were easy targets, living in small towns and cities, with only Chinese officials to guarantee their safety. The Boxers were practitioners of various forms of Chinese martial arts, and each group chose for itself a name that usually reflected its teacher or style of martial arts. Some of the groups' names were Red Lanterns Rising, Plum Flower Boxers, Spirit Boxers, and the Society of the Righteous and Harmonious Fists, from which, along with their martial arts moves, the Westerners coined the name Boxers.

Reading letters to the various mission boards and missionaries' letters home in the period leading up to the Boxer violence, such as Eva Jane Price's *China Journal, 1889-1900: An American Missionary Family during the Boxer Rebellion*[17] and *The Chinese Recorder* for the time, one senses the growing violence in the countryside and against Chinese Christians and missionaries.[18] Reading these accounts more than a century later, one has the tremendous urge to shout "RUN" as we know what will happen. But, of course, the missionaries could not run as the streets outside their compounds were filled with great mobs of armed men, Boxers, milling about. In the case of the Price family, the parents learned that their children, who had been sent to another mission station deemed to be safe

---

17. Eva Jane Price, *China Journal, 1889-1900: An American Missionary Family during the Boxer Rebellion: With the Letters and Diaries of Eva Jane Price and Her Family* (New York: Collier Books, 1990).
18. *The Chinese Recorder* was an ecumenical Protestant publication issued in Shanghai from 1867 to 1941. It circulated to all mission stations and to supporters at home. (See chapter 6 for more on *The Chinese Recorder*.)

from the Boxers, had been killed along with all the others at that station.

Before the Boxer Uprising was suppressed, in part by the invasion of foreign troops, two hundred thirty-nine missionaries (one hundred eighty-nine Protestants including their children and forty Roman Catholics) had been killed. No one counted how many Chinese Christians were put to death.[19]

As a result of the Boxer Uprising, the foreigners once again required that China agree to their treaty demands. The Confucian examinations were suspended in north China as the foreigners felt the government officials there had aided the Boxers in their anti-foreign activities. The examinations were abolished in 1906 as the rapidly fading Qing dynasty sought to modernize the country in the post-Boxer period. The indemnity the foreigners demanded for lives and property lost to the Boxers was later determined by the foreigners to be too large, and so some of the excess funds were repatriated to China in the form of scholarships for Chinese to study in the Western countries and Japan. This was yet another way the foreigners sought to change China, until it more closely followed the pattern the Westerners preferred.

Among the many Chinese who flocked abroad for university educations on Boxer Indemnity funds were Zhou Enlai and Deng Xiaoping, both of whom went to France. According to Jonathan Spence's *The Search for Modern China*, Zhou made contact with the French Communist Party, while Deng, one of the youngest of the expatriates, spent most of his time working on the Chinese Communist Party's (CCP) newsletter, cranking it out on a mimeograph machine. Before returning to China,

---

19. Oberlin College in Ohio, alma mater for many China missionaries and their wives, erected a memorial arch to those missionaries killed by the Boxers. The commencement line, traditionally, filed under the arch until the 1970s when students pointed out that the Chinese Christian martyrs were not commemorated there.

the students created a certificate making Deng a "doctor of mimeography," so he would have a degree to show his family![20]

In the years after the Boxers were suppressed, the Qing dynasty finally instituted long-needed reforms. One of these was a government-led campaign against the opium trade and the domestic production and use of the drug. Another reform was an attempt at parliamentary government. True change in China did not come through these reforms, but the 1911 Revolution was on the horizon.

Opium: The Gigantic Roadblock

Overshadowing all issues between Chinese and foreigners in China in the nineteenth and early twentieth centuries was opium. For the missionaries it was a particularly difficult problem, because in the early years of the evangelistic endeavor in China, they had to take ship on opium vessels if they wanted to go to China. Until the widespread use of scheduled steamships on set routes between Western and Asian ports in the late nineteenth century, the missionaries relied on supportive ships' captains to give them passage to China, ideally, at no charge. It was the unfortunate fate of these early missionaries to be tightly bound in the Chinese mind to the nefarious opium that addicted many Chinese and made the foreigners fabulously rich.[21]

(Only one trader refused to deal in opium on the grounds that the trade was immoral. The reader may recall that many American families rose to wealth and prominence as a result

---

20. Jonathan Spence, *The Search for Modern China* (New York: Norton, 1990), 321.
21. See Kathleen L. Lodwick, *Crusaders Against Opium: Protestant Missionaries in China, 1874-1917* (Lexington: University Press of Kentucky, 1996) for a discussion of the missionaries and the opium question.

of smuggling opium, including that of Warren Delano, Franklin Delano Roosevelt's maternal great-grandfather.)

It is impossible to know when opium first reached China, but the fact that only Chinese smoked the drug, as opposed to Westerners who injected it in the form of morphine and Indians who ate it, the best guess anyone has is that it was introduced by traders in the sixteenth or seventeenth centuries, along with tobacco from the New World. Opium likely originated in Turkey, as both the ancient Greeks and the ancient Egyptians knew of the drug. That opium did not exist in China before Westerners imported it can be established both by its Chinese name (*yapien*), clearly a loan word from English, and, because it is not mentioned in *The Yellow Emperor's Classic on Internal Medicine*, which is the traditional Chinese pharmacopeia.[22]

Although opium was declared illegal in China in 1727, there were always people who were willing to risk smuggling, because of the great profits that could be made. One of the early Protestant missionaries at Guangzhou, Karl Gutzlaff, a Pomeranian, who was fluent in several Chinese dialects, has long been identified with helping some of the Western smugglers. The traders normally off-loaded their cargoes at Macau from seagoing vessels onto small boats that then ran up the coast of China, selling their contraband. Gutzlaff, who desired to convert the Chinese, was said to have traded opium off one side of the boat while dispensing Christian tracts off the other. Jessie Lutz in her work, *Opening China: Karl F. A. Gutzlaff and Sino-Western Relations, 1827-1852*,[23] doubts the validity of this

---

22. The Yellow Emperor is one of China's three mythical emperors from the prehistory period. There are numerous editions of this work. One is *The Yellow Emperor's Classic on Internal Medicine*, trans. Ilza Veith (Berkeley: University of California Press, 2002).

23. Jessie Lutz, *Opening China: Karl F.A. Gutzlaff and Sino-Western Relations, 1827-1852* (Grand Rapids, MI: Eerdmans, 2008).

story, but we do know that Gutzlaff sometimes translated for traders.

The Chinese certainly could not be blamed for linking the drug and the foreign religion, as the two were introduced to China at about the same time. Many Protestants who tried to preach in the streets found themselves shouted down by Chinese who interrupted them with cries of "Who brought the opium to China?" It was a question the missionaries were reluctant to answer. One of the late Qing imperial princes, Gung, the official who dealt with foreign diplomats, was reported in 1869 to have told Sir Rutherford Alcock, the British representative in China, that if the foreigners would take away their missionaries and their opium, then they would be welcome in China.[24]

After the opium trade was legalized in the 1860 Treaties of Beijing, drug use skyrocketed and spread throughout the whole of China. As addicts needed to consume more and more of the drug to produce the same effect as time passed, missionaries wrote home about families totally ruined by addiction. Opium consumption makes it difficult for the addicts' bodies to process food, and many addicts starved to death as they chose to purchase opium instead of food when their finances were so depleted that such a choice was necessary. Opium also suppresses procreation abilities, so it was often said if a husband and wife were both addicts, their line would die out with them.

Many missionaries tried to cure addicts of their dependence on the drug, as no addict was ever accepted into the church as a member, unless on one's deathbed. The missionaries certainly recognized that the pernicious drug was a huge social problem

---

24. Hosea Ballou Morse, *International Relations of the Chinese Empire,* 3 vols. (London: Longmans, Green, 1910–1918), 2:220.

in Chinese society—one that the Westerners were clearly responsible for introducing.

Among the many ills that the missionaries saw in China, opium addiction was one they believed they could cure. Virtually every missionary medical doctor tried curing addicts, and it was a rare mission compound that did not have its own opium refuge. Generally, these were small, windowless buildings outside of which one posted a completely trustworthy guard, so that no opium could be smuggled in. The addicts were fed good food and, of course, prayed over, and much to the surprise of everyone, many addicts appeared cured within three days. Unable to explain these phenomena except as miracles, the former addicts were pronounced cured and released to return to their families.

Unfortunately, the jubilation was short-lived. Family members soon reported that the addict had stopped on the way home at an opium den, or was discovered asking a household servant to purchase the drug for them. The drug was not only physically addicting; it was also socially addicting. (The craving for opium smoke by the addict gave English a loan word from Chinese, *yen*, which means smoke, but, literally, the craving for opium smoke.)

When the missionaries discovered that their miracle cure, which in the late twentieth century was referred to as "cold turkey," did not work once the addicts left the opium refuge, the medical doctors tried concocting pharmaceutical cures. All types of exotic ingredients were tried, until the doctors discovered that the most effective cure for opium addiction was morphine! So many morphine pills were made and distributed by missionary doctors that the Chinese name for them was "Jesus opium." The name appalled the missionaries. Of course, the morphine pills cured the addicts' opium addiction, by giving them a morphine addiction as a substitute! Some of the missionaries and Chinese Christians, namely Dr. John Dudgeon (London Missionary Society [LMS], Beijing), and Pastor Xi (CIM), made fortunes for themselves by selling Jesus opium pills to Chinese addicts.

Finally, at the All-China Missionary Conference in Shanghai in 1890, a group of missionaries that included medical doctors decided to take direct action against the opium trade. The British had been financing their government in India for more than a century by growing opium on government-owned land and selling it at an annual auction. The Indian opium was exported primarily to China. (Because Americans were excluded from the government auction in India, they had to deal in the inferior Turkish varieties of the drug, but still made huge profits.) The missionaries in China decided they should directly attack the British government's involvement in the opium trade on moral grounds. This they did by organizing the Anti-Opium League in China and getting the support of prominent members of British society. Many of the anti-opium activists in Britain were members of the Society of Friends (Quakers), but they also included Donald Matheson, whose family had made their fortune in the China trade (including opium) as half of the great Hong Kong trading company, Jardine Matheson.

In 1896 the missionaries in China who were active in the Anti-Opium League surveyed every Western-trained doctor in China with a questionnaire about opium's harmful properties, attempted cures, extent of use in their districts, and whether or not addicts were accepted for church membership. Of the one hundred six medical doctors who responded, the overwhelming number were in the employ of missions.

However, a few Western doctors, practicing exclusively among expatriates, responded as did a few Chinese.

Every doctor reported that opium was addictive and that use of it increased constantly as the addict needed more and more to satisfy his or her yen for it. Everyone admitted it was possible to cure an addict, but it was extremely difficult and the recovering addict needed to be kept away from sources of the drug when they returned to their families. Several Chinese doctors reported that mothers who were addicts gave birth to babies who were addicted and that the newborns needed to have smoke blown across their faces if they were to survive. None of the Western doctors were willing to admit such was the case, as their training at that time still taught that mothers and babies were separate beings, even during pregnancy. The report, William H. Park's, *Opinions of Over 100 Physicians on the Use of Opium in China*,[25] was published, providing the first documentary, scientific evidence on the nature of opium addiction.

In Britain the government was reluctant to extricate itself from the opium trade due to the burden it would place on the India Office to find alternative funds to govern that subcontinent. However, presented with the evidence that opium was truly harmful, the House of Commons first adopted a resolution calling the opium trade "morally indefensible" in 1891 and then sought the end of the trade over a ten-year period in a treaty signed between Britain and China in 1907.

The fact that the opium trade was now internationally illegal did not stop opium importation to China, and by the early twentieth century the Chinese were growing a great deal of opium themselves. Several international conferences were

---

25. William H. Park, M.D., *Opinions of Over 100 Physicians on the Use of Opium in China* (Shanghai: American Presbyterian Mission Press, 1899).

held to restrict the international movement of all types of drugs, but wiping out a social evil is never easy. Finally, during the late Qing reform movement that followed the Boxer Uprising, Chinese themselves began to agitate against the drug and some progress was made on controlling its use. Before opium was brought under control, the revolution of 1911, which finally toppled the Qing, intervened. In the chaos that followed the revolutionary violence, no government of China was strong enough to control the growth and trade of opium, so use of the drug continued. After the 1949 victory by the CCP, they relentlessly campaigned against opium and got it under control to an extent not achieved by any previous government. The missionaries had worked diligently against opium, but it was the Chinese who solved the problem in their own way.

China Missions at the Movies

Turning to an entirely different area of missions, namely Hollywood's version of them, one finds as great a variety as in the China mission itself. Perhaps it was inevitable that missions would go to the movies since both figured prominently in American life in the early twentieth century. Many of the movies, with missionaries as leading characters, were based on popular novels.

The most famous of all movies about missionaries is certainly the one based on E. M. Forster's very traditional love story, *The African Queen* (1951). In the film version, Katharine Hepburn plays Rose Sayer, a missionary lady, and Humphrey Bogart plays a boat captain, Charlie Allnut, who fall in love while floating down a river on a jerry-rigged boat. Even though that movie is not about China, the story could easily have been set there, as Africa plays only a minor part in the film.

Before movies about Christian missionaries became popular, though not before hundreds of missionaries had arrived in China, D. W. Griffith made a 1919 silent film, with no music, called *Broken Blossoms or The Yellow Man and the Girl* starring Lilian Gish. In it Richard Barthelmess plays a Buddhist missionary to England who works in the Limehouse section of London, trying to teach his religion to the folks there. Most interesting, the film has many Chinese actors in it. This film is available free on the Internet at IBDM.com.

Most of the Hollywood productions that have China missionaries as characters, have the Westerner, usually American, hero or heroine saving the Chinese from themselves. This theme appears with ethnic variations in other movies of the time, namely those set in the American West.

Both Roman Catholic and Protestant missionaries figure in the films, which, after all, were made by studios that wanted to make profits. Frequently, the scriptwriters, directors, producers, actors, etc. seemed to have known nothing at all about China or Chinese people, but ignorance never stopped them from filming their ideas of what China should be like.

Among the movies centered in China, Pearl Buck's *The Good Earth* (1937), based on the novel of the same name, is certainly the most famous. It is the life story of the amah of the Claude Thomson family, the Bucks' neighbors at the American Presbyterian Mission (APM) compound on the University of Nanjing campus. Like many movies about China, the lead Chinese are played by Westerners, in this case Paul Muni as Wang Lung and Louise Rainer as O-Lan. However, the movie does have the American actor Keye Luke, best known as Charlie Chan's Number One Son, playing the part of the Elder Son (no name given!). Luke was one of very few ethnic Chinese actors who regularly appeared in Hollywood movies in the 1930s and 1940s.

Gregory Peck plays a Catholic priest, Father Francis Chisholm, in *Keys to the Kingdom* (1944), which is based on A. J. Cronin's 1941 novel. Arriving by riverboat with a crowd of people on the dock waving a welcome to him, or so he thinks, he soon discovers they are waving at a government official who is arriving at the same time. In reality, it would have been more likely that the arrival of a government official would have sent the common folk running for cover to avoid any unpleasant contact with him or the extraction of some monetary levy for his benefit. Father Chisholm helps the Chinese as the Japanese attack, making this one of the World War II propaganda films.

Frank Capra's *The Bitter Tea of General Yen* (1933) is based on a book by Grace Z. Stone published in 1930. It has Barbara Stanwyck as a missionary, Megan Davis, who arrives in Shanghai to marry another missionary, only to learn that he has gone off to rescue some orphans from the Chinese Civil War. Stanwyck's missionary insists on going along with a group of Westerners to rescue her beloved and the orphans, only to be taken captive by General Yen, who is played by Nils Asher.

This movie is often cited by critics as a prime example of the theme "white woman threatened by evil other," be he Asian, African, or Native American, which was very popular in the mid-twentieth century. The movie contains a famous silent, bedroom, nightmare sequence in which the heroine is terrorized by a masked man, who removes his mask revealing he is Chinese; in fact, he is Yen. The white woman in distress most desires what she most fears and immediately falls in love with Yen. One can find this theme of endangered missionaries rescued by their countrymen from evil "others" running throughout almost all these films.

China missionary films were not confined to the missionary era in China, as they continued to appear not only in the 1950s and 1960s, but also as recently as 2011. The *Inn of the Sixth Happiness* (1958) starring Ingrid Bergman is based on Alan Burgess's *The Small Woman* (1957), a biography of Gladys Aylward, who was a servant in Britain, but saved up enough money to get to China via the trans-Siberian railroad, and then joined the CIM. The Chinese general in this story is only half-Chinese and he is played by Curt Jergens. With his help Bergman manages to rescue the Chinese children who had been caught up in the Sino-Japanese War of 1937–1945, leading them to safety.

Charleton Heston, Ava Gardner, and David Niven star in the 1963 film, *55 Days at Peking* [sic], Hollywood's version of the Boxer Uprising, or more, specifically, of the foreign troops that invaded China to lift the siege of the Legation Quarter, where missionaries, diplomats, and other foreigners, along with Chinese Christians, had taken shelter. One critic described this film as more of a Western than an Eastern, as the closing scene shows Heston reaching out to save a beautiful, pig-tailed Chinese girl, who he pulls onto his horse behind him. She clings tightly to the hero as they ride away into the sunset, violating many Chinese social norms for young girls!

As the Vietnam War was heating up, it was the US Navy that came to the rescue of an old China missionary and his daughter, played by Candace Bergman, in *The Sand Pebbles* (1966). Steve McQueen plays the ne'er-do-well sailor whose Yangzi gunboat steams upriver to rescue the missionaries, who, of course, do not want to be rescued. McQueen's shipmates find time to make numerous visits to a local brothel where one of them falls in love with one of the women. This film has a different ending, as McQueen's character dies, perhaps signaling to the American public that all adventures in Asia could not have happy endings.

Other movies in which China missions play a key part include: *West of Shanghai* (1937) with Boris Karloff as a Chinese warlord holding missionaries prisoner; *China Sky* (1945) with Randolph Scott as a mission doctor and Anthony Quinn as the lead Chinese character even though the film has many Chinese actors in it, such as Benson Fong and Philip Ahn; *The Left Hand of God* (1955) with Humphrey Bogart as a priest; *Satan Never Sleeps* (1962) with William Holden as a priest; John Ford's *7 Women* (1967) with Anne Bancroft as a missionary doctor; and *Flowers of War* (2011), a Chinese production about the Rape of Nanjing with Christian Bale posing as a priest to rescue some Chinese girls.

Of course, many of the movies made in the pre-1949 era made their ways to Shanghai and Hong Kong where missionaries and other foreigners and Chinese could view them. Unfortunately, the author has never found any comments the missionaries made about these films.

It is impossible to gauge the impact these movies had on Americans' thinking, but in the years before television (not to mention the Internet), millions of Americans regularly attended the movies. In whatever manner the movie makers chose to show China, and particularly foreigners in that country, the films certainly had some influence on the viewers' ideas of China.

While the movies portrayed a certain view of missions in China, at the present time, some Chinese have adopted a certain view of American holidays. Given the complete secularization of Halloween and the close-to-complete secularization of Christmas, it should not be surprising that folks in other countries have taken to celebrating both holidays. When the author pointed out to some young Chinese that both these holidays were Christian, they replied they did not care, because they were fun to celebrate.

Halloween is a great excuse to dress in outlandish costumes; something young Chinese seem to enjoy given that they usually wear their school uniforms like hundreds or thousands of their schoolmates.

Santa Claus, in China, is the jolly elf in a red suit, with ruddy cheeks and white hair and beard, unlike the one becoming common in India, who wears a white mask to make him look like a Westerner. China's jolly elf has for years decorated some shop windows all year round, so it is obvious not everyone associates him with Christmas.

It remains to be seen if the Chinese will decide to celebrate Christmas as the Japanese do, by eating what they believe is the typical American Christmas dinner, Kentucky Fried Chicken! If one wants this typical American Christmas dinner in Japan, one must order weeks in advance and even then stand in long lines to pick up one's order. (The unfortunate employees in the restaurants are worked beyond exhaustion!) The author knows several Japanese who were astounded to discover, upon moving to the United States, that Americans not only do not eat KFC on Christmas, the stores are actually closed. Probably one could trace the origin of this tradition in Japan directly to the marketing department of KFC, which has been quite successful in selling their product as the typical American Christmas dinner!

Missionaries' Lifestyles

Returning to the missionaries, those who chose to go to China had to decide how each of them would live there. Some sought, as much as possible, to maintain their Western lifestyles, even to the point of importing virtually everything they ate, except rice! Others like the Roman Catholics with their vow of poverty, and the CIM, as a result of the eccentric policies of its leader, James Hudson Taylor, tried to live as much like the Chinese as possible.

Culture shock caused many missionaries, particularly but not exclusively in the early years of the missionary endeavor, to suffer mental breakdowns. It was not uncommon in many early mission stations for only the missionary and his wife to be in residence, meaning they were each other's total means of emotional support. With family and friends half a world away, the necessity of learning a new language and eating new foods even as they tried to cook dishes familiar from home, the emotional stress proved to be too much for some.

It would be difficult to estimate how many missionaries or their wives suffered from serious emotional stress, as the illness was often concealed. Both men and women suffered mental illnesses, but the precise numbers of those afflicted are impossible to determine. The more remote the place one served, the more likely one was to suffer mental problems, but that is not to suggest that those in large cities and in mission compounds housing many foreigners did not also suffer.

Missionaries' obituaries in *The Chinese Recorder* rarely mentioned mental illness, but they sometimes listed as the cause of death such maladies as "softening of the brain" and "delirium," which might have meant emotional problems.

In the LMS station at Beijing in the late nineteenth century, the missionaries seemed to take turns suffering mental collapses. Dr. Dudgeon and the Reverends Joseph Edkins and James Gilmour all suffered: Dudgeon frequently argued with the Chinese and took his disputes to local officials; Edkins sometimes harangued his colleagues on the streets, telling them they needed to repent and change their ways; and Gilmour suffered a total collapse while working alone in his very isolated field of Mongolia. Gilmour was sent home on furlough, only to report he had recovered by the time his ship reached Britain. Of course, on the voyage home, Gilmour had many people he could talk with.

In the APM on Hainan, the first wife of the mission pioneer, the Reverend Frank P. Gilman, suffered a total breakdown. Her husband took her home and left her, pregnant, with his family, while he returned to China. She was dead before he reached his station.

In the same mission after the Japanese army invaded Hainan in 1937, the Reverend John Steiner became mentally unbalanced to the extent that his colleagues feared he was compromising their safety. They conspired with the local Japanese officers, with whom the missionaries were on good terms, to refuse Steiner permission to return to Hainan, leaving him in Hong Kong where he was confined after Pearl Harbor. Clearly suffering from post-traumatic stress syndrome, Steiner committed suicide after being repatriated to the United States in 1942.

One of the difficulties missionaries faced was they did not always have separate living quarters for each family, particularly in the beginnings of a new station. Many families shared houses, eating together, and trying to rear their children in the ways each family preferred. As there were more women than men in China as missionaries, it was not unusual for single women to have a room in a married couple's home. (Obviously, this caused great confusion among some Chinese, who could not understand why the foreigners opposed concubinage among the Chinese, but practiced it themselves!) Some of the larger stations eventually provided a single women's home where the women lived as sisters in the fictive families they created.

There were usually several families and children and single women at each station, so they tended to create fictive families, many of which tended to last decades after the missionaries left China. Indeed, unrelated adults became fictive or courtesy aunts and uncles and the children were expected to obey them as they did their parents. Often these ties became quite close. Buck, in describing her childhood at the APM compound in Nanjing, writes that the missionaries tried to maintain an American lifestyle within their compound, but it was the only American community she had ever encountered in which every mother was a college graduate. (The APM required that missionary wives be college graduates prior to their appointments to China.)

Depending on their age, their location in China, and the policy of their mission board, many missionaries' children were home schooled. Sylvia Melrose Ryan, whose grandparents and parents served the APM at Nada, Hainan, once told this author that Dr. Esther Morse, M.D., ate lunch with her every Thursday during the school year as the doctor's contribution to Sylvia's education. Each week Sylvia announced what she wanted to talk about and the doctor related what she knew of the chosen topic.

After the establishment of the Shanghai American School in 1912, which took both boarding and local students, many missionaries sent their children there. There was also a smaller, ecumenical boarding school at Guling, Jiangsu, which was a popular place for missionaries to spend their summer vacations as it was in the mountains.

The Chinese Churches of the Early Twentieth Century

By the early twentieth century some Chinese Christians resented the control the foreigners exercised over the church in China. The missionaries never consulted any of their converts on issues related to their work. When the missionaries planned their budgets for the coming year and requested the money they needed from their home boards, they did not consult their converts, not even those who were ordained. Every mission paid their ordained Chinese ministers only a tiny fraction of what the missionaries were paid. Yet, these men frequently itinerated with the missionaries, built and led new church communities, and preached to thousands. In fact, the Chinese clergy were so badly paid that their children were frequently taken as scholarship students at the mission schools.

Ideally, missionaries should have been working themselves out of their jobs, because if they were successful in converting the Chinese to Christianity, then the Chinese would have their own churches. Several factors worked against this: first, for the missionaries, working in China was how they earned their livings, so to give up and return home meant starting all over for themselves and their families. This was a particular issue during the Great Depression of the 1930s when mission contributions fell off as the Western economies declined. Many board missions had to decrease, or not increase, the salaries they paid the missionaries, and they sent fewer new people to the field in these years. Very few missionaries resigned during this period because they knew it would be difficult to find employment at home.

Second, mission boards functioned as established parts of the church institutions, with separate budgets, often collected, in part, on mission Sundays in the churches. If the Chinese took over their churches, these funds would not be available to them.

Third, cultural superiority caused many of the missionaries to believe that they had a better understanding of Christianity, because they had been born and raised in a Christian society. Furthermore, many missionaries believed Western civilization was clearly superior to China's. (The reader should recall that Social Darwinism, the misapplication of Darwin's scientific theory to the social environment, was at its height during the heyday of the mission movement in China.)

Fourth, missionaries who recalled the Taiping fiasco were reluctant to allow Chinese to take control of the local churches.

Yet several changes in Chinese society forced the missionaries to reassess the role of Chinese in the churches. As Chinese students returned from studying abroad they brought with them new ideas about their country and how they wanted to change it. (The term *returned student* was a specific one used in China to refer to someone, usually a man, with a foreign education, who had spent time abroad.) Among the best known of these students was Sun Yixian (Sun Yat-sen), a native of Guangdong province, who was educated at Iolani School, a mission institution in Honolulu. Later Sun became a Western-trained medical doctor in Hong Kong, but then he devoted himself to toppling the Qing dynasty by revolution. American missionaries liked to call Sun "the George Washington of China," making the mistake of confusing the Chinese Revolution of 1911 with the American Revolution of 1776.

While most of the returned students concentrated on modernizing the Chinese government, some focused on establishing a Chinese Christian church. The best study of the indigenous Chinese church is Xi Lian's *Redeemed by Fire: The Rise of the Popular Christian Church in China*.[26] By the early twentieth century some Chinese who had encountered Christianity through foreign missionaries and by experiences overseas began to think that perhaps Christianity could be interpreted differently, without so many of the trappings of Western culture. However, many of these Chinese church leaders were not very analytical in their plans to develop a new church. Some were only interested in evangelism.

It seemed logical that if Christianity were a revealed religion for all people for all time, then certainly Chinese could proclaim their own understanding of it. In the milieu of the early twentieth century when Chinese nationalism swept the country, in the aftermath of the collapse of the Qing dynasty, many young returned students sought to change China in ways they thought were necessary. No longer were foreigners allowed to tell the reformers what to do: the Chinese had their own goals.

Thus the crusade against opium took on new dimensions as Chinese led the fight against the pernicious drug. There was an attempt at a parliamentary government, which did not succeed, but few countries successfully implement that reform the first time they try. There were calls for education that was truly for the masses, and writing in the vernacular to make the printed word accessible to the common people. Gradually, these reforms coalesced into the May Fourth Movement, which took its name from the Beijing University student protest of

---

26. Xi Lian, *Redeemed by Fire: the Rise of the Popular Christian Church in China* (New Haven, CT: Yale University Press, 2010).

4 May 1919, against China's treatment at the Versailles Peace Conference and in the treaties that came from it. In international affairs, China was clearly not considered an equal of the Western countries and Japan who negotiated the treaties.

Chinese Evangelists

In this period of social and cultural ferment, several young Chinese emerged on the scene preaching their doctrines of Christianity. Among these leaders was John Song (Song Shangjie) (1904-1944), a returned student active with the Bethel Band in China, who became the best-known evangelist in China in the early twentieth century; Wang Mingdao (1900-1991), who dabbled with Pentecostalism early in his career, and later denounced foreign missionaries and groups like the Young Men's Christian Association (YMCA) which he deemed too liberal; and Ni Tuosheng (Watchman Nee) (1903-1977), who founded the Little Flock and preached the Second Coming of Christ. (See chapter 5 for short biographies of Song, Wang, and Ni.)

Each of these Chinese challenged missionary Christianity and produced a different version of the religion, uniquely suited to China in this time of political turmoil and emergent nationalism. Distancing themselves from the Social Gospel then being advocated by more liberal churches and groups such as the YMCA and the Young Women's Christian Association (YWCA), these Chinese clergy preached instead a more fundamental view of Christianity. As their ideas spread among China's Christians, they moved the Chinese indigenous church to the Fundamentalist side of the controversy with the Modernists. (See chapter 6 for a discussion of this controversy.)

In the period after 1949 Christians were forced to join the Three-Self Patriotic Movement (TSPM) for Protestants or the Patriotic Association (PA) for Roman Catholics. For the Protestants this was not a major doctrinal issue, as the various denominations had different leaders at different times; and no one congregant was considered to be an authority any more than the next congregant, but it was a major problem for the Roman Catholics.

The Reverend Wu Yaozong (1893–1979), who had a long association with the pacifist organization, Fellowship for Reconciliation (*Wei Ai She*), before the Mukden Incident (1931), turned to the Social Gospel for a time, but by the late 1930s was associated with the CCP, and specifically with Premier Zhou. Wu became the first leader of the TSPM.

The aim of the TSPM was to unite the Protestant churches into one group that was self-governing, self-supporting, and self-propagating. No foreign contributions were allowed. Protestants who did not join the TSPM were forced underground, and eventually formed into house or underground churches. Although it has never been a written requirement, in practice, all nongovernmental organizations in China after 1949 have had members of the CCP as their leaders, but the person in the second position need not necessarily be a Party member. From this practice some scholars determined that Bishop Ding Guangxun (1915–2012), the longtime leader of the TSPM, was a member of the CCP.

In 1950 a group of Chinese churches, along with the YMCA and the YWCA issued a Manifesto, signed by as many as four hundred thousand Christians, acknowledging the authority of the CCP government. The document, which was written by the Reverend Wu, a Congregational clergyman, denounced the United States as imperialist and the Chinese churches as tools of that imperialism. The TSPM was organized in 1951 and sought to align the churches with the new government through patriotism.

The Chinese Roman Catholics were faced with a more serious choice when the PA was established in 1957. Under the PA the Catholic churches were allowed to operate, but were required to sever all contact with Rome. This was a blow many Catholics felt they could not tolerate. Those who obeyed the government's injunction and joined the PA and those who refused to obey, staying loyal to Rome and going underground, split the Chinese Catholic church asunder.

Even today the two groups have many differences and the Vatican is caught between them. While those clergy and congregants who were members of the PA continued publicly celebrating the Mass, the clergy they ordained and all actions the PA took were, to the loyalist faction, illegitimate. This situation put the Vatican in a difficult situation because it did not want to lose contact with either group. The Holy See announced that the clergy ordained by the PA and all rites it administered were "valid" but "illicit." This fine theological distinction meant that in ordinary circumstances the PA Catholics were not a part of the Church in Rome, but in emergency situations their rituals would be accepted. In 2000 the Vatican greatly offended the government of China when the pope released the names of one hundred twenty new saints, eighty-seven Chinese and thirty-three missionaries, on 1 October, the Chinese national holiday—that year being the fifty-first anniversary of the Communist Revolution.

Many older, foreign Roman Catholics have reported that attending PA masses in China is somewhat of a shock, immediately transporting them back to their childhoods, because the 1957 split with Rome meant the Chinese Catholics missed Vatican II, and as a result one can still hear the Latin Mass said in some churches in China today. However, Mandarin and various Chinese dialects are also used, and in Shanghai and Beijing foreigners can usually find a service in English.

Although it is both difficult and dangerous to generalize about churches in China, John Craig William Keating's *A Protestant Church in Communist China: Moore Memorial Church, Shanghai, 1949-1989* is an excellent account of how one large urban church managed to cope during the first forty years of the Communist era.[27]

The church's huge neon cross, atop its building, has long been a landmark in central Shanghai. Keating, an Australian whose wife's family are members of Moore Memorial, interviewed many members of the church and was given access to many documents other scholars have not seen. Keating concludes that Moore Memorial's members are Christians who are trying to negotiate an extremely complex relationship with the Chinese government.

Perhaps even more complex is the relationship of the Christians in the city of Wenzhou, Zhejiang, where they constitute 10 percent of the population and have about two thousand church buildings. Christians call the city "the Chinese Jerusalem." The best book on the Wenzhou church is Cao Nanlai's *Constructing China's Jerusalem: Christians, Power and Place in Contemporary Wenzhou*.[28] Cao writes that the Christian population of the Wenzhou area very much emulates both Chinese Confucian society and today's emphasis, throughout the society, on connections (*guangxi*) for getting anything done

---

27. John Craig William Keating, *A Protestant Church in Communist China: Moore Memorial Church, Shanghai, 1949-1989* (Bethlehem, PA: Lehigh University Press, 2012).
28. Cao Nanlai, *Constructing China's Jerusalem: Christians, Power and Place in Contemporary Wenzhou* (Stanford, CA: Stanford University Press, 2011).

from obtaining a job to getting attention from a medical doctor. Cao writes that the Christian "bosses" function within the church community as clan heads did in the past or as party cadres do today. Throughout the Wenzhou churches women are relegated to subordinate roles, with young women serving as greeters when male church members hold meetings or banquets.

Lian thinks the contemporary Chinese church will continue to be most popular among the marginalized people in Chinese society as Buddhism had been in earlier centuries. He also thinks the Chinese church will have little impact on achieving any great political reforms in the country, because of the small numbers of Chinese who follow Christianity and because of their marginalization. The fact that some, but certainly not all, Christians in China are members of ethnic minority groups only complicates the problem.

(See below in the section on Chinese Christians Today, for more on the Wenzhou churches.)

The Cultural Revolution, 1966–76

The only way to explain the period of the Cultural Revolution in China in the decade between 1966 and 1976 is to say that the society went mad. It might seem impossible for a billion people to go mad, simultaneously, but similar episodes have happened elsewhere: Germany under the Nazis, Cambodia under Pol Pot, Iran under the ayatollahs, the United States during the McCarthy era, and on a smaller scale in Salem, Massachusetts, at the time of the witch trials.[29]

---

29. The author recalls hearing a story at a regional Association for Asian Studies in the 1980s about Arthur Miller's visit to China where his play *The Crucible* was staged in Shanghai. As with virtually all entertainment in China, the opening night was sold out, but the audience clearly did not understand the play and three-quarters of them fled the theater at intermission. Those who remained moved to center themselves in

Various scholars have tried to explain what happened in China during the Cultural Revolution. Their theories include the middle class trying to reassert itself, Mao Zedong trying to hold onto power which he thought was slipping away, and the lower, agricultural class asserting itself, to name just a few. The many monographs of this period, by former landlords, by government officials and their children, by Christians, by foreigners who lived in China at that time, by former employees of foreign firms, by professors, etc. all testify to the madness of the population. The author once remarked to a Chinese colleague that the books about this period all have one other thing in common: food—there was not enough of it. The Chinese friend's surprise was immediate and his response was that he needed to rethink the subject. Yet, there could be some validity in the idea that the Cultural Revolution was caused by a food shortage, as it closely followed the disastrous Great Leap Forward of 1958 that tried to industrialize the country overnight, and the famine of the early 1960s. Farmers, who were required to attend numerous political gatherings during the Cultural Revolution, obviously had less time to actually farm.

During the Cultural Revolution anyone who was perceived as different from what the masses thought Chinese should be, was the object of harassment and violence. Obviously, a billion people could not resemble one another very closely, but traditional Chinese values extolled being like others, a part of the group or clan. Individualism or being different was seen as harmful to the social order and thus not well tolerated. During the years of the Cultural Revolution certain people were

front of the stage and watched in silence. Near the end of the play there was a sudden, huge gasp from the audience, and a wild ovation as the play ended. What the audience finally realized was the Salem witch trials were an allegory on the Cultural Revolution. Subsequent shows were sold out and everyone stayed until the play ended.

thought to be separate from the group. If one had foreign books, knew a foreign language, or had been abroad, that were enough to prove the person was not totally Chinese—thus justifying an attack by the Red Guards. If one were a landowner one automatically exploited the lower classes and that was reason to attack the person. If one were a government official or one's father or grandfather had been one, that too was a good enough excuse to be denounced and attacked. If a member of one's family were a Christian or, worse, an ordained member of the Christian clergy, that was reason to attack them.

In this period of madness, Christians were obvious targets, as they followed what most Chinese considered a foreign religion, many spoke a foreign language, and others had been educated in foreign (mission) schools. All churches were closed and the public practice of any religion was forbidden in these years. Attacks on religion had been frequent after the 1949 revolution, and they were not exclusively against Christians. Indeed, there seems to be no evidence that Christians were singled out and persecuted any more severely than anyone else thought to be different; they were simply easy targets, because neighbors knew they were Christians.

Many Chinese suffered because they followed other religions. Muslims (*Hui* in Chinese), most of whom lived in the far west, suffered; Buddhists and Daoists were also subjects of persecution as the government attempted to diminish their influence over society and bring them under governmental control. In the late 1950s and continuing through the Cultural Revolution, Buddhist monasteries and temples were closed and monks were forced to rejoin the larger society and be productive, if not imprisoned or killed for their beliefs. *Bones of the Master* by George Crane[30] is a harrowing account of the persecution of one monk who was forced to flee his monastery in 1959, and his painful, perilous journey to survive. It is also the story of his return to the location of the monastery, in the company of an American, a left-over 1960s hippie, whose sole goal in life was to never have a full-time job. As they embarked on their journey, the monk insisted upon taking a statue of the Buddha as carry-on luggage. Encased in a wooden box, as it traveled through the pre-9/11 airport X-ray, the attendant, saw the statue, and yelled, "Jesus Christ." The monk replied softly, "Similar." The monk and his American friend did manage to locate the bones of the monk's master on a mountain in Inner Mongolia, even though they lacked government permission to travel in that area.

While religion in China was under attack during the Cultural Revolution, so were intellectuals for similar reasons. Many had been abroad, had been in contact with foreigners in scholarly exchanges, or knew foreign languages. Russian had been taught in many schools between 1949 and the split with the Soviet Union in 1960, so many of the educated knew that language.

All schools were closed during these years, which caused many problems. China had never had a problem with teenage gangs until then, when gangs became an acute problem, particularly when parents were sent to labor camps or farms and children were left to fend for themselves.

Post-1972 Western Contacts with Chinese Christians

Westerners renewed their contacts with China in the 1970s as both the United States and China saw each other as a

---

30. George Crane, *Bones of the Master: A Journey to Secret Mongolia* (New York: Random House, 2001).

counterbalance to the power of the Soviet Union. Yet many of the Americans eager to resume connections with Chinese seemed unaware that the situation was not the same as it had been before 1949. In the 1980s, after American diplomatic relations with China had resumed, one wealthy charitable organization in the United States, that had funded theological education in China prior to 1949 and in the intervening years had turned its attention to Southeast Asian countries, quickly reestablished its ties in China. It seemed as though the group had learned nothing during the long years of cultural misunderstandings that had accompanied so many of the missionary attempts "to change China" in the two previous centuries. This group almost immediately sought to have the TSPM agree to a statement of belief that was drafted by the Western Christians! It was quite obvious that the Americans thought they could still dictate what Chinese Christians believed, and it is also likely that the Americans making the request had no idea what the relationship was between the TSPM and the CCP at that time.

Indeed, many Americans who rushed to China as tourists in those years took Bibles they sought to give to Chinese Christians. Those who managed to make contact with TSPM or underground churches were often politely told to take the Bibles home with them when they left, since the government printed Bibles for the churches. Clearly, the foreigners were ignorant of the situation in which they might place the Chinese Christians if these gifts were accepted.

Many Western church leaders who encouraged Chinese Christians to seek theological education in America, which the CCP agreed to as a means of improving relations with the United States and European countries, seemed never to realize that the students sent all had good connections in China. How closely the encouragement of Christianity in China was linked to United States-China diplomatic, cultural, economic, etc. relations appears to have passed under the radar of many American church leaders, who seemed to think China had changed little since 1949! Just to see what answer the author would get, she once asked an official of the organization that wanted the Chinese church to sign a statement of faith, why the Chinese did not take advantage of the extensive Christian theological seminaries in Southeast Asia, which this group had been supporting since the early 1950s. The official replied that the Chinese did not seem to be interested in Christianity elsewhere in Asia; they only wanted to study in the United States! This man, whose organization was supporting many Chinese students in the United States, was totally oblivious to the possibility that there might be any geopolitical reason behind the Chinese government's decision to send students to the United States to study Christianity.

The author once heard an American attendee at a professional meeting ask participating scholars to what extent they thought Christianity in China was linked to United States-Chinese relations. The answer the scholars gave suggested that the person look at Falun Gung that had no extra-China support and how rapidly, and totally, the government had moved against it.

In the past, Chinese Christian contacts with foreign Christians sometimes have harmed both individuals and the Chinese church. For foreign Christians it is nearly impossible to know when contacts with Chinese Christians might be helpful or harmful; they can only look to Chinese Christians for clues and guidance, and then proceed with caution.

In the 1990s Bishop Ding made what many considered a farewell trip to the United States. The stated purpose of the trip was to thank the surviving missionaries and their children and grandchildren for their service to China. As this author was then working on the papers of the Presbyterian mission on Hainan and knew the surviving missionaries and many of their children, they insisted the American organizers invite the author to the meeting they would attend. (There were several such meetings in various cities.)

At the gathering, the author was only one of two non-missionary or missionary offspring in attendance; the other was a Chinese-born American in the employ of one of the ecumenical organizations with long ties to China. It is human nature to hear what one wants to hear, and in that context, the bishop's tour was a success. He had come to America to thank the missionaries and their children for their service to China, and those in attendance were most grateful that Ding acknowledged their families' contributions in his talk.

The problem was that Bishop Ding had said absolutely nothing about the missionaries, their children, or their work in China. Instead, he spoke about the Nestorian Monument, and presented a rubbing of it to the institution hosting the meeting. When the author privately asked a representative of the ecumenical organization what was going on, his reply echoed her thoughts—those in attendance heard what they wanted to hear! Clearly, as in the centuries past, the Chinese Christians and the Western Christians were speaking to one another, but each heard and understood only what they wanted to.

That the late Bishop Ding was protected from harm during the Cultural Revolution, on orders from Premier Zhou, was no accident. Zhou, the ever-urbane, educated diplomat who was savvy about the West, knew that Christian connections could be used to China's advantage in dealing with the Americans.

Exactly where Ding spent the years of the Cultural Revolution has never been revealed, but it should be noted that his house was attacked by Red Guards several times in his absence.[31]

Since the 1970s many people have asked the author if there are missionaries in China today. She always answers, "No, it is illegal for them to be there"; then asks how many of these nonexistent missionaries they think the author has personally met or heard about, including a cousin of the Mennonite man who redid my kitchen floor! Most of the missionaries in China today are there as English teachers, but when asked privately, they admit to having used biblical references or other Christian materials in their classrooms. At one meeting of scholars studying the missionary movement, one scholar stated that there were probably more missionaries in China today than there had ever been before 1949. Statistics are impossible to come by, but no one disputed the contention.

Chinese officials are certainly not naïve enough to believe Western Christians would not want to proselytize once China was open to having foreigners live in their country. The problem for the officials is to control the situation as much as possible, while maintaining good relations with the Western governments.

What the relationship between the church in any one location might be with the local Religious Affairs Bureau (RAB) or after 1998 with its successor the State Administration of Religious Affairs (SARA) depends largely upon what year it is, what the position of the CCP is toward Christianity at the moment, if there are serious power struggles taking place within the central or local governments, and if there are local issues between officials and church leaders.

---

31. This situation has been discussed among American China scholars many times in the years since the Cultural Revolution, but no one has come up with an answer.

In 1988 when the author first visited Hainan, she arrived on a Sunday morning and asked at the hotel the location of the nearest church, using the words for Protestant church, knowing there had been only an APM mission on the island. Leaders there welcomed the author and inquired if she had been to the RAB and when she replied she had not, having just arrived, they agreed to accompany her to the RAB the following day. Personal relations between the three church leaders and the RAB personnel seemed to be quite cordial, and one RAB man told the author she could go anywhere on the island she wanted to, except where there were soldiers. Everyone laughed when the author replied she had no interest in soldiers.

The RAB officials later telephoned the clergyman in the interior town of Nada to alert him that the author would be visiting there. At Jiaji, the other interior town where a mission station had been located, the church elders had not been notified of the author's impending visit, probably because there was then no clergyman serving that church. Nonetheless, they too welcomed the author, showing her the old mission compound and the church.

In 2002 when the author again visited Hainan, she asked if she needed to go to the SARA to alert them about her visit. An official of the government tourist board replied, "Oh, no, no one bothers with that these days." The author's presence was certainly no secret as she visited Hainan University, and was also interviewed by the local newspaper, as the author of the only book in English about Hainan, albeit about the Presbyterian missionaries who had served on the island!

On both these visits and on others to various parts of China over the past thirty plus years, the author has visited several TSPM church services that had many children in attendance.

One church even displayed government-approved blueprints for a new building that included Sunday school rooms for children. As the constitution of the government of China forbids the teaching of any religion to anyone under the age of eighteen, the author decided it was probably best not to ask any questions. This was certainly a Chinese issue on which a foreigner's questions might prove embarrassing or detrimental.

Likewise, on one of these visits the author was given the name of a woman who was the leader of the underground church in her city. Arriving in the city on a Sunday, the author went to the local TSPM church, and the first person who approached her was the woman she had been told led the underground church there. As the author observed the service and the interactions of those attending, it was obvious that this woman was a well-respected leader of the congregation. Again, the author did not consider it appropriate to question the situation.

It is important to remind readers that the underground church in China is not in any sense "underground." Typical meeting places are members' homes, but sometimes other buildings are used. Returning from one of his trips researching the indigenous Chinese churches, Lian reported that he had visited one underground church that was housed in a four-story building, the interior of which was like a stadium.

The Chinese government has also allowed some Christian groups, specifically the Amity Foundation, to establish themselves in China. Amity is located adjacent to the main gate of the University of Nanjing. In one case related to the author, this group funded the living expenses of a Muslim student who was from extreme Western China. His family was so poor that they had no money left to give him for food after they had purchased him a bus ticket to travel to the university. After a few days his roommates discovered he had a huge sack of flatbread, out of which he carefully rationed several pieces, for his daily meals. Alerting faculty members to the situation, they contacted the Amity Foundation for assistance, which then provided the man a grant so he would have proper food each day.

Non-Christians' Views of Christians

Today some non-Christian Chinese authors have turned to writing about Chinese Christians, simply because they find them to be interesting subjects. Liao Yiwu and Da Chen are but two examples.

Again, it is dangerous to generalize from the experiences of individuals, but the author will cite examples of two Chinese Christians whose stories are included in Liao's excellent work, *God Is Red*.[32] Liao, many of whose works have been banned by the Chinese government, found kinship with those who had also been persecuted.

God Is Red includes the story of Wang Zhiming, who was executed in 1973 and was recognized as one of the ten martyrs of the twentieth century whose statues stand above the Great West Door of Westminster Abbey. A member of the Miao minority in the mountains of southwest China, Wang's family was converted by two missionaries—one Australian and one British—in the early twentieth century. Educated in Christian schools, Wang served as the clergyman for the Liao, Yi, and

---

32. Liao Yiwu, *God Is Red: The Secret Story of How Christianity Survived and Flourished in Communist China.* Translated by Huang Wenguang (New York: HarperCollins, 2001). The book won the 2001 Book of the Year award from the evangelical publication, *Books and Culture*. The author is indebted to Dyron Daughrity for this information: see http:www.booksandculture.com/articles/webexclusives/2001/December/favorite books2001.

Miao people, many of whom had become Christians. Early in the Communist period Wang was sometimes imprisoned and sometimes used as a role model for other reactionaries, while being denounced publicly. During the Cultural Revolution, Wang held church services in caves, where he baptized many of the local people. Finally arrested in 1969, he was executed in 1973 although he was never formally accused of any crime. Instead, he was informally accused of being a lackey of the foreign imperialists, a counterrevolutionary, and a spy, among other charges.

Liao also related the story of Dr. Sun, who practiced medicine among the extremely poor minority Christians in the mountains of southern Yunnan. He obtained a medical degree in Beijing and served for a time as an emergency room doctor, before being made a hospital administrator. As a bureaucrat he abolished the custom of hosting lavish banquets for his employees and sold his state-provided automobile to give the money to the hospital. These reforms angered so many of his colleagues that he was eventually forced to give up his position.

In the meantime, in the early 1990s, he made contact with some foreigners who were visiting and obtained a Bible from them. He became a Christian, but shortly thereafter, one of his students betrayed his new belief to Party officials. He was then asked to join the Party, and refused citing his belief in Christianity. After a sojourn in Thailand working in a Burmese refugee hospital, he returned to Yunnan in 1999 to work at a small hospital. When treating impoverished patients he prescribed the cheapest, most effective medicine, alienating the hospital managers and their pharmacy colleagues because this practice cut into their profits. Eventually, he left the hospital and began doing medical mission work among the tribal peoples who were Christians, treating them for free.

Liao published an article on Dr. Sun on an overseas Chinese website, which resulted in the doctor being invited to the United States by a Chinese church to talk about his work. After that visit Dr. Sun was refused permission to return to China, because Yunnan government officials accused him of undermining the state hospitals by treating people for free. At the end of his account of Dr. Sun, Liao writes that the doctor was then studying English in California and hoping for a job as a medical missionary in Africa.[33]

Da Chen in his autobiography, *Sounds of the River*, relates meeting a Norwegian student at the Foreign Language Institute in Beijing in the 1970s who was asked to leave because of his Christian activities. Before the man left he gave Chen, a non-Christian, an English Bible with Jesus's words in red. Chen gave it to the Christian woman in his village who had taught him such good English that he scored first in a nationwide exam for college entrance. The woman had lost her Bible, during the Cultural Revolution, to Red Guards who threatened to cut off her hands if she did not relinquish it. She was overjoyed that Chen had thought of her when he was offered the Bible, which she treasured.[34]

Chinese Christians Today

In 2014, news reports from China indicated that the government demolished a church in the city of Wenzhou. While church members were able to physically prevent equipment from reaching the structure on several occasions,

---

33. Liao, *God Is Red*, 96.
34. Da Chen, *Sounds of the River* (New York: HarperPerennial, 2003).

action was taken between three and six o'clock in the morning and the building came down. The twelve-year-old building apparently had no structural problems, as is common with many older churches, and no reason was given for the destruction. Several scholars have recently told the author that some of the many recently-built church buildings in and around Wenzhou are much larger than the size authorized on their official government plans, suggesting some connivance between the builders and the officials. If this proves to be the case, then one can only guess that the issue has little or nothing to do with Christianity, but is part of a larger struggle for control either within the province or in the CCP.

The news also reported that the government removed two crosses from churches in an effort to limit visible symbols of the foreign religion. While it is impossible to know what prompted the action, one can guess it was a local issue. The future of the Chinese Christian church resides in the hands of the Chinese Christians and the way in which they are able to negotiate their existence and beliefs with the governmental authorities. The informal, foreign missionaries in China today will likely have little impact on the growth of the Christian church, but if care is not taken, they might do damage to their co-religionists by their ignorance of local issues, by their mere presence, or by their actions.

2

Denominationalism

Denominationalism was not an issue among the Protestant missionaries in China in the nineteenth and twentieth centuries as it was in their home countries. Ecumenism guided all the Protestant missionaries from the earliest days of their endeavor until the 1920s when the Fundamentalist-Modernist controversy which had started in American churches finally shattered the cooperation that had characterized the China missions. (See chapter 6 for the Fundamentalist-Modernist issue.)

There were several reasons why the China missionaries paid so little attention to the denominationalism that was common in their home countries. The sheer size of the Chinese population they hoped to convert overwhelmed new missionaries immediately upon disembarking in China. Another reason for ecumenism was the isolation of many mission stations, where a traveling missionary was a welcome guest, whatever his or her denomination. The absence of hotels the foreigners approved of in China's interior meant that mission houses became de facto hotels. Yet another spur to ecumenism was the success of the missionary secondary schools and the inability of the missions to send every bright and promising student abroad for further education. Each denomination realized it alone could never support a university in China, so the solution was to cooperate with others denominations to establish a Christian university. Eventually, there were thirteen ecumenical universities in China.

The Early Missionary Character

In the early years of the Protestant endeavor in China, a missionary definitely needed a call to mission work. The nature of the call differed greatly for each person. However, it usually involved some feeling, perhaps first recognized in church or at a revival, that God wanted that individual to go to China to spread the Good News. (Many missionaries revealed their thoughts on their work when they sang their words to the hymn "Bringing in the Sheaves," i.e., "Bringing in Chinese.") In the period before the 1890s it was common to have applications to mission boards from single women, perhaps in their thirties or forties, who wrote that as their parents were now dead they were freed from family responsibilities and so they felt the call to China. This was particularly true if the applicant were an only child or faced the possibility of living with a sibling's family. Indeed, the few alternatives available to single women in the United States and Britain in the nineteenth century undoubtedly caused many adventurous women to consider joining a mission. Even into the twentieth century many single women, such as Wilhelmina (Minnie) Vautrin of the United Christian Missionary Society (UCMS), who worked at Ginling College in Nanjing, chose to stay at the college as the Japanese approached the city in 1937, simply because they had no other homes.[1]

In the nineteenth century some Protestant boards asked applicants if they were entering mission work "for life, God willing." The American Presbyterian Mission (APM) was among those asking missionaries to make this commitment, which was similar to joining a Catholic religious order. Yet, questions on applications changed over the years and this particular one seems to have been removed from most boards' applications by the beginning of the twentieth century. As men who went to the mission fields needed ordination by their various denominations, it was assumed that they had dedicated their lives to Christ, but for women, boards wanted to know why they were choosing a career in missions.

From many scholarly studies on Protestant women missionaries done in the last quarter-century or so, it is clear that women missionaries went to work in overseas missions largely to escape the limitations of careers open to them in their home countries. One could teach at home, but one could teach and head a school on the mission field. Women medical doctors in mission service headed up their own hospitals and in many institutions the woman was the only doctor in residence. Mission boards even recruited those with secretarial and bookkeeping skills as missions became bigger and more complicated to administer, so that those who taught or evangelized or did medical work did not need to also purchase

---

1. Ginling College had been founded in 1913 and was the only Protestant college for women.

goods, keep records and books, send reports to the boards at home, etc.

Clergymen in both in the United States and Britain in the nineteenth century had generally attended some type of post-secondary institution where they had studied for their chosen profession. Except in the earliest years of the mission venture, when men with little education were sent to China as mission printers and carpenters, nearly all of the missionary men were ordained. Many mission boards required that medical doctors also be ordained, but when the increase of missionaries demanded more and more doctors to care for them, most boards abandoned the ordination requirement since medical doctors with both qualifications were extremely hard to find.

The culture shock the missionaries experienced upon arriving in China cannot be underestimated. China's population was crowded onto the narrow, cultivable plain of the coastal area, into the lowlands of south China, and along the Yellow and Yangzi Rivers. Cities had grown in China, as they had elsewhere in Asia, around governmental centers, so before the Industrial Revolution had produced great cities in the West, China already had many cities with populations exceeding one million. (Marco Polo mentions four cities of that size.) Many early missionaries commented on the density of the population, as well as the dirt they saw everywhere.

By the mid-1890s, with the growing professionalism in the Western countries, missionaries needed credentials for the jobs they were to do. It was no longer enough to have a "call" and lend one's hand to whatever needed to be done on the mission field; now one needed to be a credentialed teacher, a trained bookkeeper, or a licensed medical doctor, etc. Of course, clergy had always been ordained, but the days of the laymen who went abroad to proclaim the gospel were now past, except for some of the faith missions such as the China Inland Mission (CIM).

Yet, even with this growing professionalism, most missionaries knew little about China when they set out for their life's work. Few institutions of higher education in the West taught anything about Asia, save those few that had granted professorships to returned missionaries, like James Legge in his post at Oxford.

Protestant Methods and Practices

Methods and practices of the Protestant missionaries for converting the Chinese to Christianity were far different from those of the Jesuits in the sixteenth and seventeenth centuries, yet, some issues were the same. Coming from the religious environment created from the Great Awakening, the American Protestants sought to convert the Chinese to their ideas of Christianity, which were heavily laden with Western cultural practices. Rather than accommodate themselves to Chinese society, as Matteo Ricci had tried to do, the Protestants set out to change China and make it more like the West. Accordingly, they set up mission stations, generally, walled compounds set apart from the surrounding Chinese, where they lived a totally Western lifestyle, but with the help of Chinese servants.

The only group that tried any assimilation was the CIM, whose eccentric leader, James Hudson Taylor, required all his missionaries to wear Chinese clothing and the men to have queues, using fake ones pinned to their caps until their own hair grew! (Blonds and redheads must have had special problems.) Such superficial accommodation likely amused most Chinese who encountered these foreigners.

Protestants Face the Same Problems as the Roman Catholics

When the Protestant missionaries arrived in China, they too were faced with how to convert the Chinese to Christianity, just as the Roman Catholics had been in earlier centuries. The sheer size of the Chinese population daunted even the most determined. The first missionaries realized they could do nothing without the help of educated Chinese, who would teach them to read and write both the classical language, which China's educated elite used in their writings, and the local vernaculars, the multiplicity of which staggered the foreigners.

Because of the necessity that Protestants be able to read the Bible for themselves, many of the nineteenth-century missionaries decided the only way they could educate their potential converts was to render the Chinese dialects into the Latin alphabet. Those who sought to do this were, of course, not linguists, as indeed, linguistics did not yet exist as a formal discipline of study. (In fact, in many parts of the world it was missionaries who first transcribed into written forms the many languages they encountered.) Although the China missionaries were certainly aware that the spoken languages of China were tonal, very few tried to render the tones into their romanized versions of Chinese, making their efforts unintelligible to Chinese listeners who had not been missionary trained.

The Wade-Giles system of romanization, along with the modifications done by the Chinese Post Office, came into widespread use after 1892. (Wade and Giles were both British government officials in China.) Using the Wade-Giles system produced Canton for Guangzhou, Peking for Beijing, Sun Yat-sen for Sun Yixian, Mao Tse-tung for Mao Zedong, and Jehol for

Rehe. Unfortunately, this system denoted the tone of the word by a final consonant, the purpose of which was soon forgotten, resulting in many mispronunciations by foreigners. Of course, a missionary's attempt at romanizing Chinese depended on the sounds in that person's native language, and even the British and the Americans had slightly different romanizations.

Before the missionaries gave up their romanization schemes, much ink had been spilled on their efforts. Many women missionaries proudly reported to home mission boards that they had taught a number of previously illiterate women to read the Bible in a romanized form. Those taught in these systems were only able to read the Bible and the few tracts the missionaries had published in that system; otherwise they were still illiterate in Chinese.

The other problem the Protestants faced, as had the Catholics centuries earlier, was how to render the theological terms of Christianity into Chinese, when the entire concept was foreign and there were no equivalent words to convey ideas. Unfortunately, all the missionaries ended up using theological terms that the Buddhists used. As had the Catholics, the Protestants argued over how to render God into Chinese characters. Like the Catholics, this controversy caused a major split in the Protestant group. Lacking any leader, like the pope, who could ultimately solve the problem, the Protestants quickly devised a solution. Bible translators gave up arguing about the issue, and the printers set their Bibles in Chinese type with the word for God missing. Then as one group or another ordered Bibles from the Shanghai printers, they specified which "god" they wanted, and the appropriate character was inserted and the Bibles printed!

Roman Catholics in the Nineteenth Century

Roman Catholic missionaries also joined the nineteenth-century task of converting the Chinese. The 1860 Treaties of Beijing permitted the teaching of Christianity in China, and allowed foreigners to own land in the country. The Roman Catholics' methods had changed in the centuries since Ricci and they tended to live closer to the Chinese they sought to convert, than did the Protestants, primarily because they had no families to support and because of their vows of poverty. No American orders joined the Roman Catholics in China in the nineteenth century, because the Vatican considered the church in the United States a mission field until 1906. Prior to that time, the only way an American Roman Catholic could go to China as a missionary was to join a European religious order and pray the order sent one to China. The Catholic Foreign Missionary Society of America, better known as the Maryknoll Fathers, was founded in 1911 and was the first American order to send priests to China. They were quickly followed by those who belonged to American branches of the various European religious orders—Jesuits, Dominicans, Franciscans, etc.

Nuns, too, went to China as missionaries, but as many in the nineteenth century lived sheltered lives in cloisters, they had little contact with everyday Chinese life. (This author was once told by a devout Roman Catholic, albeit from Hanoi, that he had seen the face of a cloistered, European, Carmelite nun, the mother superior, only once, when she had sent for him to arrange for the sisters to flee to the south in 1954, even though he had talked to her weekly, throughout his adult life, through a screen.) The nuns in China tended to run orphanages or to teach in schools that had been established in their compounds.

It was unusual to find nuns working outside their convents in the local community.

Becoming a Missionary

Why one became a missionary to China varied with the individual, and whether one was Catholic or Protestant. Each person was likely a fervent practitioner of Christianity, although even this trait did not apply to everyone. Adele Fielde, who worked in Siam and later in China with the American Baptist Missionary Union (ABMU), announced upon her retirement that she would not accept a pension from the mission board, because she had never believed the Baptists' teachings! And Pearl S. Buck recorded that her mother, who had spent all her married life in China, cursed Christianity on her deathbed because of her suffering and the loss of her children in China. (See chapter 5 for short biographies of Fielde and Buck.)

Much was made in the mission movement, and by its supporters at home, of the call missionaries were supposed to have had. Many of the recent scholarly works on Roman Catholic missionaries point to the impact of martyrs of one's particular order as powerful, and effective, recruiters for those who joined the overseas missions. Portraits, and later photographs, of the martyrs were prominently hung in the orders' quarters to remind the residents of their colleagues' sacrifices.

Those Protestant mission boards that required missionaries to send regular reports (some quarterly, some annually) soon found that they had piles of reports that said simply, "Taught at the girls' school in Jinzhou" or "Did evangelization work in Lingzhou district." Roman Catholic priests seem to have done better in their weekly or monthly letters to their home orders, as they tended to describe social and political conditions in their districts. (These archived reports are gold mines of information for scholars of both secular conditions and the work of the missions.)

The impulse for the growth of both Roman Catholic missions and the Protestant evangelistic movement to spread Christianity throughout the world in the nineteenth and early twentieth centuries was closely related to the imperial ventures of the various Western countries in these years. The European colonies in Africa, India, and French Indochina drew missionaries to those places, but it was China, never any Western country's colony, with its vast population, that attracted the most mission agencies and the most missionaries. (Likewise, China attracted a large commercial class bent on selling the Chinese every product the industrialized West could produce, in exchange for the luxury products of China, namely, silk, tea, and porcelain.) Although China was never colonized, the Europeans, but not the United States, claimed great swaths of eastern China as concessions where the foreigners claimed special privileges. The US Open Door policy, which originated in the British Foreign Office before being suggested to the Americans, was an effort to open all the concessions to all trading countries. To the Chinese all foreigners were viewed as exploiting China, even though many Americans long held the belief that the Chinese viewed them differently than they did the Europeans. This erroneous belief caused serious misunderstandings between Americans and Chinese on many occasions.

Board vs. Faith Missionaries

The Protestant missions were divided into two distinct groups: those supported by mission boards at home and those who relied on faith in God to provide for them. The largest of the mission boards, most of which operated throughout the world, were the London Missionary Society (LMS), the Church (of England) Mission Society (CMS), the American Methodist Episcopal Mission (AMEM), the American Southern Baptist Missionary Society (ASBMS), and the APM. In time many of these would have affiliated women's boards, which many historians now cite as the beginnings of the feminization of Christianity in the West. (See chapter 6 for more on the feminization topic.)

The largest of the faith missions was the CIM, which relied on God to provide all its needs. In practice this meant it recruited from among wealthy families in both Britain and America, that is, it accepted those who could fund their own sojourns in China. Of course, some folks without personal funds for support joined the CIM, which then had to find money to support them, which often came irregularly. Thus the CIM was quite unlike the board missions, which financially supported the work of the carefully selected people they sent to China.

Antagonisms sprang up between the two groups with the board missionaries saying that the faith missionaries relied on the board missionaries for their support! Yet, it must be noted that in times of hardship missionaries were generous to their fellow workers. At the time of the Boxer Uprising missionaries of all groups huddled together with diplomats, businessmen, and Chinese converts in the Legation Quarter in Beijing and worked together for their mutual survival.

During World War I when the German missionaries were cut

off from their boards and other benefactors at home, other missions supported the Germans' work. When World War II began in China in 1937, the task of caring for refugees was so great that many missionaries simply banded together, wherever they were, to relieve the suffering, realizing that theological differences were meaningless when bombs were dropping and tens of thousands of refugees were at the door needing food, shelter, and medical care.

In addition to differences between board and faith missionaries, there were differences along nationalistic lines, rather than distinct differences between denominations. In the early twentieth century when Pentecostals, Holiness Christians, Seventh Day Adventists, and Mormons arrived in China, they did form distinct groups that tended to separate themselves along lines of belief, and they had little to do with the missionaries whose agencies had been sending personnel to China for decades. The Fundamentalist-Modernist controversy also drove wedges between and within groups, as did the appearance of indigenous Chinese Christian sects. (See chapter 6 for a discussion of the Fundamentalist-Modernist controversy.)

Being Selected and Sent

There were always exceptions, but, generally, the mainstream Protestant board missions had similar requirements for missionaries. Although some boards accepted only married couples without children, others permitted those with children to go to the mission field. It was generally assumed that the couples would have children on the mission field.

When ordained or medical men became missionaries to China in the early nineteenth century they were required to be married, or at least engaged, to a woman who was willing to support the work of the mission and lend a hand to whatever needed doing. Often this meant taking on a full-time, but always unpaid, job, teaching English in the mission school, if nothing else.

In the early years, even medical doctors were required to be ordained, as their work was seen as converting the heathen, while looking after the health of the missionaries and their families. There was no thought or plan in the early years that mission stations might have clinics or hospitals and treat Chinese—that came later after medical doctors actually arrived in China and saw the need for their services. The issue of medical care for Chinese was resolved at the 1877 All-China Missionary Conference in Shanghai, when the delegates decided medical care was a legitimate part of the work of their missions.

Early in the evangelical Protestant missions' work, more men than women were assigned to the mission, but that soon changed as mission agencies were willing to send single women to the mission, but not single men. The underlying assumption of the male-dominated mission boards was that single women would be able to have full-time jobs and take care of their homes, but single men could never manage such tasks! It was also assumed that women would be less likely to marry local men, whereas men would not be able to resist local women! In fact, both men and women missionaries married Chinese Christians, and the reactions to such marriages ranged from expelling the missionary from service to welcoming the Chinese spouse into the mission community.

Single women who were recruited were, generally, assigned to teach in the mission schools and to work toward the conversion of local women, tasks to which mission boards discovered married women, especially those with growing families, could not do full time. As hospitals and orphanages were organized, some single women worked in them as administrators, doctors, and nurses. Most of the boards that sent single women to the field in the early years denied those same women the right to vote on local mission matters. But by the time of the 1877 Conference, the men who organized the meeting decided that since women's work in China was an essential part of their mission, they would allow three women to speak at the meeting on the issues they faced. This was certainly a great concession to the missionary women, as many of the denominations they represented did not allow women to speak in their home churches.

Accurate statistics are always elusive when discussing China missions, but it is evident there were more women than men on the field. Many married women missionaries died in childbirth, and with the availability of single women, widowers did not remain single for long. (Unfortunately, it is impossible to know if deaths in childbirth were higher among the missionaries than they were in the home countries in these years.) Boards generally accepted Cupid's work among the missionaries, particularly if folks chose to marry within their own denomination, or at least a closely related one. But there were some protests, particularly in the nineteenth century, when say a Congregationalist married a Lutheran without first gaining permission from local colleagues and the board at home.

By the twentieth century, denominationalism in China had faded so far into the background that usually no fuss was made when missionaries married across denominations. Sometimes, courtships happened on the Pacific crossing, and when it did it was customary for the mission the wife was joining (men almost never joined the wife's mission) to reimburse her original board for the cost of her passage.

More than one application for appointment by a mission board contains phrases like "I'm already here," when a newlywed wife was asked why she had selected a certain mission as the place where she wished to serve. Second, even third, wives were common among the Protestant missionaries, but the prize for the most wives certainly belongs to the Reverend E. C. Lord (ABMU), who had six wives while he lived in China. Sometimes women missionaries married into the expatriate business community or into the diplomatic service, but when that happened records about them generally disappear from the mission.

Beginning in the 1890s many American missions required that all those appointed as missionaries be college or university graduates. Some even required that wives have college degrees, although exceptions were sometimes made. The faith missions continued to take anyone who thought they had a call and, preferably, could finance themselves.

Among the board missions in the United States and Britain, the process for becoming a missionary was basically this: a man needed to be ordained or at least studying at a theological seminary when he contacted the board of missions of the church to which he belonged. Boards required some evidence of good health, as it was extremely expensive to send anyone to the far reaches of the globe where mission stations were located. The missionaries needed to be able to physically endure both the trip and the trials of living in a totally different environment than the one at home. This was, of course, long before cultural differences were recognized and called such. Westerners generally made cultural judgments, measuring China against the Western cultures that most missionaries believed were the most advanced and thus the superior ones. (The reader should note that this was the heyday of Social Darwinism, a misguided attempt to apply Darwin's scientific theory to explain the social world, when many theories abounded about the superiority of certain nations and peoples, specifically Western ones. The fact that those supposedly superior people were the least numerous, by far, among the world's population groups, contradicted Darwin's statement that the most fit would be the most numerous, but this was conveniently overlooked by those espousing Social Darwinism.)

Generally, most mission boards asked for a statement of personal beliefs and why the applicant wanted to become a missionary. After the establishment of the Student Volunteer Movement for Foreign Missions (SVMFM), many American college students signed the SVMFM pledge to become a missionary at one of their campus rallies or at their summer conferences. These pledges were then forwarded to the church board of the denomination to which the student indicated he or she was a member. (See chapter 6 for more on the SVMFM.)

The applicant was also asked to provide letters of recommendation, and these generally came from a college president or professor, the minister of the applicant's church, and a longtime friend or perhaps a prominent member of his or her home community. If the applicant were an ordained minister, letters from the president of his theological college or a prominent professor were often submitted. If the person were a medical doctor, letters from the medical college's professors or president were included.

A requirement for all missionaries, which boards could not assess, was their sense of adventure. Even if single women entered mission work because of the few opportunities available to them in their home countries, they still needed to have a sense of adventure, if not outright courage, particularly in the early years of the missionary endeavor. In the days of sail, shipwrecks were fairly common and more than one group headed for China experienced them, particularly if one's ship were caught in the South China Sea during typhoon season. Some missionaries were shipwrecked more than once on the coast of China, before they reached their destinations. It is not hard to understand why they thought God wanted them in China, after such experiences. In the days when communication with folks at home took months, and one needed the board's permission to leave a station, going off into the unknown was not for the timid or faint of heart.

It would be difficult to determine the criteria mission boards used to accept applicants. However, several scholars who have worked extensively in applicants' files conclude that very, very few applicants were rejected, except for medical reasons. The other exceptions were those American men who applied to become missionaries as soon as the draft was instituted in the United States at the time of World War I. At that time, board applications added a question for men requiring them to state their status with their draft boards.

The Presbyterians rejected at least one woman medical doctor who applied to serve in China, because she was Chinese! Judy Tzu-chun Wu's monograph about Margaret Chung, *Doctor Mom Chung and the Fair-Haired Bastards: The Life of a Wartime Celebrity*,[2] states that Chung, a native Californian, was raised by her Presbyterian parents who attended church regularly. At her local church, the young Chung was influenced by the women's missionary society, and decided quite early to

---

2. Judy Tzu-chun Wu, *Doctor Mom Chung and the Fair-Haired Bastards* (Berkeley: University of California Press, 2005).

become a medical doctor so that she might serve in China. Once she obtained her medical degree, she applied to the APM, only to be rejected on the grounds that she was Chinese! After all, the Board recorded, where would she live? It was unthinkable that a Chinese, even one born and educated in the United States, might actually live with the non-Chinese, that is, white American missionary women! One wonders what the APM members would have thought had they known, as Wu writes, that Chung was a lesbian, although letters in the mission board's archives indicate she would not have been the first lesbian to join the mission. (Chung opened a medical practice in San Francisco's Chinatown, and during World War II she entertained crowds of US Navy men of all ranks at her home on Sunday nights. They called themselves "Mom Chung's fair-haired bastards.")

Medical Doctors in the Missions

Medical doctors were always in short supply in the mission field, and board missions did not send anyone to serve in stations where a mission doctor was not in residence. The doctor's first responsibility was to take care of the missionaries. Of course, the doctors quickly discovered that taking care of their colleagues was not a full-time job, hence, the establishment of mission hospitals.

In the case of the APM on Hainan Island, which the author has studied extensively, the board rejected one medical doctor because he was single, he had sent one of his poems with his application, and one of his references termed him "a dreamer." After working with an immigrant community in North Dakota for several years, he was accepted as a mission doctor and sent off to China, finding a wife, who was returning to an AMEM school in India, during the Pacific crossing.

In another case in the same mission, the board was so desperate for doctors at the time of World War I that they took a medical doctor, although his wife had only two years of elementary schooling (recall the qualification for wives was a college degree); his letter from his medical school stated that their records revealed he had attended their school—no one seemed to remember him; and another letter was from the local hardware dealer/undertaker, who wrote he thought the doctor was a Baptist! A note in his file mentioned that he owned the largest home in his community. His wife's health broke down, perhaps in part due to having to share their mission home with another family, and they resigned from the mission in less than a year.

Of even more concern to those on the New York board was their discovery that mission doctors sometimes worked beyond the mission, for money. Haikou, Hainan, had become a treaty port under the unequal treaties China had been forced to sign. Accordingly, the China Imperial Maritime Customs Service, staffed by foreigners, controlled shipping at the port, and their regulations required that a Western medical doctor inspect all coolie ships leaving a Chinese treaty port. (Hainanese men had been going overseas to seek their fortunes, particularly at Penang in present-day Malaysia, for at least a thousand years, so coolie ships frequently called at the port.) As the mission doctor at Haikou was the only one within sixty miles, he was recruited as inspector and the money he earned was placed in the mission treasury.

The mission board at home was astounded to discover this side job of the doctor, but then they were told the doctor also treated members of the British and German diplomatic missions at Haikou. This came to light at the board's offices when the missionaries reported the British diplomats requested their government pay the doctor for his medical services and also purchase him a microscope to thank him for his help. The board at first fumed upon learning this news and demanded the doctor not accept fees from foreigners. Again, they relented when the doctor and his missionary colleagues informed the board that the doctor could not refuse to treat those who came to him for help as he had taken the Hippocratic Oath, and that the patients ordinarily paid as they would have done at home, but in this case the doctor deposited his fees into the general revenue account of his hospital, as he did with fees received from Chinese patients.

One cannot help noting that no one on the mission board at home objected when they learned that one of the ordained men of the Haikou mission had baptized the infant son of one of the British diplomats, but then that was a different matter!

Traveling to China

If one wanted to go to China as a missionary in the early years of the great evangelistic movement, one had to sail on a trading ship, as commercial passenger ships did not yet exist. Missionaries and agencies often prayed for free passage. Unfortunately for the missionaries, all of the ships calling at Guangzhou, the only port opened by the Chinese for foreign trade prior to the Opium War, traded in opium. Arriving in China on an opium ship was a situation that was to plague the missionaries throughout the nineteenth century.

(In fact, the international banking system was invented by the China coast traders when they convinced their London bankers to issue letters of credit, ending the necessity of sending out ships laden with gold and silver.)

After the advent of regularly scheduled steamship service between the United States and China and European ports and China, the trip changed significantly. Missionaries no longer had to rely on the kindness of ships' captains, but now mission boards had to purchase tickets. (Readers are reminded that the Suez Canal, opened in 1869, was built to shorten the trip to Asia, and Matthew Perry went to Japan in 1854 seeking coaling stations for Americans for their new oceanic steamships.) Some transpacific liners had a special rate for missionaries, as did many railroads in the United States. Missionaries always traveled second class, and in 1927 when so many people wanted to avoid the political turmoil in China, some ship companies invented "steerage, second class," that was offered to men only. It offered sleeping accommodations in steerage, but meals in second class.

On coastal or river steamers in China, missionaries had their own etiquette. If a mission couple were occupying the only cabin and another couple or a single woman boarded, the man in the cabin automatically gave his bed to the woman who was boarding. Only on the smallest boats on China's interior rivers did women missionaries sleep on deck, and even some of these boats had a cabin of sorts made of a woven mat.

Mission Finances

It was the task of the churches' mission boards to collect and dispense funds for their missionaries throughout the world. With the increasing professionalism and the adoption of business methods by churches in the 1890s, most boards standardized the methods under which they operated. This coincided with the growth of women's missionary boards in various churches, which frequently were able to collect far more money, through their special collection plate appeals, than were the male-dominated church mission boards.

Mission boards received letters directly from missionaries with requests for funds until early in the twentieth century, when most board missionaries organized committees in China to decide priorities for funding requests. Reading the nineteenth-century letters of the Reverend James Gilmour, the LMS's representative to Mongolia, one can only imagine the discussion the Board members in London had as they considered his request to purchase a camel. His letters detailed the difficulty of hiring camels and drivers, the various sicknesses camels were subject to, and how much each animal could carry. Presumably, there were similar letters from other parts of the world for horses, donkeys, etc.

Requests were also made for stoves to heat houses; boats for river transportation—usually declined in favor of hiring local boats; mosquito nets; screens for houses and other buildings; and on and on, whatever the expatriates needed. The demands on the boards always far exceeded their resources. Though missionaries always referred to the work as "much more valuable that gold," in reality there was never enough money to fulfill the demands.

The question of what missionaries were paid depends upon the time referred to and the mission one wants to cite. Faith missionaries had no set salaries, so it is necessary to eliminate them from this estimate. In the nineteenth century when the Reverend Gilmour was sent to Beijing to open the mission in Mongolia, the LMS paid him a salary fairly close to what a clergyman of a large, urban church in Britain might be paid. Both, of course, had housing provided, and for the missionary, in addition to salary and housing, they received expenses for trips to and within the mission field. In Gilmour's case this was for his yearly trips to Mongolia.

The missionaries also had their medical and dental expenses covered. Some boards paid a lump sum for the missionary going to the field for the first time so they might equip their homes, and, generally, a man's salary was increased following the birth of each of his children. Some boards increased the children's allowances at set ages, and nearly all boards gave grants to pay the missionary children's college expenses. Single women missionaries were given a certain portion of a male missionary's pay—two-thirds was, probably, an average amount.

Salaries for medical doctors were also set by the mission boards, but it seems few doctors were willing to accept the low payments boards offered and, given the difficulty of getting medical doctors to serve in the missions, most negotiated considerably more money for themselves.

Readers will recall that married women were expected to serve the mission, but were never paid salaries. The only exceptions were those women who were widowed on the field and chose to remain in mission work. They were given the salary of a single woman, though they might negotiate for more if children were involved. Some widows were rejected because they had too many children, who were costly for the boards to support.

By the 1930s a guaranteed salary from a mission board was often better than a smaller salary at home. John F. Cady, who was the author's mentor, in 1935 was teaching at a small church college for a salary of sixteen hundred dollars a year, when the college could get it, and faculty were allowed to go through the cafeteria line after the students to take any left-over food home for their families. When asked to go to Burma, in accordance with his SVMFM pledge signed when he was an undergraduate, he was told that the salary was fifteen hundred dollars a year guaranteed, plus passage to Burma, housing, and medical expenses. He agreed immediately, but as a widower he had to find a wife to accompany him, which he readily did. They departed for Burma immediately after their marriage ceremony, and the marriage lasted more than sixty years!

Those missionaries who tried to resign during the 1930s were warned that it was extremely difficult to obtain work in the home countries and that the boards would be unable to assist anyone with job hunting. Obviously, mission boards suffered declines in their revenues in these years and some had to cut missionary salaries, or more commonly, salary increases were not given.

Communication Problems

Trying to communicate with the local population was a major problem for every missionary. The everyday tasks of purchasing food, getting from place to place by any means of transportation, and the multiplicity of daily matters all required talking to Chinese. If missionaries were to make headway in converting the Chinese to Christianity, they needed to learn Chinese. This was the first problem every missionary faced, from the first to arrive in China until the end of the missionary endeavor there. *The Chinese Recorder,* a Protestant nondenominational, monthly periodical issued at Shanghai, in one of its early issues, related the story of a missionary on his way to China whose ship had anchored in the Straits Settlement (roughly the region along the Straits of Malacca). The writer reported that the missionary could not speak with the "half-naked heathen" he saw working on the docks, but wanted to tell them they needed to be "washed in the blood of Christ," so took off his shirt and rubbed it vigorously between his hands. The writer commented, if anyone had seen the good Reverend's actions, that person might have concluded that the man was looking for someone to do his laundry! Such were the common everyday opportunities for miscommunication.

Not only did the missionaries have to learn to read and write Chinese characters, they also had to learn to speak the local dialect which was largely unintelligible to those living in other, distant parts of the country. This was certainly a big reason why missionaries tended to stay in the region where they had first settled. Speaking only a local dialect became a major problem in 1907 when the Protestant All-China Missionary Conference in Shanghai was conducted in Mandarin, a northern dialect soon to become the official language of the country, so that Chinese attendees who knew that dialect might participate. Of course, the missionaries who knew Mandarin understood, as did those who spoke closely related dialects, but some missionaries who had been in China for decades and spoke other dialects needed an interpreter to understand what was being said.

Some missionaries, especially those from the faith missions who had dabbled with Pentecostalism, thought the Holy Spirit would grant them the gift of tongues, or at least the gift of Chinese, once they set foot in China. They soon discovered that the Holy Spirit did not confer knowledge of Chinese, so they set themselves to the difficult task of memorizing characters and attuning their ears to tones. At least one scholar of the missionary movement and charismatic Christianity, Murray Rubinstein, thinks the practice of speaking in tongues originated with the influence of returned China missionaries who had failed to learn Chinese, which they thought were the rambling sounds of some supernatural force.[3]

In the early years of the mission movement, China's Qing dynasty (1644–1911) did not want the Westerners—traders or missionaries—to settle permanently at the warehouses in Guangzhou, so it greatly restricted how long the foreigners could reside there each year. All the foreigners were required to retreat to nearby Macau each summer, once the trading season had ended. The government also strictly forbade the teaching of the Chinese language to foreigners.

Just as sailors had developed a language of the high seas, the Guangzhou traders developed a language they used on the China coast. Pidgin, a corruption of the word "business," is basically a vernacular of Chinese grammatical structure with English words. Over time, China coast pidgin contributed such words as *coolie, catsup,* and *typhoon* to English, along with the phrases "look-see," "chop-chop," and the unforgettable "no tickee, no washee." Eventually, despite the law, a Chinese scholar undertook to teach Chinese to some of the foreigners. It was reported that he always brought a shoe to the lessons and placed it on the table. Should any Chinese official inquire as to what he was doing, he could convincingly reply that he was selling shoes.

Well into the twentieth century, Margaret Moninger of the APM in Hainan wrote home that one of her recently arrived colleagues was trying to deliver his first sermon in the Hainan dialect. The man wanted to tell his listeners that Jesus would hold them safely in his arms, but used the wrong tone and said Jesus would drag them along by a rope looped through holes in the top of the staves of a bucket as a bail. Moninger's only

---

3. Author's conversation with Murray Rubinstein, New York, March, 2010.

comment was "the Chinese will always be better at preaching than foreigners."[4]

Becoming a Christian

Baptism of Chinese was a difficult issue for the missionaries. Some, like the CIM missionaries, baptized anyone who seemed remotely interested in Christianity. For example, Pastor Xi presented many members of local cults to the CIM missionaries, who baptized them. Yet, most of the mainline missions working in China would not baptize any Chinese until they could recite a long catechism designed to explain various concepts of Christianity, such as the Virgin Birth, the Crucifixion, the Resurrection, the Trinity, the Divinity of Jesus, etc. Converts needed to memorize these words, but who could say what anyone understood of them? In fact, becoming a church member in China during the years of the missionary endeavor was much more difficult than becoming a member of most of the Protestant churches at home.

Once a Chinese became a Christian, most missionaries discouraged marriage to non-Christians, although they were, of course, powerless to actually prevent it, particularly where families had pledged children to marriage partners years earlier. Those denominations that practiced infant baptism, baptized the babies of Christian parents. If only one parent were Christian, baptism could still take place, if the other parent did not object.

Several years ago at a professional conference, some scholars of the missionary movement in China began

---

4. Moninger, *Papers*. Of course, such things did not happen only in China. One is reminded of a Czech friend who related the story of a priest, newly arrived in post-Communist Prague from Italy, who at mass one Sunday exhorted his congregation to avoid sin, but used the grossest, most vulgar term possible. The grandmothers gasped, while the teenagers giggled into their prayer books!

discussing what the Chinese converts actually understood of Christianity. Most of the ethnic Chinese, many of whom were Christians, thought most Chinese converts had no real grasp of the nature of Christianity until the third generation of a family had been raised in the faith and daily practiced its beliefs. However, some of the non-Chinese scholars, many of whom were not practicing Christians, thought that at least some of the first converts completely understood the nature of the religion. Alas, this is one of the questions about the missionary enterprise in China, and elsewhere, that will never be answered.

The question itself became further confused during the Communist period after 1949 when it was illegal to teach any religion to any person under the age of eighteen, even though the law was regularly ignored by many Christian families, particularly in the more liberal years of the 1980s and after. It was once said that Christianity had survived in the Soviet Union because its teachings were whispered by grandmas each night into their grandchildren's ears, in the dark, after they had gone to bed, and no government can ever control what grandmas whisper to children in the dark. Perhaps the same was true in China.

Also, in the twentieth century many Chinese called themselves cultural Christians, meaning they followed the Christian ideas of honesty, truthfulness, monogamy, caring for others, etc., but did not necessarily accept any or all aspects of theological Christianity. Whether or not these folks should be called Christians, particularly in statistics, is a difficult issue.

Missionaries' Lives in China

For the missionary in China, and elsewhere, in the late

nineteenth or early twentieth century there was always the question of how to maintain the lifestyles they had had at home, while living in a foreign country. Many missionaries transported furniture including beds, stoves, desks, chests of drawers, tables, chairs, sofas, pianos, and pump organs, with them to China, but by the twentieth century these items were sometimes purchased in Shanghai or Hong Kong.

All China missionaries employed local Chinese to assist them in their houses and with the upkeep of the mission station. For the pioneer missionaries it was essential to hire a Chinese helper to assist in purchasing land, not to mention food for each day. The Chinese assistant also supervised the building of a house for the missionary and later a church, a school, a hospital, and all other buildings the foreigners needed. It was the norm for missionary women to have several household servants to help them maintain their homes. In fact, many missionary women reported that their most difficult times were when they were home on furlough and had no servants, so had to do all the shopping, cooking, cleaning, laundry, etc., as well as taking care of their children. Husbands often spent furloughs traveling to various churches to speak about, and collect funds for, the missions, leaving many wives as single parents.

The Montgomery Ward catalog was a staple in mission homes, and orders were generally placed yearly for those items the missionaries thought they could not do without. Buck, ever the knowing mission child, correctly guessed two single missionaries were about to wed when she saw them studying the Montgomery Ward catalog together![5]

Inevitably, the question arises: "Did the missionaries dress for dinner in the jungle?" The answer is an emphatic "YES."

---

5. Pearl S. Buck, *Fighting Angel: Portrait of a Soul* (New York: John Day, 1936), 156–57.

One China missionary who went out in 1930 explained to the author that while it was extremely difficult to maintain one's lifestyle in China, formal dinners were one way to do it. This was the age when a formal dinner meant men in tuxedos and women in floor-length gowns. Most board mission stations had these dinners on a regular basis, say monthly. Of course, the CIM was an exception.

This writer's mentor, mentioned earlier, was sent to Burma in 1935 to teach European history at Judson College. He once told the author that he wore his wool tuxedo more often in the tropics than he ever had at home. When he left Burma he gave the suit to one of the local Christians, who was more than happy to have it, since he could then dress as a proper Westerner!

At the 1890 All-China Missionary Conference in Shanghai someone noted that perhaps three-fourths of the attendees were wearing Chinese clothing. Of course, the more remote one's mission station, the more likely one was to wear Chinese clothing as few tailors far in the interior were knowledgeable about how to make Western-style clothes and the distance involved made it difficult to obtain clothing from Shanghai or Hong Kong. Those missionaries who served in very remote places were frequently surprised at the fashions they saw when they journeyed to the coast. One commented that in Hong Kong she had been surprised to see foreign women wearing hats as "big as washtubs."[6] Of course, all the representatives of the CIM were wearing their customary Chinese garb.

Later, many missionaries transported their sewing machines with them to China and made many of their own clothes. If they were not able to make their own clothes, and had adopted

---

6. Women's Occidental Board of Foreign Missions, San Francisco, *Annual Report*, 1908–9, 40.

Chinese clothing for everyday use, missionary women were mindful that they needed proper clothing to wear home on furloughs. Rare was the missionary woman who arrived home in any dress that was not many years out of fashion. An unfortunate few had to go home in their Chinese clothing and endure the stares of strangers.

The related question of what the missionaries ate depended on where one lived in China and the mission one belonged to. Faith missionaries, who were more likely to spend their time itinerating, seem to have eaten more Chinese food than did their more settled colleagues. Most mission houses had gardens in their yards where Western vegetables were grown. Since the missionaries were in China before environmentalists were concerned about introducing nonindigenous plants to any area, the Westerners planted seeds from home and, after the Americans established an experimental tropical plant nursery in the Philippines, those in the tropics obtained plants from there.

Even though the missionaries employed Chinese to cook for them, they rarely ate Chinese food. They taught their cooks to produce Western dishes. Thus the missionaries' usual dinner might include fried chicken with mashed potatoes and gravy, along with carrots or green beans. The cook also baked bread and made Western-style desserts, including ice cream, if ice were available. The menus for the missionaries' holiday dinners included all the traditional foods one would have eaten at home even though one had to plan months in advance for the ingredients to be brought in from Shanghai or Hong Kong.

Except in the earliest years of the China mission endeavor, missionaries were sometimes invited to dine in the home of Chinese, where they were treated to various delicacies, which some truly enjoyed. From reading mission letters, the author would guess that Western men in China were far less likely to eat and enjoy Chinese food than were Western women, although the reason for this is unclear. Even though it is not about China, perhaps the best account of these types of cross-cultural culinary adventures is Lizzie Collingham's *Curry: A Tale of Cooks and Conquerors*.[7] A scholarly study of what the British ate in India in the days of the Raj, it is also a hilarious account of various cross-cultural encounters, particularly the attempts to cook Western food in India, and curry in Britain, once the foreigners returned home and began to long for it. To accommodate this need, one enterprising Indian invented and bottled curry powder, specifically for foreigners at home, since Indians ground their own spices each time they cooked and had no use for an already-prepared spice blend. Included in the monograph is an account of how the British convinced the Indians to drink tea, after the British had stolen the tea plants from China, planted them around Darjeeling, and then needed to develop a local market. Foremost, however, it is an account of how the food of the "other" was perceived in the nineteenth century.

Cross-Cultural Ideas and Practices

Western missionaries living in China in the nineteenth and early twentieth centuries constituted the largest, longest-lived, cross-cultural experience the world has ever seen, and no one planned it, much less directed it. To the Chinese the missionaries not only introduced a Western religion, but daily demonstrated, to those with whom they had contact, a totally different way of family life, housing, and childrearing, as well

---

7. Lizzie Collingham, *Curry: A Tale of Cooks and Conquerors* (Oxford: Oxford University Press, 2007).

as Western science, mathematics, medicine, government, philosophy, etc. They taught the promise of a better life in Heaven, after death, for Christians, and yet were astounded when, in the mid-twentieth century, many Chinese decided they preferred the better life the Chinese Communist Party (CCP) promised for everyone here and now.

John King Fairbank, and other scholars, tried to explain the mission movement in China by suggesting that Americans would have a better understanding of the view of the Chinese toward missionaries if they could imagine the American reaction to a similar series of events in the United States. What if, about 1850, hundreds of Chinese had arrived at New Orleans, fought a war with the Americans and, having won, extracted all kinds of privileges in their treaty settlements? As a result the Chinese then took great chunks of New Orleans and began to govern that area, requiring everyone there to live under Chinese laws. Then the Chinese ventured up the Mississippi and all its tributaries, settling in any town or city they chose, and constructing buildings that did not blend in with those of the area. These Chinese preached Buddhism or the Confucian tradition on the highways and byways while claiming that the American social system had no value and needed to be replaced with a system like China's. Next, these Chinese opened schools, recruited young Americans to them, and taught foreign subjects and Chinese. They also established Chinese-style hospitals, claiming that American medical practices were superstitious and backward. As a result of all this, the Chinese managed to convert a number of Americans to their teachings, thus alienating them from the mainstream of American society.

Missionaries Change Their Home Countries

The contributions of the Protestant China missionaries to Western countries also radically altered those cultures. The missionaries produced the first Chinese-English dictionaries, along with primers for learning Chinese. They introduced knowledge of Chinese culture to Westerners, and some of the more scholarly missionaries wrote the first academic accounts of China's history and culture. As missionaries learned about the social structure of the Chinese and the role of Confucius in it, along with Chinese traditional religious beliefs, as well as Buddhism and Daoism, they transmitted this information to the West. Some missionaries who returned home introduced the academic study of China both to great universities and to tiny Bible colleges.

Perhaps one of the more unusual cross-cultural interchanges was identified by the British Museum. In a 1980s exhibit on Chinese ivory, the curators contended that the missionaries introduced pornographic ivory carvings to the Chinese, who misunderstood the use of the naked baby Jesus in the manger!

Pistol-Packing Mamas and Papas

China during the late Qing dynasty and particularly in the republican period often suffered episodes of unrest and lawlessness. Westerners bound for China in the nineteenth and twentieth centuries often took firearms with them, particularly after the Taiping Rebellion, during which guns had flooded into China from the Western countries, especially after the Crimean and the American Civil Wars. Some American diplomatic personnel actually advised missionaries to take guns with them to China for their protection.

Exactly how each missionary made the decision to include a weapon in his or her luggage is impossible to say. The author cites several cases of the APM on Hainan Island in the hope that as a mainline American church its mission might be typical of others in China.

The Reverend Frank P. Gilman, the first ordained man to serve on the island, had a shotgun that he often referred to in his letters and diaries. He and his Chinese assistant took turns carrying it while itinerating, and they sometimes used it to shoot birds for dinner.

One of the earliest single women to serve in Hainan, Katherine Schaeffer, who spent her adult life in the mission, also had a shotgun. Moninger, a teacher who sometimes lived with Schaeffer, reported to her family at home that they had been robbed one night. Although the women did lose a few things, including Moninger's extra pair of glasses, Schaeffer dealt with the situation by firing her shotgun off the second-floor balcony of their house to scare off the thieves.

One of the missionary children, the Reverend Robert Thomas, told this author that his father had been advised by the US Department of State to take a gun with him to China. He did, but he kept it in the station's safe which was in a building across the road from their home!

Mrs. Margaret Melrose, who had been widowed in 1898 a few years after arriving in Hainan, carried on her work as a single woman for more than thirty years, having taken her two young sons home to be raised by relatives in Iowa. Melrose's son Paul and his wife later joined the mission. According to Paul's daughter, Margaret's granddaughter, Sylvia, her grandmother not only carried a pistol on her itinerating trips, she regularly demonstrated that she knew how to use it, after an incident.

On one itinerating trip Mother Melrose and her Chinese

assistant planned to stay a night at a Chinese inn where everyone slept in one room, or if lucky, in a separate room that offered some privacy. After retiring for the night Mother Melrose heard several Chinese men, in the adjoining room, making plans to rob her. She leapt to her feet, announced in the Hainan dialect that she had a gun, and asked if the men wanted a demonstration of her ability to use it. According to Sylvia, after that incident whenever her grandmother went itinerating, accompanied always by some Chinese who worked for the mission, they adopted the practice of finding their nighttime accommodations, then Mother Melrose would go outside, line up a series of rocks at a considerable distance and take target practice. She was so expert at hitting the rocks that she and her assistants were never bothered by brigands! However much this image of a sixtyish, kindly missionary woman emptying her Colt .45 at rocks before retiring for the night goes against the picture most Westerners have of missionaries, others who served or grew up in that mission all say this is an accurate account.

Other missionaries also had guns. One CIM missionary son told the author that he was not sure his father ever converted anyone to Christianity, but he did do a lot of hunting, which he greatly enjoyed. A Methodist missionary in a mountainous location gained local fame when he shot a tiger that had been bothering a village. And, the Tianjin Incident in 1870 was provoked when a German diplomat fired his gun into a crowd, demonstrating that at least some diplomats too had guns.

Missionary Children

Many of the missionary children, although they grew up in walled mission compounds were nevertheless, more exposed to another culture than were their contemporaries at home. In adulthood many of the missionary children were considerably more liberal than their parents and many came home to lead liberal causes, while a few others were famous for their conservative ideas. In the latter category was Henry Luce, who grew up in Shandong, and returned to the United States to found *Time, Life*, and *Fortune*, and become a big supporter of Jiang Jishi and the Nationalists during World War II and the Chinese Civil War. The more liberal of the missionary children included Buck, certainly one of the best-known of the China mission children. John (Jack) Stewart Service and John Paton Davies were also well-known missionary children, because they were blamed by US Sen. Joseph McCarthy for "losing China," after 1949. Service was the author of *Golden Inches* about his family in Sichuan, and he is the subject of Lynne Joiner's book, *Honorable Survivor: Mao's China, McCarthy's America and the Persecution of John S. Service*.[8]

For memories of a China childhood no one can equal John Espey's outrageously hilarious account, *Minor Heresies, Major Departures: A China Mission Boyhood*.[9] Espey reports that he and his sister were the only mission children at an APM compound in Shanghai. This was surely an unusual situation, especially for an APM compound in a large city, as it was one of the biggest of the missions working in China. Typically, three or four families with children lived in the compounds of the larger missions. These children, in effect, became de facto cousins maintaining their relationships the rest of their lives, in many cases.

---

8. John S. Service, *Golden Inches: The China Memoir of Grace Service* (Berkeley: University of California Press, 1989); and Lynne Joiner, *Honorable Survivor: Mao's China, McCarthy's America and the Persecution of John S. Service* (Annapolis, MD: Naval Institute Press, 2009).
9. John Espey, *Minor Heresies, Major Departures: A China Mission Boyhood* (Berkeley: University of California Press, 1994).

Some families, of course, tried sending their young children to the mission kindergarten or elementary school so that they could learn the local dialect, sometimes with unexpected results. Espey relates that he and his sister learned a Mandarin Christmas song at the mission's Chinese kindergarten. As they sang "Gau lei tzu mei li jen loo mung" their mother howled with laughter, and finally convinced them they were not singing in Mandarin, but rather singing "God Rest Ye Merry, Gentlemen" in English as their Chinese teacher had heard it!

In his chapter *Le Scouting en Chine*, Espey describes being a Boy Scout in early twentieth-century China. When the boys went on a camping trip, their coolies did all the work—carrying the boys' backpacks, pitching tents, cooking, etc. None of the Scouts even tried to earn the camping badge. Later, while attending the mission school at Guling, Espey and his fellow Scouts worked as message runners for Jiang Jishi, who was visiting the resort, although generally, there were no messages for them carry. However, one day on a path he met a man in a Russian military uniform and greeted him as "Mr. Borodin." The man smiled, but only later did Espey realize that a better greeting might have been "Comrade." (Mikhail Borodin [1884–1951], the Comintern agent in China, was a Russian Jew by birth who migrated to the United States, attended the Lutheran Valparaiso University in Indiana, and worked at Jane Addams' Hull House before becoming Russia's Comintern agent in China in the 1920s.)[10]

Espey also reveals the hierarchy of the various Protestant churches, as established by the mission children, as well as living with a collection of single women missionaries, his Courtesy Aunts, and all their eccentricities.[11]

---

10. Jonathan Spence, *The Search for Modern China* (New York: Norton, 1990), 337.
11. Espey, *Minor Heresies, Major Departures*, 36–37, 116, 181, 227.

Very young children were the easiest to care for because a Chinese amah could be employed, at a low sum, to take charge of them. As children reached school age, the need for education was solved in various ways. Many American families relied on the curriculum of the Calvert School in Baltimore, which provided everything the child needed to have an American education, at home. The social life of mission children was fulfilled by the other children, both foreign and Chinese, on the compound.

Scholars who have worked in the mission archives have encountered cases of "missionary divorce." These were situations where the wife returned home with her children "to attend to the children's education." In some of these families the wife remained at home even after the children enrolled in college. Alvyn Austin called the unhappy marriages among CIM members the "deepest, darkest family secret." As soon as two people became engaged it was Taylor's policy to send them to separate stations, so the couple hardly knew each other at the time of their marriage. As soon as the children were old enough for school, many mothers and children departed for home.[12]

Many of the American denominations ran colleges in the United States, and mission children often attended them. Some, like the Presbyterian Wooster College in Ohio, even had local homes that boarded mission children while in high school so that they might have something of an American education before attending college. Some missionary children attended Yale, Stanford, and Harvard, suggesting their home schooling in China or education at the mission boarding schools was

---

12. Alvyn J. Austin, *China's Millions: The China Inland Mission and Late Qing Society, 1832-1905* (Grand Rapids, MI: Eerdmans, 2007), 233.

comparable to what their contemporaries in the United States had received.

In the twentieth century the missionaries established two American-style boarding schools in China, both co-ed: the Shanghai American School (SAS) and the Guling School. SAS was the larger and better-known school and it accepted non-mission children. Some of the SAS alumni remember Borodin's two sons attending the school. They always ate lunch together and never associated with the other students.

During the nineteenth century, the CIM established a boarding school for the children of its members at Zhifu, Shandong. Although it was co-ed, boys and girls were strictly segregated. The school was organized along the lines of a British boarding school and was not concerned with advanced education for its alumni.

The CIM: Interdenominational and Eccentric

Any discussion of the Protestant missionary movement in China would be incomplete without some attention to the CIM. The biggest of the faith missions, it was destined to be the largest mission operating in China. It was reported that the CIM had as many missionaries in China as all the other organizations put together, but given the secrecy that characterized the CIM, it is impossible to confirm this claim.

The CIM was founded by Taylor, a Yorkshireman who had been influenced by the Methodists of his family and various groups of Brethren and Quakers in England. Taylor decided he had a call to China and sought to join the Chinese Evangelization Society (CES), which had been founded by the independent Pomeranian missionary, Karl Gutzlaff, in 1850.

Gutzlaff published Christian tracts in Chinese characters and hired local men to travel to the interior distributing them. Although this was the first attempt at the indigenization of the mission work, the CES and Gutzlaff's methods were discredited when it was discovered that the men he employed had not distributed their tracts anywhere; instead they had accepted their salaries and discarded the literature.

Taylor was a highly secretive, eccentric Britisher with little education, but a desire to convert Chinese to Christianity. On his first trip to China, he decided that Gutzlaff's CES was doomed because it was led, in Taylor's words, "by businessmen," so Taylor decided not to join it. While in China Taylor married his first wife, Maria Dyer, who was reputed to be the richest woman on the China coast. (After bearing nine children, she died in China in 1870.)

Returning to Britain, Taylor began to study medicine, supported by one of his many benefactors. They thought medicine would be a way of reaching Chinese with the gospel message. Despite being in poor health during the five years Taylor spent in London, he completed his medical studies and was ordained. He never gave up his plan for a mission in China and in 1865, following a vision he experienced while visiting Brighton, he actively began working toward his goal.

The CIM was the result, and its principles set forth by Taylor were: no solicitation of funds or missionaries; no guaranteed salary; no debt; faith in God alone to supply one's needs; and nondenominational in membership. These guiding principles appeared in every issue of the CIM's publication, *China's Millions*. Taylor was fortunate that early in his quest to start a mission in China he gained the support of the Guinness family. Yes, *that* Guinness family. Missionaries tended to be teetotalers, so this support was unusual. Perhaps Taylor did not object to the making of ale, or maybe he did not consider it as bad as hard liquor. One member of the Guinness family, Geraldine, married Taylor's son and worked with him on publishing books about the CIM's work.

China's Millions, Alvyn Austin's excellent study of the CIM and its work, primarily in Shanxi, states that Taylor's principles meant that nothing appeared in the CIM archives concerning funds and denominational issues.[13] Indeed, dissension within the CIM was so widespread by the 1890s that Taylor instructed his son Howard and daughter-in-law Geraldine, who were just finishing up an official history of the CIM, to purge the archives of any materials that did not conform to what they had written. As a result of this secrecy and the purging of the archives, historians view the CIM records, periodicals, and histories with the utmost caution.

As soon as the first CIM volunteers came forward, it became obvious they would not be a harmonious group: Anglicans and Dissenters argued over baptism, communion, and church government; Quakers and Brethren differed with other sects over all sacraments; premillennialists argued with postmillennialists; and those pious souls who gave up jobs as printers or carpenters or farmers to save the heathen Chinese were looked down upon as illiterate bumpkins by the university graduates fluent in Greek and Latin, who also were off to convert the Chinese. Likewise, British diplomats in China, all of whom were from the ranks of the upper classes at home, voiced their opposition to having the CIM's "illiterates" trying to convert the Chinese.

The first CIM group of thirty volunteers argued all the way to China over every possible subject, including, according to Austin, a pair of stockings. Taylor baptized several of his helpers who had decided that their earlier baptisms were not

---

13. Austin, *China's Millions,* 16.

valid, performing the rites while in Java to avoid criticism of the Anglican missionaries they would later need to work with in China. The extremely quarrelsome journey ended with their ship being caught in several typhoons in the South China Sea. That they arrived in China with no deaths nor serious injuries or illness was itself something of a miracle![14]

Taylor feared that if the dissension among his "helpers," as he called them, became known to his supporters in Britain, contributions would cease. As Taylor was the sole head of the organization, he decreed that nothing negative about the CIM would ever appear in word or print in Britain. In this he became the forerunner of twentieth-century spin doctors, cleverly changing any negative into a positive before releasing the news to the public.

Usually the faith missions, and particularly the CIM, insisted that their missionaries live as close to the local lifestyle as possible. One of the issues the early CIM missionaries argued about was whether or not they should wear Chinese clothes. Even Taylor's wife opposed her husband on this issue, donning a Chinese outfit only at the specific request of her husband in order to be a model for the other women sailing with the first CIM group to China. Mrs. Taylor thought that Western clothes set Western women apart from their Chinese sisters, whom she knew were not highly regarded by the men of their society. Even some members of the British diplomat community thought it best that Western women wear Western dress. But Taylor's view became a CIM requirement: among the Westerners in China his missionaries were distinct by the clothing they wore. No other mission had such requirements. Nevertheless, even CIM missionaries eventually set up houses

---

14. Austin, *China's Millions*, 114.

with Western furniture, where they ate Western food; it was simply too much for Taylor to control what his helpers ate.

For Taylor, anyone who felt "the call" was acceptable to his mission, especially if they could find funds to support their work. He was not concerned with education for his missionaries and many had little formal education.

Because of the secretive nature of the CIM and Taylor's reluctance to reveal much of the workings of his mission to the public, scholars know very little about this largest of the missions in China. Austin relates that once *China's Millions* published the account of an incident that had actually happened two years earlier! With this kind of secrecy, we do not know how the CIM transmitted funds, but the best guess is through one of the international banks with an office in Shanghai. Taylor was known to have had a bank account in London, but of course, he alone knew how much was in it and he reported to no one.

The CIM was also the only mission ever to have its headquarters in China, although they did have an office in London, and later ones in Canada and the United States. In fact, the CIM headquarters was anywhere Taylor happened to be. Taylor ran his mission almost single-handedly, and drew recruits from all conservative church groups. Denominationalism meant little, if anything, to Taylor, although he did subscribe to a fundamentalist view of Christianity and eventually withdrew from the Church of Christ in China, an all-China body that had formed out of the mission conferences.

Austin details the early years of the CIM that were fraught with arguments over the issues of wearing Chinese clothing and eating Chinese food, to disagreements about theological beliefs and methods of missionary work. The CMS missionary, the Reverend George Moule, opposed Taylor because of the baptisms Taylor had performed in Java, and he was particularly outraged that Taylor and his wife housed the single women missionaries in their home. Moule felt that practice gave Chinese the wrong impression, as all missionaries opposed concubinage.

Taylor's ideas about what he and his mission could do in China promptly involved him in a diplomatic dispute. Possessing both letters from the local Chinese official and directions from the British Minister in Beijing, Taylor attempted to establish the CIM in the city of Yangzhou in the summer of 1868. Unfortunately, the local folk opposed the missionaries in their city, and a mob, estimated to be as large as ten thousand, attacked the missionaries.

The local magistrate knew that the ringleaders were community leaders, and therefore had no desire to oppose them. The situation was further complicated by the fact that one of China's leading statesman, Zeng Guofan, who vigorously had opposed the Taiping, was governor-general of three provinces, including Jiangsu where Yangzhou was located. Zeng was strongly anti-Christian and local officials had no wish to antagonize him.

Taylor and the CIM members fled to Shanghai where they reported the incident to the British consul, asking that their extraterritoriality privileges be enforced. As a result, a British gunboat with a detachment of marines was dispatched to Yangzhou, the issue was discussed in Parliament where opinion was divided over whether missionaries should precede or follow the flag, and Taylor became even more secretive about the CIM.

Communications between Shanghai and London were slow, but Taylor never told his home representative exactly what had happened, leaving that man to deal on his own with criticism from CIM supporters. The incident made Taylor decide that whenever his missionaries were persecuted they should not seek help from Chinese officials nor should they appeal to their diplomatic representatives, even in the event of the death of CIM missionaries.

Unlike board missions, which generally offered their missionaries an expense-paid furlough every seven to ten years, the CIM had no furlough policy; funds were sought to convert the Chinese, not to finance missionaries' visits to their families. Later on, CIM workers were given a paid furlough every ten years. However, many CIM missionaries, like Evangeline and Francesca French and Mildred Cable, financed their own work in China, so the CIM could hardly refuse them furloughs whenever they wanted to return home. (See chapter 5 for short biographies of the three women.)

Because it was an interdenominational, faith mission, the CIM tended to accept anyone who wanted to go to China to save the heathen. It does not appear that the CIM ever required letters of recommendation, as church-related board missions did. The CIM policy of accepting anyone with a desire to be a missionary resulted, over the years, in the mission including more than a few in their ranks who would have been rejected by other missions on the grounds of mental instability!

Austin reported that there were three known suicides in the CIM, but none of them were recorded in the CIM archives or reported in *China's Millions*.[15] Because of the CIM's secrecy, no one knows how many suicides the group suffered. One of the few accounts of a CIM suicide, from an outsider in China, was that of Eva Jane Price, American Board of Commissioners for Foreign Missions (ABCFM) whose letters from Shanxi in the period leading up to the Boxer Uprising are one of the best

---

15. Austin, *China's Millions*, 277.

of the contemporary accounts.[16] Price noted that she often entertained CIM folks in her home, and they told her it was one of the only places in China where they felt welcome. She had known Sara Seed Russell, one of the CIM suicides, and commented that she thought Russell would not have had a nervous breakdown and taken her own life had the CIM "thought it their duty to live in more comfort."[17]

The CIM did require that those going to China have an interview with mission personnel in London. In fact, some people identified as CIM missionaries had only very tenuous links to the organization, but rather financed themselves in China and largely did as they wished while there. Because the CIM members had no common core beliefs, there were many arguments over what to teach the Chinese, and many missionaries resigned from the organization. Austin states that more than fifty people resigned from the CIM in Shanxi in a fourteen-year period in the 1880s and 1890s, largely over doctrinal differences. Other people simply could not tolerate Taylor's dictatorial methods, which extended to prohibiting a marriage on at least one occasion, and the lack of a regular salary.[18]

Shanxi, where the CIM concentrated its early work, had been devastated by a famine in the 1870s, and following it, many farmers planted opium because it was a quick-growing cash crop. Chinese estimated that 80 per cent of the province's population was addicted to opium. According to Austin, some villagers remarked that "eleven out of every ten people were addicted." One CIM missionary noted that Shanxi with its "opium drugged" population was the most difficult place in the

---

16. Eva Jane Price, *China Journal, 1889-1900: An American Missionary Family During the Boxer Rebellion* (New York: Scribner, 1989), 108, 110.
17. Price, *China Journal*, 60.
18. Austin, *China's Millions*, 272-73.

world to try to make converts, while another commented that it was like trying to convert drunkards.[19]

During its beginnings in Shanxi the CIM had close contact with opium addicts, some of whom became converts. This was the result of the missionaries coming into contact with the leader of a Chinese indigenous cult, who practiced exorcism, and was also an opium addict. Known as Pastor Xi, he took the name Shengmo (Overcomer of Demons) after he claimed to have been converted and cured of his addiction to opium. Xi had at most two months' contact with the CIM missionary David Hill, as Xi was known to thoroughly dislike the foreigners and preferred to work by himself.

Xi read the Bible on his own and devised his own explanations of it. For example, he had grown both tobacco and opium until he decided they were evil. He also adopted a kosher diet, which was not unknown in the part of Shanxi where he lived, as it was home to many Muslims. Xi carefully studied the treaty rights foreigners held in China and after one village dispute he took his complaints to the local governor, claiming that Chinese Christians were protected under the unequal provisions of the international treaties, because they were followers of a foreign religion. This was to cause much misunderstanding and confusion in the future, and the idea appalled the foreign diplomats in China who did not know what to make of such a claim. As a result of such claims the Chinese government stripped Xi of the Confucian degree he had earned in the government examinations, but after protests in which Xi enlisted the help of the British missionary, the Reverend Timothy Richard, Baptist Missionary Society (BMS), the degree was reinstated. Apparently, the local official

---

19. Austin, *China's Millions*, 174, 270. He quotes Mrs. Howard Taylor's *Pastor Xi* for the comment "eleven out of every ten."

decided Xi, who stayed mostly to his tiny village, was not teaching the heterodox ideas of the Taiping, and was therefore fairly harmless.

Austin states that Mrs. Geraldine Taylor's biography of Pastor Xi is the first attempt by a Westerner to explain Chinese exorcism for a Western lay audience. While Mrs. Taylor mentioned that CIM missionaries had witnessed exorcisms, and some even participated in them, most missionaries were afraid to reveal to other Westerners that they had been a part of such rites. Austin relates that one Chinese pastor working with the CIM explained that there were no demons in the West, because the Christians had been casting them out for two thousand years, with the result that they had all settled in China!

Scholars now think the ritual of casting out demons was practiced more among farmers than those the missionaries came into contact with in small towns. There is also the possibility that inquirers and converts did not wish to mention this practice, which was widespread throughout China, to the missionaries.

Pastor Xi famously cured several women, including his second wife, of demon possession by exorcism and when his power became known his fame increased. His home was quite far from the CIM mission station, and, about two years after converting to Christianity, he established his own Gospel Hall or Hall of Happy News, on his own land. The CIM missionaries were skeptical of his actions and soon split into pro- and anti-Pastor Xi groups. Xi then moved into the business of opium cures, which many missionaries had been trying to perfect in order to aid Chinese addicts. Xi's red pills came in three different doses: Life-Emparting, Life-Establishing, and Health-Restoring, and most probably contained some derivative of opium. Xi's followers grew in number, and he eventually had at least forty opium shops dispensing his pills.

Unfortunately for Xi, another man challenged him for leadership of the sect. The CIM records refer to this man only as Mr. Fan. He lived perhaps twenty miles from Xi and was a leader of the Secret Religion, a sect that practiced vegetarianism, idol worship, and had a series of daily devotions that members were expected to follow. Eventually, some of the CIM missionaries decided to work with Xi while others chose Fan, but not before they held a mass baptism of two hundred fourteen people. Several years later they had to report that most of those baptized had disappeared, had become backsliders, or had resumed their opium habits.

Around 1879, the CIM women in Shanxi began using a wordless book of colored cloth—black, red, white, and yellow, to "gossip the Gospel" as they sewed with Chinese women. Austin notes that it was in Shanxi, five thousand years earlier, that the five colors (*wuxing*) of the Chinese cosmology had been developed. The CIM's wordless book was invented in 1866 in Britain by Charles Spurgeon as a means of converting children to Christianity. It is uncertain if the CIM women knew that the colors they were using were an important part of Chinese cosmology and that each color had a special meaning. The foreign women also used their fingers to teach Chinese what they needed to know of Christianity. Similar efforts were being used at the same time by missionaries in Africa.[20]

As the CIM recruited new members, Taylor decided to stir up some publicity by sending to China seven recruits, who had attended Cambridge University together. Upon reaching China, three of these men went on a long trip in Shanxi and Sichuan while praying that the Holy Spirit would give them the

---

20. Austin, *China's Millions*, 270.

gift of tongues in the form of Chinese. (Pentecostalism among the CIM eventually caused Taylor to expel those who practiced it.) Others of the group went to Beijing for two months and spent their time praying and planning for their work, never once visiting any of the city's great sites.[21]

After the experiences of those who tried to learn Chinese through the Holy Spirit, Taylor decided he needed formal language classes for his new recruits. F. W. Baller (CIM), who was skilled at languages, created a six-year language course that was required for all CIM people arriving in China. In time the CIM established a language school for women at Yangzhou and one for men at Anjing. CIM people were soon known to be the most linguistically skilled of all the missionaries, and Baller's course was eventually used by many mission societies as well as by nonmissionaries.

Common Ignorance of China and Its Culture

It was not only the CIM missionaries who were ignorant of China and its culture. Few, if any, mission boards prepared their people for life in China. One Presbyterian missionary told this author that she had graduated from a church-related college and her husband had also been to theological seminary after college, but it was only on board a ship bound for China in 1930 that they first learned of Buddhism. A returning missionary on board loaned them a book on the belief, which many Chinese subscribed to. The woman also told the author she had not known that China was ruled by a dynasty until 1911, or that it was then struggling to find a method to rule its people.

In addition, most missionaries did not understand the

---

21. Austin, *China's Millions*, 222.

Chinese cultural requirement that one have a son to carry on the family name and that sons, whoever their mothers were, were always accommodated into the patriarchal family. Missionaries, and other foreigners, could rarely distinguish between secondary wives or concubines, and women slaves who resided in a family's house. In particular, they did not comprehend why all the children called the first wife "mother" regardless of which woman had given birth to them.

It was many years before the missionaries recognized that for a Chinese, becoming a Christian meant one became an outsider in most families and, thus, had no claim on the family for housing, land, food, etc. It was for this reason that secondary wives and slaves who wanted to escape their roles or those who had already left their homes were easier than others to convert. The mission might offer these women a place to live, and possibly, a position as a mission employee. If one were skilled in learning what the foreigners were teaching, a place as a Bible woman was a possibility. Such women would undoubtedly have considered attending church services, where one could sit quietly a few hours a week, a reasonable exchange for escape from an abusive husband or family. The widespread use of Bible women in the China missions was one of the bases for the feminization of Christianity, which is dealt with in chapter 6.

Conclusion

Clearly, the missionaries in China in the nineteenth and early twentieth centuries understood little about the history and culture of the country in which they lived, and many things that they did understand they denounced as contrary to

Christian teaching. Though converting Chinese to Christianity was not an easy task, many persevered.

Most of the missionaries gradually came to their own understanding of China, but some, of course, never saw anything noteworthy or good in the culture. Those who understood something of China often transmitted what they knew to people at home, but what they told others was colored by the missionaries' own cultural value judgments and by their acceptance or rejection of what they saw in China and its people.

3

Sociopolitical

Protestant missionaries in the early nineteenth century had difficulties deciding how they would explain Christianity to the Chinese and how they would translate certain key Christian words into Chinese, just as the Jesuits had had in earlier centuries.

The Protestants also had to decide who they should target for their conversion efforts. Because of the basic Christian teaching of the equality of all in the eyes of God, one's social status, theoretically, should not have concerned the missionaries. However, for the Protestants it was crucial that their converts be able to read the Bible for themselves, so they hoped to convert people who were literate. Unfortunately, literate inquirers and converts were few and far between.

Learning to communicate in Chinese is never easy and China in the early nineteenth century had no national language. The educated elite wrote in Classical Chinese which, was unintelligible to those who were not schooled in it, but like everyone else the elites spoke the dialects of their home provinces. Writing in the vernacular was not widespread until the modernization movements in the early twentieth century.

For the reader unfamiliar with the Chinese language, there is only one written language, but a multiplicity of regional dialects. Thus for two literate Chinese, one who speaks and understands only the Yunnan dialect and the other who speaks and understands only the Shandong dialect, writing whatever they want to tell each other is the only way to communicate. After the 1949 Revolution the Chinese government legalized a form of shorthand, by which extremely complicated characters are rendered in fewer strokes as are very common words. The government also required that all education be in Mandarin, which means the dialect problem is no longer as big an issue as it was previously.

The question of who in China was literate in the premodern era has taxed many scholars. Most current thinking puts the rate probably close to those in Western countries. Government and clan schools for the education of boys were widespread throughout China. They were studying to one day take the Confucian examinations, which were abolished in 1906. The examination system began at the local level, and those passing had certain privileges, but were not automatically appointed to office. It was common for men passing this level of the examinations, which gave them the title *shengyuan*, to work for someone, most likely a relative or close friend who already had a government job, to learn how the government operated. Men who passed the first level of the examinations could take the second level at the provincial level. If successful they were designated *juren*, and could then try the top examinations, at the national level. Those passing at the national level were designated *jinshi*. The man who came in first at the national level had his name publicized throughout the empire and received an immediate posting. When the various titles were used, following a scholar's name, it was customary to note the person's age when he had passed the examinations. There were many subgroupings of these classifications of ranks, and over the years the number of scholars increased markedly.

Benjamin A. Elman estimated that in 1400 (Ming dynasty), when China's population was perhaps sixty-five million, there were about thirty thousand *shengyuan* degree holders or one for every two thousand two hundred people, but by 1700 (Qing dynasty) when the population was perhaps one hundred fifty million, there were half a million *shengyuan* degree holders or one for every three hundred people. He also estimated the odds for passing all three levels of the examinations were only one in six thousand.[1]

As very few men were intelligent and skilled enough in the memorization necessary to succeed at the examinations, there were thousands of men who yearly dropped out of the schools, but who were literate enough to manage the finances of great households or clans, or to operate businesses ranging from mining, salt processing, and distribution, to engineering and banking, etc. In the premodern period, some Chinese women, usually from elite families, were also literate, having been taught at home along with their brothers.

After the Protestants arrived they endeavored to reach as many Chinese as possible, at all levels of society, as is evidenced by just a few of the organizations they started, including the Society for the Diffusion of Christian and

---

1. Benjamin A. Elman, "Changes in Confucian Civil Service Examinations from the Ming to the Ch'ing Dynasty," in *Education and Society in Late Imperial China, 1600-1900*, ed. Benjamin A. Elman and Alexander Woodside (Berkeley: University of California Press, 1994), 117.

Scientific Knowledge, the Society for the Diffusion of Christian and General Knowledge Among the Chinese, the Society for Female Education in China and the East, the Mission to Buddhists, the Mission to Deep Sea Fishermen, the Mission to Lepers, the Mission to the Chinese Blind, the Mission to Ricksha Coolies in Shanghai, and the International Postal Telegraph Christian Association. The work of these groups was in addition to the day-to-day evangelistic work the missionaries did in the places they lived and operated schools and hospitals, along with their churches.

The missionaries who lived at established stations generally had contact only with a limited number of local folks who lived nearby or frequented the station and those who worked for the mission or the missionaries. Some missionaries, of course, practiced street evangelization and they had various methods of attracting crowds to hear their messages. The musically talented played trumpets or other Western instruments, while others sang hymns, to gather an audience.

Interestingly, the Protestants attracted to their compounds both the outcasts and the elites of the society. Each group saw something they needed in the foreigners' mission compounds and used them to improve their lots in life. In any society there are always some people who have fallen to the lowest level of the social strata. In China such people were usually, but not exclusively, women. Girls could become outcasts at birth if the family felt it could not afford to support them, and consequently gave them away, sold them as slaves, or committed female infanticide. Many missionaries found themselves the caretakers of such girls. If the compound ran an orphanage, the girls lived there, but few mission compounds had orphanages and it was more likely that an infant was cared for by a mission family or by one of their servants. If a family could not support an older girl she might be sold to a wealthier family as a concubine or as a slave, and sometimes the missionaries took in such girls.

Some girls were sold to brothels, such as Lalu Nathoy, later Polly Bemis (1853–1933), whose life in China and Idaho is the subject of Ruthanne Lum McCunn's *Thousand Pieces of Gold*.[2] The presence of Chinese women in gold camps in the American West in the late nineteenth century was fairly common, as evidenced by the poignant gravestone found in Tombstone, Arizona's boot hill—"China Mary, Born in China, Died in Tombstone." One can only wonder at the life between those statements. In the case of Bemis, she survived to become one of the longtime, highly respected members of her community, but countless others lived out their lives as "China Mary" or "China Polly," unknown by any other names.

Elite Chinese, such as those in Judith Liu's *Foreign Exchange*,[3] saw the foreigners' compounds as safe havens for their daughters in time of civil disorder. (See below, "Education for the Chinese," for a discussion of this work.)

Bible Women

When some of the older girls or women learned of the presence of foreigners in their communities, they sometimes tried to find refuge with the missionaries. Some of the Chinese women who had converted to Christianity, particularly those who were widowed or middle-aged, were recruited by the missionaries to be Bible Women. All the Protestant missions employed Bible Women, and each mission trained their own,

---

2. Ruthanne Lum McCunn, *Thousand Pieces of Gold* (San Francisco: Design Enterprises of San Francisco, 1981).
3. Judith Liu, *Foreign Exchange: Counterculture behind the Walls of St. Hilda's School for Girls, 1929-1937* (Bethlehem, PA: Lehigh University Press, 2011).

but there was a remarkable similarity in their training and tasks. To be baptized one had to know and be able to recite basic Christian beliefs, and further knowledge gained one church membership. For those women who progressed through these steps there was the possibility of being employed by the mission as a Bible Woman. (One must remember that in the first century of the missionary endeavor these women would have had bound feet.) Indeed, some of the women might previously have been employed by the missionaries as a household servant, a cook, a wash-woman, or an amah.

The Bible Women traveled around to people's homes to discuss Christianity with them. There were several advantages to this system. First, the Bible Women could speak the local dialects. Second, they frequently knew or were related to the people they visited. Third, the employment of Bible Women greatly expanded the number of people who could be evangelized. Fourth, the Bible Women usually accompanied the missionary women when they went itinerating, making it more acceptable for the foreign women to travel. Jessie Lutz's edited volume, *Pioneer Chinese Christian Women: Gender, Christianity, and Social Mobility*,[4] contains a number of excellent essays on Bible Women and their roles in the spread of Christianity in China.

The vast majority of Chinese, even if they knew foreigners lived within their midst, had little or nothing to do with them. Even in the years after the Cultural Revolution, as Da Chen writes in his memoir, *Sounds of the River*,[5] the Christian woman who lived in his village lived apart from her non-Christian

---

4. Jessie G. Lutz, ed., *Pioneer Chinese Christian Women: Gender, Christianity, and Social Mobility* (Bethlehem, PA: Lehigh University Press, 2010).
5. Da Chen, *Sounds of the River* (New York: HarperPerennial, 2003).

neighbors. Although she attended a party his family held to celebrate his return from Beijing, she did not stay long. As he says, she did not fit with his friends, meaning she was more refined than they were. (See chapter 1 for more on Chen's work.)

Education for the Chinese

Although missionaries did not keep statistics of the social classes of their converts, one can assume that most inquirers and converts were students at the mission elementary and secondary schools. These schools had a tremendous influence on modern Chinese society. Whether or not the missionaries realized what they were doing, and in most cases they did not, they managed to introduce into their curricula a modern concept of nationalism, based on identity with the Chinese government, that is, the Nationalists in the 1911 to 1949 period; their native land; their culture; their history; their language; their belief systems; and their traditions.

Once the missionaries had determined, at the 1877 All-China Missionary Conference, that education for Chinese, including Chinese women, was a legitimate part of missionary work, schools increased in number. In the early years of the missions it was common for any missionary or missionary wife to teach in a mission school. While the Qing dynasty was still in power, the missionary schools stood in sharp contrast to Chinese schools; the former imparted knowledge of the West while the latter prepared men for the Confucian examinations. In the twentieth century the schools more closely resembled each other in many parts of the curricula, and mission teachers sometimes taught part time in government schools.

Getting Chinese to attend the mission schools was a problem

for most of the early missionaries. Eliza Bridgman started a school in her home, but few wanted to be students. Mrs. Bridgman discovered that paying students to attend and providing them with food and clothing attracted some students, but they did not stay long. Many other missionaries would also discover that students who came for the food and the clothing soon left.

Most Protestant missionaries thought schools were necessary to their work of converting the Chinese, because they needed to read the Bible for themselves. The missionaries also hoped that their students would become converts, and would want to work with the missionaries to convert others to Christianity. Although some of the students followed this path to a job with the missionaries, most did not. Some of the early missionaries taught English in their schools, so that they might better communicate with their hoped-for converts.

Unfortunately, just as the missionaries were getting themselves established, the Western merchants were increasing their trade with China. Most of the merchants were in China only to make money, or what the nineteenth-century folks called their competency, that is, enough money to return home and retire to a comfortable lifestyle. Few merchants were interested in spending long years in China, so they had no interest in learning the language. However, not only linguistic knowledge, but also knowledge of local customs, banking, and products was essential to the foreign traders. For this knowledge, the merchants came to rely heavily on the Chinese they employed. A Chinese loan word to English, *taipan*, was applied to the chief Chinese in the employ of foreigners, and many taipans became incredibly rich. Knowledge of some English was essential for a Chinese to work for a foreigner, who knew no Chinese. Consequently, as soon as students at mission schools learned some English, many left the schools and went off to Shanghai in search of their fortunes.

It should also be noted that *The Chinese Recorder*, which began publishing in 1867, early in its run detailed the history of each mission then operating in China. Some of the early missionaries were men who were sent to China to work primarily as printers or other skilled laborers. Many of them left the missions after a short time "to go to Shanghai." The reports never included the obvious: they, like the English-speaking students, were off to make their fortunes with the businessmen in the treaty ports.

Having experienced this loss of students to the business community, some mission schools eliminated English from their curricula. Exactly what was taught in any of the mission schools is hard to determine. Some schools, at the elementary level, were for those with no previous education, while others took only students with some basic level of literacy in Chinese and introduced Western science, mathematics, philosophy, etc. Until the mid-1890s when board missions began recruiting credentialed teachers with expertise in specific areas, the subjects taught in the mission schools tended to be what the resident missionaries felt comfortable teaching.

As the missionaries were in China to convert the Chinese, the basics of Christian belief were always taught. Missionaries were very concerned that their inquirers and their converts give up all aspects of their previous belief systems, which the missionaries termed heathen. China's major annual festival, Chinese New Year, is calculated by the lunar calendar, and comes in late January or early February. Chinese who had left their natal homes to live elsewhere, for whatever reason, felt a great necessity to return to their native places during this celebration. Although the early Communist government called the New Year holiday the "Spring Festival," people still flocked home to observe what the government termed a feudal custom. Today, all means of transportation are vastly overbooked for weeks before the holiday.

Preparations for the holiday involved paying off any debts one might have before New Year arrived, getting new clothes made, posting slogans or pictures of gods at entrances to homes, honoring one's ancestors and the eldest living members of one's family, burning paper money and pictures of everyday objects for the use of the ancestors during the coming year, eating special foods with family and friends, and, for children, receiving a red paper packet containing money. The missionaries objected to the holiday, noting it cost a lot of money, and they were particularly opposed to honoring one's ancestors and parents as this involved kowtowing to them. Somehow, an early, unknown, missionary termed this practice "worshiping one's ancestors," thinking that kowtowing to the names of one's ancestors written on a slip of wood or paper was akin to worship in a Christian context. Despite the missionaries' opposition to the holiday, mission schools routinely dismissed classes for a week or two at Chinese New Year so that the students could return to their families!

However, the mission schools were in session on all Christian holidays. Christmas and Easter holidays were times of great celebration at mission schools and some even developed the custom of having the students awaken the missionaries by singing carols on Christmas morning and Easter songs on that day. After the 1911 Revolution mission schools celebrated Double Ten Day (10 October), the Nationalist holiday celebrating the beginning of the revolution, with ceremonies in the schools, but when that day fell on Sunday, the celebration was postponed until the following day. Of course, the customs the Westerners followed baffled more than one Chinese, since Christmas and Easter were never postponed a day.

Missionaries quickly learned that Chinese New Year was not a good time to go itinerating to outlying areas, as few Chinese were willing to welcome strangers, much less foreigners, into their homes at that time. Some mission stations recognized Chinese New Year as a good time to hold their annual station meetings or go off to Shanghai or Hong Kong to have a vacation, do their necessary shopping, and visit a dentist or an optician. Dentists did not exist within the mission world, but there were some foreign dentists practicing in Hong Kong and Shanghai, whom missionaries could see. The same was true for opticians, although mission doctors could take care of eye diseases. In rare cases, one might find either profession among the diplomatic community and make use of their services.

Missionaries also had a very difficult time conveying to the Chinese that Sunday was a day when they were supposed to rest. *The Chinese Recorder* published a story of one missionary who was in his study on Sunday afternoon and heard a tennis ball hitting the outside of his house and the voices of two young men from the mission school. The missionary went outside to admonish them for not keeping the Sabbath, but when he saw the great camaraderie they were enjoying, he went back to his study to rethink his ideas of what one should do on the Sabbath!

Most mission schools had great difficulty finding teachers of Chinese. The person needed to be highly literate to teach the students, but that usually meant the person would have passed the Confucian examinations, in the years before they were abolished. Anyone with such qualification certainly would not take a job with foreigners, until after the collapse of the Qing dynasty. There were, of course, many men who were educated but had failed the government examinations, and they were sometimes hired as the missionaries knew many of these men taught in Chinese village or clan schools.

Missionaries quickly discovered reasons to reject many of these candidates. The two most common reasons were that the man had more than one wife or he was an opium addict. Hostility to Christianity or xenophobia were also reasons to reject possible Chinese teachers, if the missionaries detected these ideas. Finding teachers was never an easy task, especially in the early years of the mission endeavor. In those years there were few converts who had the education necessary to become teachers of Chinese history and literature, although in later years converts did fill many of these positions.

Educating Chinese Women

Why Chinese were willing to send their daughters to mission schools is quite a different matter from educating sons. Some Chinese had always educated their daughters at home with tutors. Other Chinese saw their country changing and thought their daughters might have better marriage prospects if they had attended a school. While these might have been the most common reasons girls attended mission schools, there was another, perhaps more important, reason—mission girls' schools were known to the Chinese as safe places for young women to live. In any traditional society, particularly one wracked by warfare and disease, families can break down and need to reorganize themselves in new ways. For example, if a young girl had lost her parents and siblings and had only an aged uncle or grandfather to look after her, the mission school might offer an alternative place for her to live. If by some mishap a young teenage girl suddenly found herself being taken care of by relatives who had, say, four teenage boys at home, they might consider the alternative of the mission girls' boarding school.

Liu's account of her mother and aunt, who were placed in the American Episcopal School, St Hilda's, in Wuchang by their wealthy parents for safekeeping after the violence of the Northern Expedition reached the Wuhan area in 1927, is also a study in cultural differences. (The Northern Expedition was the movement of the Nationalists to the north to consolidate their power.) The girls' family was not interested in Christianity, but saw the American mission as a safe refuge for their teenage girls.[6] The missionaries were known to be extremely protective of all females in their care. Although Shirley Garrett was writing about men in her history of the YMCA in China, *Social Reformers in Urban China: The Chinese Y.M.C.A., 1895-1926*,[7] her assessment of the YMCA could also apply to girls' schools. Garrett writes that many traditional families, Christian and non-Christian, permitted their sons to move to the large cities on the coast, because they could live at the YMCA where there was no smoking, no opium, no drinking, no gambling, and certainly no prostitutes, thus an atmosphere where the parents' hoped their sons would not go astray.

Most girls' schools refused to allow men on their premises; the sole exception, if there were one, was likely the elderly gatekeeper who enforced the rules. Indeed, many mission schools refused to allow female students outside the school compound unless a male member of her family, or an elderly, trusted male servant, came to escort her home. Of course,

---

6. Liu, *Foreign Exchange*, 51–52.
7. Shirley Garrett, *Social Reformers in Urban China: The Chinese Y.M.C.A., 1895-1926* (Cambridge, MA: Harvard University Press, 1970).

there were exceptions. In Hainan the schoolgirls often traveled home in groups, even at night, without a male chaperone.

Just how determinedly the missionary women defended the sanctity of their girls' schools was illustrated by Margaret Moninger in Hainan in 1918 when a Cantonese army invaded the island. Moninger reported to her family that when she saw the men entering the school compound, she went out and informed them "politely but firmly . . . that this is a girls' school where no men are allowed," adding that they could go to the boys' school if they wished. Moninger added, "It's funny how ten or a dozen big fellows with their guns move when I speak." She concluded that she did not think the soldiers would have left if a Chinese servant had talked to them. She also wrote that one of her colleagues living in Hoihou, Mrs. Olivia Kerr McCandliss, had disarmed a group of Chinese soldiers who had entered the mission compound.[8]

While schools were quite costly, most of those in China started small, often in the missionaries' homes. As the Western schools became more popular because of the subjects they taught, the missionaries appealed to their boards for funds to build separate school buildings. Although costly, few boards refused funds for schools, in the hope that the students would become leaders of the new indigenous church.

Mission schools soon developed their own traditions, based on what the missionaries remembered of their school days at home. Most schools had outdoor calisthenics each morning, although according to Liu many Chinese believed that strenuous exercise would cause young girls to lose their virginity! Set classes in various subjects filled the students' days. After-school activities included various clubs according to the students' interests, but generally, there were some

---

8. Margaret to People, 3 Nov. 1918, Moninger Papers.

Christian clubs and classes and self-help groups. Some schools even had bands that played Western musical instruments.

Coming as they did out of the late nineteenth and early twentieth centuries, the missionaries thought that vocational education was a good subject for their schools. Accordingly, they taught woodworking, farming, etc. to boys while the girls learned housekeeping, cooking, and sewing. Again, this indicates how little the missionaries understood of China's culture. Jobs involving manual work were not for the educated members of Chinese society, and certainly not for anyone who had attended a foreign school!

There were numerous other cultural misunderstandings among the mission teachers and their students. Liu relates that when her mother was at St. Hilda's, the school principal decided she had broken too many rules so could not attend graduation, apparently the worst punishment the principal could think of. However, Liu's mother was overjoyed to be sent home from school early, because at home she needed to do no tasks like making her bed or keeping her clothes orderly as she had servants to do such tasks. Additionally, she could lie in bed all day, if she chose, and ask the servants to cook her favorite foods![9]

Mission Higher Education

As missionary secondary schools produced more and more graduates, missionaries began to think about university education for their best and brightest students. In the early years of the Protestant mission endeavor, the best students were sent to the United States for further education. The first of these was Rong Hong (Yung Wing), who graduated from

---

9. Liu, *Foreign Exchange*, 125–26.

Yale in 1854. Rong, a native of Guangdong, had been sent by his father to study with Mrs. Bridgman in the hope that he might learn something useful. Rong eventually became quite influential in Chinese-American educational, diplomatic, and business ventures in the late nineteenth century. (See chapter 5 for a short biography of Rong.)

Mission Universities in China

Sending every talented student abroad for years was not a realistic, long-term solution to higher education for the Chinese, but missionaries quickly realized no one mission board was going to be able to finance a university in China. While missionaries knew that an interdenominational or a nondenominational university would be the solution to their problem, they also knew that their supporters at home were unlikely to give money for such an institution. Folks in the pews of the home churches wanted to support their own denomination's schools, not those of other churches. The China missionaries were far ahead of the church at home in embracing ecumenism, which would sweep the mainstream churches at home in the late twentieth century. The missionaries went ahead with plans for an ecumenical university, first convincing their boards at home that it was the only way to fund higher education. Eventually, there were thirteen mission universities in China, one of them for women, Ginling in Nanjing; several seminaries; and the Rockefeller Foundation's medical school and hospital in Beijing.

Ginling College and the Rape of Nanjing

World War II began in China in 1937, and in December the Japanese army took Nanjing, then China's capital, precipitating the Rape of Nanjing which lasted three weeks. The government along with schools and an estimated quarter million people fled the city ahead of the onslaught. Foreign diplomats had urged their nationals to abandon the city, and most did, but a few remained largely to protect the missionary schools and foreign business properties.

Minnie Vautrin, acting head of Ginling College, was one who stayed. She was probably the only foreign woman to remain in the city and she did so to protect her students who had not fled the Ginling campus. Besides her students many women, young boys, and elderly men sought refuge on the campus. The college was part of the International Safety Zone established by foreigners in and around the University of Nanjing and Ginling College, which were adjacent to each other.

The Japanese army was highly disciplined, and most scholars think their rampage in Nanjing was only possible because the officers acquiesced in it. Except for a fortunate few who were hidden, some scholars think every female over the age of eight, who was left in the city, was raped; many thousands were killed. The rampage did not attract outrage in the West at the time it happened, partly because the Western countries were not then at war with Japan, and partly because events in China were not of much interest to Western governments and people.

Because of the continuing neutrality of the United States, Japanese pilots bombing Chinese properties were quite careful to avoid those owned by Americans. Missionaries who remained in China after the fighting began reported prominently displaying their flags on their compounds, and many saw Japanese pilots make large curves in their flight paths so as not to fly over neutral property, lest they drop a bomb by accident. (Readers will recall that it was also in December 1937 that the Japanese attacked the USS *Panay*, a naval ship, in the Yangzi River, killing three of its crew. The Japanese government quickly acknowledged the mistake and paid two million dollars in compensation to the American government. It was after the attack on the *Panay* that President Franklin D. Roosevelt made his famous "trial balloon" speech to ascertain American attitude toward war, and immediately learned the vast majority of Americans clung to isolationism.)

In the 1980s an American filmmaker, visiting the site in Nanjing where the museum to the memory of the victims of the Rape was being built was approached by three elderly Chinese women who wanted to know if he were American and if he knew Vautrin. He said he was American, but did not know Vautrin. The three told him they visited the site daily to pay homage to Vautrin, as she had saved their lives during the Rape by hiding them in her house.

The story of the International Safety Zone in Nanjing is detailed in John Rabe, *The Good Man of Nanjing: The Diaries of John Rabe*.[10] That story was unearthed after a German globetrotter published a book of his 1936 world tour, mentioning meeting Rabe in Nanjing. The Rabe family then remembered their grandfather's papers in the attic! Rabe was the Siemens representative in Nanjing for thirty years, but had never learned any Chinese, relying on pidgin for communication. He had joined the Nazi party on one of his rare visits to Germany in the 1930s, because friends advised that membership would help him gain government support for a German school he ran from his home, which adjoined the University of Nanjing campus. In 1937, as a card-carrying Nazi, he wrote Adolf Hitler asking him to prevail on the Japanese not to harm any Chinese noncombatants when the Japanese army took Nanjing, noting

---

10. John Rabe, *The Good Man of Nanjing: The Diaries of John Rabe* (New York: Knopf Doubleday, 2007).

that the Chinese were his friends. Siemens fired Rabe for staying in Nanjing after they ordered him to leave, but he thought by staying he might save some of his Chinese friends in the city. After the war he could find no employment in Germany because he had been a Nazi, so some of the Chinese he had saved helped support him. Although it is rare to have public statues of foreigners in any country, today there are three statues of Rabe in Nanjing: at his home, now on the University of Nanjing campus; across the city at the museum to the victims of the Rape; and at the Siemens office.

(Visitors to Nanjing should certainly visit the museum to those who died in 1937. To enter the building one must walk in the footsteps of some of the survivors, and along the pathway one is joined by sculptures of other survivors who display broken bones and other wounds. The museum shows home movies of the Japanese atrocities, taken by some of the missionaries who remained in the city. Overall, the museum's tone is that the world testifies as to what happened in Nanjing in December 1937. The issue continues to be a volatile one between China and Japan, which surfaces from time to time. Today, Nanjing is a city of nearly four million, but according to Temur, the author's friend there, it was eerily quiet on 13 December 2007, as the population silently remembered the Rape of seventy years earlier.)

Who Converted?

In a country the size of China it would be difficult to generalize about which people became Christians and why they made that decision. Some scholars think it was those groups who were already alienated from the mainstream of their society who became converts, such as those who belonged to various vegetarian sects. Nanjing was one of the centers of vegetarian groups, so perhaps there was some overlapping membership, as the city became a major center of Christian activity.

It seems that many who converted to Christianity were already alienated from their families or society. Many a mission hired as amahs women who had been concubines or household slaves, but for some reason had left or been cast out of the families where they served. Some converts were orphans for whom the mission compound became something like a fictive family. Of course, some converts came from among the patients in the mission hospitals and others from the students in the mission schools. Although most missionaries did not require their household servants to be at least inquirers within the church, employees were encouraged to attend church and many did, probably thinking their jobs depended upon such activity. But then many missionaries had longtime servants who repeatedly said they would convert at some time in the future even though that time never came. Espey's account of his childhood includes the story of one such servant, who worked for his family, and was always going to convert in the future. It seems the missionaries cared more about having honest servants who were accustomed to the way the foreigners lived, than about having servants who were Christians.

Banditry

Unfortunately, civil disorder was common in China in the waning years of the Qing dynasty as the central government had less and less control over the countryside, and conditions grew worse after the 1911 Revolution. As the government lost control of the country, authorized officials had less power and lawlessness increased. Many missionaries were robbed when traveling between the coast and their interior stations, or even between the outposts of their stations. Early in the history of the Protestant missions, it became common knowledge among Chinese that missionaries carried cash with them when they traveled! Generally, travelers in China, missionaries included, packed their possessions and perhaps trade goods and money in coins in baskets that were carried by porters. (Folks at home always enjoyed the pictures of Chinese babies transported in these baskets.)

Missionaries did not understand how Chinese traditionally transported their money, or if they did, they were reluctant to trust that system, which worked on couriers and letters of credit between merchants. As a result, missionaries carried many pounds of silver dollars whenever they traveled. There were many currencies in use in China in the late nineteenth and early twentieth centuries, but the favored one was the Mexican silver dollar, because of its purity. These coins were minted in Mexico and had been transported to Asia by an annual galleon that made the journey from Acapulco to Manila from 1565 to 1815. If other types of silver coins were presented for a debt, the person receiving them had to "ring" every one to make sure it was not counterfeit, as that was a huge problem.

Missionaries along the China coast reported the currencies in circulation that they used daily were pounds sterling, US dollars, Bland (or American) trade dollars, Customs Service dollars, Vietnamese piasters, French Indochina dollars, Philippine pesos, Japanese yen, Chinese dollars, Hong Kong dollars, Hong Kong postal currency, Straits Settlements dollars, and Shanghai or Customs Service taels. Of course, there was always pure gold and silver. Using any currency could result in change being given in a different one, and more than one mission treasurer reported he or she was never exactly sure how much money they had in their accounts! Exchange rates changed daily, but generally, two Mexican silver dollars equaled one US dollar. How unreliable the Chinese banking system was, and how great the risk of robbery in the early twentieth century, was demonstrated on one occasion when Chinese government officials gave Mother Melrose, one of the senior members of the APM in Nada, Hainan, a thousand dollars in coin for safekeeping, probably assuming the mission safe was one of the more secure places in town to keep money![11]

When missionaries were robbed, depending upon the local circumstances, and, if the Chinese accompanying the missionaries could identify the robbers or their home villages, they sometimes tracked down the culprits and demanded their possessions be returned. This was a much quicker solution than appealing to consular officials who could take months to resolve a problem.

Some bandits robbed the missionaries of their clothing. In Hainan, the Byers family lost one shoe of each pair of their daughter's new shoes and Mrs. Byers's wedding dress, which a bandit was wearing, minus its lace, when the missionaries caught up with him and recovered the dress, but not the shoes![12] Eyeglasses were also a favorite of thieves.

Murders of Missionaries

If mayhem included the death of a foreigner, then the incident did become a consular matter. Sometimes the missionaries

---

11. Margaret to Daddy and Louise; Margaret to Louise, both 8 Dec. 1929; Moninger Papers.
12. Kathleen L. Lodwick, *The Widow's Quest: The Byers Extraterritoriality Case in Hainan, China, 1924-25* (Bethlehem, PA: Lehigh University Press, 2003), 29.

provoked violence against themselves, as when in 1903 the Reverend Edward Machle (APM) in Guangzhou broke idols in a local temple and was subsequently attacked by a mob. His wife and daughter were hidden by local Christians in a cave, but were found and killed. He survived because his Chinese guide took him to another part of the cave, by mistake.[13] Of course, most violent deaths of missionaries took place at the time of the Boxer Uprising, which is dealt with in several excellent monographs. (See chapter 1.)

Two cases involving the murders of missionaries in the 1920s demonstrate the differences in how the deaths of a Presbyterian clergyman and of three Roman Catholic Passionist priests were dealt with by the diplomatic community. These two cases are that of the Reverend George D. Byers (APM), killed by a well-known local bandit at the interior town of Jiaji, Hainan, in 1924, and the Passionist fathers—Clement Seybold, Godfrey Holbein, and Walter Coveyou—killed by bandits, probably for causes related to some local struggle for power, in Huajiao, Hunan, in 1929.

The case of the murder of Byers is dealt with in the author's monograph, *The Widow's Quest*.[14] In Hainan it was customary for missionaries to take their yearly required in-country vacation when schools finished for the summer. It was also the custom to leave one mission family at each of the stations, to look after the compound. Accordingly, in 1924 all the missionaries at Jiaji, except Byers, his pregnant wife, and their four children, left the town for the port of Haikou, where there was another mission station, and where they would await a coastal steamer to Hong Kong.

In Jiaji, a public road cut through the mission land, with the

13. *Chinese Recorder*, "Deaths," 36:651–52.
14. Lodwick, *Widow's Quest*.

homes of the missionaries on one side and the schools, the church, and the hospital on the other. Byers had just finished the evening church service, and was crossing the road on his way home, when he was attacked by three men who slipped a noose around his neck. News stories of attacks on missionaries had been frequent in recent months, and in an astounding coincidence, the Reverend Rex Ray (ASBM), husband of the daughter of the founder of the Hainan mission, had been kidnapped and later released in Guangdong province just a few weeks earlier. The Hainan missionaries learned of that kidnapping through the Hong Kong newspapers which arrived regularly at Haikou. As they discussed the incident, Byers, who his colleagues described as a tough, determined individual, had stated he would never allow himself to be kidnapped for ransom.

Unfortunately, the men who captured Byers were intent upon collecting a ransom, as a written demand was found on the mission compound the morning after the attack. Apparently, Byers struggled against the three men, and one shot him in the stomach in the ensuing mayhem. Byers had shouted to his wife in the nearby house and she reached him just before his death. The Chinese hospital assistant also arrived, surveyed the wound, and informed Mrs. Byers that no doctor could have saved her husband.

There is no indication that the killing of Byers was planned or even that it was an anti-Christian act, as a dead foreigner was worthless to the bandits. Killing a foreigner meant government officials would become involved, and there would be no ransom paid. The culprits had fled into the night. Mrs. Byers was able, after quite a bit of difficulty, to use the recently installed military telephone to call Haikou and inform the other missionaries of the murder. Several of the missionary men from Haikou set off for Jiaji at daybreak.

The nearest American consular official was resident at Guangzhou, a two-day journey by boat, but Great Britain had a consulate at Haikou, which adjoined the mission compound. The British took care of American interests on Hainan, so the consul there was informed of the murder. He, as well as the missionaries, communicated with the American consul in Guangzhou by letter.

The ensuing diplomatic matter lasted over a year. The American diplomats at Guangzhou were clearly irritated that a missionary had been killed, as one informed the American officials at Beijing that such incidents "interfere with the work of this office."[15] Clearly, the American diplomats considered their work to be helping businessmen increase their trade, and profits, in China, not in pursuing an extraterritorial case on the remote island of Hainan that involved a dead missionary! (It is probably safe to assume that such an attitude was common among consular officials elsewhere in China.) At one time the British official on Hainan wrote to his counterpart in Guangzhou, "in case you might still be interested," the main suspect in the case had just been executed![16]

Under the extraterritorial provisions of the treaties between China and the Western countries, the foreigners had the right to demand compensation for the loss of the life of any of their citizens, and all the diplomats knew that if they did not pursue those rights in every case that arose, they would lose them simply because they did not take action.

(Likewise, China had the right to demand compensation for

---

15. Douglas Jenkins to Jacob Gould Schurman, 1 July 1924, National Archives, US Consulate, Canton, *Despatches from US Consulates in Canton 1790-1906*. Washington, DC, Microfilm.
16. National Archives, H. H. Bristow to Jenkins, 6 Oct. 1924.

the loss of the lives of their citizens through violence in the United States. They made a claim after the 1885 Rock Springs, Wyoming, incident in which twenty-eight Chinese were killed and fifteen others were injured. The Chinese government worked through their diplomats in Washington and in 1887 the US Congress voted the compensation.)

At the time of Byers's death no Presbyterian missionary anywhere in the world was required to have life insurance, a policy that changed as a result of his death. Mrs. Byers and her supporters in China and in the United States pressured Congressmen to get the State Department to act. First, the commander of the US naval fleet in China waters insisted that he had no boat to send to Hainan, though he quickly found one when told that a consular official was being sent to the island. Although the gunboat was quite small and had to leave Haikou's notoriously poor harbor quickly and the vice consul assigned the task was only twenty-seven years old, he managed to extract an indemnity from a warlord on the mainland, adjacent to Hainan, who claimed the right to govern the island.

The matter dragged on for a year, but the APM Board in New York, which at first had opposed the collection of an indemnity from the Chinese, eventually decided to accept it, since the US government was going to collect an indemnity regardless of what the APM Board wished. The members of the Board finally realized if they were to accept indemnity, it would lessen the amount they would need to provide Mrs. Byers. The APM Board had voted a pension for life to Mrs. Byers, which included assistance for her children until they completed college.

The aftermath of the murder of the three Passionist priests in Hunan, five years after Byers's murder, was quite different. This case was dealt with by Father Robert Carbonneau, a Passionist, in his Georgetown University dissertation, *Life,*

Death, and Memory: Three Passionists in Hunan, China, and the Shaping of an American Mission Perspective in the 1920s.[17] As with the Byers case, there is no evidence to suggest that the priests were killed because they were Christians.

Most foreigners killed in China during these years were victims of the lack of a civil society. The Roman Catholic missionaries in China, as well as their supporters at home, always thought martyrdom was a possibility; indeed, it was seen as the first step toward sainthood.

All the Passionists had fled Hunan in 1927 as the troops of the Northern Expedition approached, and Holbein later wrote home that since the fathers had fled in the time of greatest danger, if they returned to Hunan in a more peaceful time and then were killed, the Chinese would not view their deaths as martyrdom. In fact, Holbein had pondered what martyrdom meant in such circumstances.

The killing of the three priests took place on 24 April 1929. The night before they had stayed in a Chinese inn in the town of Huajiao, and during the night, gunfire was heard in the area. By morning, the local militia reported the area was safe and the priests and some of their converts started off on their own via a different road than the one they had planned to use, having been unable to obtain a military escort in the town. Once out of the town they were confronted by bandits, suggesting that someone in the town had told the bandits of the group's new route. Led a short distance down the road, the priests were shot and killed within minutes of being captured. Their bodies were dumped down an abandoned mine shaft. The eleven Chinese accompanying the priests were nearby when the

---

17. Robert Carbonneau, *Life, Death, and Memory: Three Passionists in Hunan, China, and the Shaping of an American Mission Perspective in the 1920s.* PhD diss., Georgetown University, 1992.

murders were committed, and afterward they were set free. They returned to the town to report what had happened.

A 1990 study of the murders by the Passionist Father Caspar Caulfield determines that the Communist forces were behind the murders, as they had been active in that region of Hunan. (Caulfield's book,[18] and particularly its conclusion, is thought by many scholars to have been written to start the three Passionists on the road to sainthood. Carbonneau recently told the author that he now believes, based on further archival studies by several scholars, that the deaths of the men were part of the widespread violence in the area rather than an anti-Christian incident, because there is no clear archival evidence of any Communist participation in the murder.)[19] There was no indication that the priests were captured to be held for ransom, because they were killed within minutes of being taken captive.

News of the murder of the three priests reached the Passionists and the National Catholic Welfare Council (NCWC) in the United States before the US State Department received official word of the incident. A Passionist in China cabled his brothers in Baltimore, Maryland, on 27 April 1929, about the deaths and they informed the NCWC by telephone. The NCWC then telephoned the State Department's Division of Far Eastern Affairs to report the deaths, which the government officially learned about two days later.

After consulting with the Maryknoll fathers, who had been the first American priests to work in China, the Passionists decided not to seek an indemnity. Later the US government also decided it would not seek an indemnity for the deaths of

18. Caspar Caulfield, *Only a Beginning: The Passionists in China, 1921-1931* (Union City, NJ: Passionist Press, 1990).
19. Author's conversation with Fr. Robert Carbonneau, Washington, DC, 6 March 2004.

the three priests. The case was complicated by the fact that the Holy See had sent an Apostolic Delegate to China in 1922. While the Delegate tried to maintain his distance from the French and Italian diplomats, who had previously looked after the affairs of Catholic missionaries, he was received by the Chinese president and thus recognized as part of the diplomatic community in China. The Delegate had been sent, in part, because the Vatican during this time was emphasizing the need to ordain Chinese clergy and to appoint them to positions of authority, which was not looked upon favorably by some of the foreign orders that had long been active in China.

The question of extraterritoriality was a subject of discussion within the US Department of State in these years. In the case of the Passionist fathers the US government decided not to collect an indemnity, but the Vatican representative told the Chinese government if they wished to establish a hospital or a school as a memorial to the priests, there would be no opposition to that.

The differences between the Presbyterians' decision to accept an indemnity for the death of one of their missionaries and the decision of the Roman Catholics not to collect an indemnity for the loss of three of its missionaries was based primarily on the fact that the Presbyterian had a wife and four, soon to be five, children who needed to be supported, and the Roman Catholics could not request any compensation for their deaths because the priests were members of a religious order, and thus did not support their families. (Likewise, when foreign children were killed in China, no indemnities for their lives were sought because they had no one to support.)

Conclusion

The vast majority of Protestant missionaries traveling to China to convert the Chinese to Christianity, well into the twentieth century, had little or no knowledge of the country in which they were to live. Virtually all men and single women were required to be college graduates in order to be accepted by mission boards. Some boards even insisted that wives be college graduates, although there were some exceptions. Many of the missionaries were graduates of small, church-related colleges that taught nothing about Asia. (In fact, Asian studies in Western colleges and universities was first taught by returned missionaries. Some scholars think this situation is related to the fact that all the East Asian scholars love the countries and cultures they study, whereas Russian studies in the West was pioneered by emigrés from the Russian Revolution of 1917, producing a very different perspective on the part of scholars of that country.)

The difficulties inherent in learning to speak the local Chinese dialect and to write Chinese characters took up much of the missionaries' time in their early years in China. Some of the wives, especially those with young children, never progressed beyond a very rudimentary skill.

Communication was necessary not only to preach Christianity, but also to successfully negotiate living in a foreign country. One woman who had been a missionary in Hainan in the twentieth century told the author that she considered the squeeze her coolie took when he made purchases as the price she paid for living in China, but that another of her colleagues demanded that her coolie account for every coin given, spent, and returned, as well as every stick of firewood, can of food, and bar of soap on the shopping list. Not surprisingly, that colleague also frequently denounced the Chinese as dishonest. Such were the many cultural misunderstandings between Chinese and Westerners.

When the missionaries established schools in China, they replicated the ones they had attended in their home countries. Some schools taught English, while others either abandoned it or refused to even try teaching it, because the missionaries learned fairly quickly that Chinese who knew some English tended not to become Christians or, more important, evangelists for the missions. Instead the students went off to Shanghai or Hong Kong to seek their fortunes with the Western businessmen.

Under the treaties the Western governments had forced the Chinese to accept in the nineteenth century, all foreigners had extraterritorial rights in China. In some cases these rights were reciprocal.

The murders of the American missionaries, Byers, a Presbyterian, and the three Passionist fathers in the 1920s demonstrate how the responses of the APM Board differed from that of the Passionists and the NCWC. The responses were different not because extraterritorial rights were different (they were not), but because Byers left a widow with five children, and the Passionists were members of a religious order and thus had no dependents. As far as the missionaries and extraterritorial rights were concerned, nothing was ever simple.

4

Geographic

Geographic concerns were never an issue for the China missionaries as they were in say India and Africa, because, during heyday of the missionary movement, China was ruled by a central government, and was not colonized by a foreign power in the nineteenth and twentieth centuries. It is the norm in human civilization for large empires not to last too long as, for example, Alexander's empire, the Roman Empire, the Carolingian empire, the Mongol empire, the Zimbabwe empire, the Ottoman empire, etc. Within this model of human government, so widespread in time and place, China is clearly the exception.

How China was able to preserve the immense size of her territory as succeeding dynasties, both Han Chinese and foreigners, conquered the land where the Chinese lived is not easy to explain. Various reasons historians have given to explain China's separate path include early widespread literacy with a uniform written language; the early adoption of Confucian precepts as a model for society, from the imperial institution to family organization; the infusion of new blood as dynasties were established by non-Han peoples; the terrain of China, which confined most people to the coastal plain, the lowlands of the south, and river valleys, with mountains and deserts on the periphery as natural boundaries; and, for much of history, no strong neighboring states to challenge China's power.

The vast population of China, currently about one and one-third billion, lives on the coastal plain and in the valleys of the Yellow and Yangzi rivers. Until modern times, the main routes of travel were along these rivers and their tributaries and via the Grand Canal, built in pieces but much of it during the Sui dynasty (581–618), which stretches from Hangzhou in the south to Beijing in the north, a distance of eleven hundred miles. The Grand Canal was primarily used to transport tribute grain from the rich farmlands of the south to the capital in the north.

Early in their history, the Chinese developed agricultural systems that allowed for population growth. In south China the major grain was rice, but in the north, which received less rainfall, wheat, barley, millet, and sorghum were the grains grown. Over the years crop failures and floods caused widespread famines. Those who study the history of food and how it influenced various countries have written that both tea and the diet the Chinese devised enabled them to survive famines and plagues. Making tea required that water be boiled, fortuitously killing many waterborne, disease-carrying organisms. The Han people also developed a style of eating that saw a grain, a vegetable, and a meat combined in various ways. This diet has been called famine-proof, because if meat were not available, or affordable, the grains and vegetables would sustain life. Likewise if vegetables were unavailable, life could be sustained on the grains alone, and if grains were in short supply they could be thinned into gruel. The Chinese styles of cooking—flash frying, steaming, and boiling—preserved the vitamins in the food. Also, the utilization of the water, which had been used in steaming and boiling, as soup meant more nutrients were consumed. Bamboo steamers and metal woks, like the ones used in Chinese kitchens today, have been unearthed from many ancient archaeological sites in China, demonstrating how long these styles of cooking have been in existence.

China's Past

To better understand the country the missionaries sought to convert, a brief look at China's past should prove helpful. Humans have been living in the territory now called China for thousands of years, but the first dynasty that historians recognize as unifying the country was the Qin (221–206 BCE). Qin Shi Huang-di gained worldwide notice and fame with the discovery of his tomb in 1974. (See chapter 1.) The Qin dynasty was a very short one, having only two emperors, but it helped organize the state that allowed the Han (206 BCE–220 CE) to consolidate its power and control China's territory for four hundred years. There was a brief interregnum between 8 and 23 CE when Wang Mang, a relative of the royal family, seized power. The Han is thus divided into the Former and Later Han, but the rulers were from the same clan.

Culture under the Han reached such a high point that to this day ethnic Chinese refer to themselves "Han people." During the Han the arts and the sciences flourished. Among the technological developments of the Han were the invention of an early seismograph, a water-powered mill, paper, and porcelain. Han Chinese astronomers knew about sunspots. The country also benefited from the standardization of weights and measures that the Qin dynasty had established. Philosophy also flourished during the period. The central government became better organized and exercised control over the population.

The Han was the first of the strong dynasties, usually numbered as six, counting Former Han and the Later Han as two. Following the Han, the strong dynasties were the Tang (618–960); the Song (960–1279); the Ming (1368–1644); and the Qing (1644–1911). Historians consider as major dynasties those that controlled the eighteen provinces of China proper, that is, those south of the Great Wall after it was built during the Ming, and lasted a considerable length of time, usually several centuries. In between these major dynasties there were shorted-lived dynasties such as the Yuan or Mongol (1271–1368), those that were unifiers such as the Qin which preceded the Han and the Sui which preceded the Tang, and others that controlled some territory, but not the whole of China. The Yuan dynasty lasted in China for only a century, but its territory was far larger than that of the other dynasties. The Mongol empire, whose leaders were elected, reached as far west as eastern Europe; the so-called Golden Horde reached present day Iran and surrounding territories. During the years of the Mongol empire, many foreigners traveled back and forth throughout their lands because it was relatively safe to do so under the unifying security of the Mongol rulers, who were often brothers or half-brothers.

China was ruled by the imperial system until 1911, when the Qing dynasty was overthrown by revolution and replaced by the Nationalist government, which in turn was supplanted by the current Communist government in 1949. As the government developed over the centuries, officials were stationed at the city or town that was the administrative seat of a province or district. Gradually, great cities grew around these administrative centers, as they did elsewhere in Asia. (The reader should note that this is quite different from urbanization in the West, which was the result of the Industrial Revolution.)

Although there were differences among the dynasties throughout the centuries, generally speaking, the central governments of most dynasties were centered at either present-day Xian or present-day Beijing. Here the emperor, his vast household, and the highest administrators of the state lived and conducted their work. Depending on the dynasty, below the emperor the next rank of officials were usually princes of the blood or military commanders, who held places as advisers to the emperor or, beyond the capital, as governors-general over several provinces. Below these men were governors of each of the provinces, and then regional officials for various parts of the provinces. At the local level the magistrates were responsible for collecting taxes, taking the censuses, and maintaining law and order. Men for these posts were selected from those who had passed the higher levels of the Confucian examinations. In actual practice, order in the towns, villages, and countryside was maintained by the heads of the most powerful clans in each area. These headmen, along with government officials, constituted China's literati, termed the scholar-official-gentry class.

Within China's society the emperor was considered as the head; followed by the literate, scholar-official-gentry class; the peasants; the artisans; and at the bottom, the merchants, who only profited from the work of others.

China was a patriarchy where the heads of families or extended clans were responsible for the good behavior of their relatives. The emphasis on dealing with problems outside the governmental structure is evident in the Chinese proverb: Do not enter the yamen gate unless your purse is full. As it was necessary to offer a gratuity to nearly every official working at the yamen, it was a wise man who could solve problems without resorting to the government.

Because of the imperial nature of the Chinese government, which each dynasty established anew, there was no part of China that was not under the control of the Qing dynasty when the foreign missionaries arrived to spread their religion. Thus it was not possible for the missionaries, who disliked the government of the area they had chosen to work, to move away to a region governed by a different regime—there was no such place in China. As China was not colonized by a Western power, there was no place where missionaries could work with full foreign protection.

The Western traders and missionaries had their difficulties with the Qing government, primarily because it operated under the Chinese legal system and not by what the foreigners considered International Law, which was, of course, only known to Westerners. When the Taiping Rebellion broke out, the foreigners thought at last China would have a government similar to a Western one. Yet after a few missionaries traveled to Nanjing and discovered the true nature of the Taiping, the foreigners decided they were better off with the Qing government, from which they had already extracted many privileges, than with the eccentrics who headed the Taiping.

Early in China's history, during the period known as the Spring and Autumn Annals (722–476 BCE) Confucius (*Kungfuzi*), one of China's greatest thinkers, described for his students what he saw in the states he said were most successful. By teaching his students, who wrote down his teachings, he established guidelines for societal success. In the best-run states, Confucius noted that people observed the obligations and responsibilities based upon their places in the family and the society. The relationships Confucius considered important were between the emperor and his subjects. The emperor had the obligations of maintaining peace in the country, making sure laws were enforced, collecting of taxes, providing assistance to famine-ravished regions, etc. The inferiors in this relationship were the subjects who had the responsibility for obeying the laws, and paying taxes, etc.

Likewise the relationship between fathers and sons had obligations and responsibilities. Fathers were to provide for their families, guide their children in the correct behavior toward others in the family and the society, teach the sons the work of the father, and educate them in the Classics, if at all possible. In return, sons were expected to obey their parents and grandparents, provide good examples for younger siblings, learn the work of the father so that sons might one day have their own families, and study diligently, if schooling were within the financial scope of the family.

There was also the relationship between husband and wife, again with each having distinct roles. Husbands were expected to provide for the wife and the family, be fair and just to family members, teach the children, especially his sons, what they need to know to succeed in life, etc. The wife was to keep the house, cook for the family, weave silk or other fabrics that could be used to pay taxes to the government, bring up the children, and, most important, provide a son so the family line would continue to another generation. The great need to provide a male heir meant that if a man's wife had no sons, the society expected him to take a concubine, sometimes more than one, until a male heir was born. In some extended families, it was not unheard of for the family to decide that one sibling with more than one son needed to give one of those sons to a brother who lacked a male heir. (Indeed, this happened in the family of Zhou Enlai, where his uncles of the Zhou clan decided his birth-parents were not raising him to the family's expectations, so they moved him to the family of one of his uncles who had no children, making him their heir. This particular extended family lived together in one large house, so the young Enlai was simply moved from his birth-parents' quarters to the rooms of his uncle and his wife.)

In addition to these three relationships, often called the Three Bonds, there were two others. There was the relationship between elder brother and younger brother. Indeed, so important is one's birth order in the family, that the Chinese language has no word for brothers (or sisters). In Chinese one must distinguish between elder brothers and younger brothers (or elder sisters and younger sisters). Because of the importance of the family surname—and in traditional times, extended families might occupy only one house—children sharing the same surname were considered as brothers and sisters. In the popular novel *The Dream of the Red Chamber,* by Cao Xueqin, written during the Qing dynasty, one of a group of teenagers who lived in a very large extended family remarked that they were so close in age they sometimes confused the names by which they addressed one another. That is, each person properly needed to call the others "elder brother (his given name)," or "younger sister (her given name)," and each person was supposed to keep track of which honorific was proper for each person.

Confucius thought the ideal family would have five sons and

two daughters, but historians and demographers now think that given the short lifespans of individuals in premodern times, the large, traditional, extended family might have been rare. A Chinese family might have consisted of as few as five people—say, an elderly mother in her forties or fifties, her son and his wife and two of their children, or elderly parents, two children, and the son's wife.

The last of the relationships Confucius commented on was that between two friends. This was the only relationship not based on familial or marital ties. The friendship might have developed because the two men had been to school together, or had passed the Confucian examinations in the same year, or were the grandsons of men who had been friends. The younger friend could always address the older person as "elder brother" if he so chose, but the elder brother would never demean the younger by addressing him as "younger brother."

As all of these relationships determined where a person fit in the society, even though one's position changed with age, marriage, death, etc., it is not hard to see how totally the Christian teaching of the equality of all in the eyes of God threatened the entire Chinese sociopolitical/cultural order.

After the 1860 unequal treaties imposed on China by the Western countries, following the wars that had begun in 1839, the Qing government had an office to take care of foreign affairs with the Western countries. From time to time rebellions or other social unrest might wrack one part of the country or another, making the central government's control in that area somewhat tenuous, but as far as Westerners were concerned they could always take their complaints directly to the central government through their diplomatic personnel, once those folks had taken up residence in Beijing.

Exclusive Territory for Each Mission

Cooperation, not competition, governed which mission worked where in China. By the time of the 1877 All-China Missionary Conference in Shanghai, those working in the country had informally agreed not to compete with one another. In the large cities, such as Beijing, Shanghai, and Guangzhou, the missionaries agreed that anyone could set up a mission station. Of course, these were among China's largest cities and there were plenty of potential converts to go around. However, inland and in smaller cities and towns the missionaries agreed there was no point in having say both the London Mission Society (LMS) and the American Methodist Episcopal Mission (AMEM) competing for converts and students for their schools, in the same location. Instead, the missionaries agreed to a "first come, first claim the field" plan. Although no one was actually keeping track of which mission was where, new mission agencies or those seeking to expand their field did not move into an area where there was already a Protestant mission at work. Throughout the missionary era, Chinese who had converted were accepted by those of different missions, based on a letter from the missionary who converted the person. All the Protestants accepted baptisms and church membership from other sects.

One place can be used to illustrate the principle: when the LMS sent the Reverend James Gilmour to work in Mongolia in 1871, largely the territory today known as Inner Mongolia, he discovered the American Board of Commissioners for Foreign Missionaries (ABCFM) had a couple, the Gulicks, living at Jiangjiakou for the express purpose of evangelizing Mongolia. In such an isolated location, one can imagine how much the Americans welcomed the arrival of the traveling Gilmour.

Indeed as Gilmour wrote the LMS board in London, they were very good friends and he had gone itinerating with the Reverend Gulick and had no theological differences with him. The problem was, while the ABCFM board in Boston wanted Gilmour to withdraw from the field, their missionaries in the field truly enjoyed the friendship of the man who had invaded their mission's territory! As with most such disputes in China, this one was resolved by health, when the Gulicks were forced to withdraw because of illness. The ABCFM, like all mission boards, never had enough people or money to fill all the needs of the mission, so they did not send replacements to staff the Jiangjiakou station, and the LMS took the field. With the death of Gilmour in 1892 the LMS did not assign anyone else to his field, probably because in twenty years of itinerating Gilmour had made no converts.

Who Went Where?

Exactly how any one missionary decided to locate a station is somewhat a mystery. After the 1842 treaties, the missionaries established themselves in the five ports that the treaties had opened to trade along the China coast. These were Guangzhou, Fuzhou, Xiamen (Amoy), Ningpo, and Shanghai. As Hong Kong had become a British territory under provisions of the 1842 Treaty of Nanjing, some British missionaries established themselves there. Within a few years the center for foreign trade had moved northward to Shanghai, partly due to Guangzhou being closed to foreigners because of a hostile environment, following the treaty settlement.

After the advent of the steamship, Shanghai was the port at which most trans-oceanic passenger liners arrived. As a result, virtually every mission organization had some type of office or home in that city, and those that did not could make use of the Mission House, which was actually a foreign-style hotel, catering exclusively to missionaries. The Mission House had a back stairway from the dining room that was dubbed "the escape stairs" for those who thought the daily devotions after meals were too long!

The outbreak of the Taiping Rebellion in south China hindered the missionaries in their desires to plant stations inland. But once it was quelled, the missionaries were on the move, penetrating the interior. Access to the Yangzi River from Shanghai was quite easy and soon missionaries were making the journey upriver to determine good places to establish their work. Generally, the missionaries tended to settle first in large cities where a Chinese governor or governor-general had his yamen. The missionaries, of course, knew they were protected by the extraterritoriality clauses of their treaties, and the Chinese officials knew of these privileges but sometimes chose to ignore them, if they could.

Missionaries leaving the coast of China for the interior first established themselves in cities or large towns along rivers, which were the main routes of transportation in China. Once a mission station was established in the river city, missionaries might discover some smaller towns or villages nearby, say within a day's journey by riverboat, foot, or sedan chair. Often a Chinese who worked at the mission station in the river city was a native of one of these towns in the hinterlands and introduced the missionaries to their clan relatives there.

When foreigners tried to purchase land in these interior places, often they found no one willing to sell to them. Totally ignorant of the social structure of China, the missionaries had no idea that an individual could not sell land, which in any case was probably not the sole possession of that person, but rather belonged to his extended clan. Missionaries new to many places soon found themselves housed in abandoned temples—clan, Buddhist, or Daoist. Other housing offered to missionaries included rundown buildings, which many of the locals thought were haunted, or those next to a cemetery or execution ground, as Chinese did not like to live in such unlucky places. One early missionary reported in *The Chinese Recorder* that he had been housed overnight in the crude attic of an opium house, where the fumes drifted up to him. Fleeing those accommodations, he then spent the entire night in a roofless shack protecting himself from a drenching rain with his umbrella. In any case, if the Chinese did not want the foreigners to stay, they were often provided with the most uncomfortable lodgings available.

The missionaries thought some provinces of China were more hostile to them than others. For example, Hunan was thought to be the province most resistant to Christianity, and it was the last part of China to have missionaries within its boundaries. Because the missionaries had little, if any, information about the people who lived in China, when they did happen on folks who were obviously not Han Chinese, they frequently concentrated on trying to convert these people to Christianity.

For example, when the Reverend B. C. Henry (APM), Guangzhou, accompanied C. C. Jeremiassen, purportedly a Danish sea captain[1] who had found religion and decided to convert Hainan, traveled to the island in the 1880s, they discovered both Hakka and aborigines living there. Henry

---

1. Jeremiassen is a rather unusual Danish surname, and the author, with the assistance of several Danes, has been unable to verify anyone with that name ever enrolled in the school for seamen or received sailing papers from the Danish government. Needless to say, Jeremiassen's daughter and granddaughters were stunned when they learned of this information. His origins remain unknown.

wrote the APM board in New York stating that he believed both the Hakka and the aborigines would be more amenable to Christianity, because they lacked the prejudices the Han Chinese had toward the religion. He also wrote to the APM board in New York that everyone on the island seemed to understand the Guangdong dialect, so language would not present a problem to the missionaries from Guangzhou. Once the Presbyterians established a mission on the island, they discovered that only migrants from Guangzhou understood that dialect, and others on the island spoke the Hakka dialect, the Loi language, the Miao language, the Fujian dialect, as well as regional variations of these dialects and languages. The island was, in fact, one of the most linguistically complicated areas in China, and it was not long before the missionaries discovered the non-Han residents of Hainan shared many of the same views of Christianity that the Han people of the mainland held.

As customs of the mainstream Han lifestyle strongly opposed any person or group who differed from the dominant tradition, some Protestant missionaries gradually turned their attentions to those already alienated from the Confucian tradition.

It was not only Protestants who thought non-Han peoples might be drawn to Christianity. Some of the French Roman Catholic missionaries in Jean Michaud's *"Incidental" Ethnographers*[2] worked among aboriginal people in Yunnan province, and the adjoining region in present-day Vietnam, which was then French Indochina. Many of those they converted were aboriginal tribesmen, often called Hmong, who had been pushed onto marginal uplands centuries earlier by

---

2. Jean Michaud, *"Incidental" Ethnographers: French Catholic Missionaries on the Tonkin-Yunnan Frontier, 1880-1930* (Leiden: Brill, 2007).

the encroaching Han people. Relations between the minority tribes and the Han Chinese were usually strained, and as the tribes were pushed higher and higher into the mountains, they had only steep hillsides with very poor soil to cultivate.

In truth, despite its huge population, China was not a field where folks flocked to the religion of the foreigners. Missionaries often wrote home about both their converts and their "almost converts," that is, people who might one day convert, but hesitated to do so usually because of family and cultural concerns. Many people who had contact with the missionaries fell into the latter category.

After the Protestants discovered how few Han Chinese were interested in Christianity, some decided to try to convert the aboriginal tribes who lived in southern China. The province of Yunnan is home to an estimated 44 percent of China's ethnic minorities. (The present government of China recognizes fifty-five distinct ethnic groups in the country.)

T'ien Ju-K'ang's *Peaks of Faith: Protestant Mission in Revolutionary China*[3] details the early mission work in Yunnan. In the first decade in the twentieth century, the British United Methodist Mission pioneered work among the tribal peoples there, but they soon asked the CIM to take over work in part of the province. The Methodists converted many of the Miao people, while the CIM concentrated on the Yi tribes. Wars between the Miao and the Qing, in the waning days of the dynasty, had generally ended with the Qing victorious and the confiscation of Miao lands by the Han people. The CIM missionaries helped the Miao by providing funds to purchase back their former lands, because the foreign missionaries thought the Miao living in villages would be easier to convert than if they migrated seasonally.[4] The CIM also had some

---

3. T'ien Ju-K'ang, *Peaks of Faith: Protestant Mission in Revolutionary China* (Leiden: Brill, 1993).

success among the Lisu people, who also lived in Yunnan. Other groups that were the objects of missionaries' attention were the Lahu and the Wa, the latter having many settlements in what is today Myanmar. T'ien reported that the converts numbered about one hundred thirty thousand, by 1949, but among the Han, who constituted 40 percent of the province's population, there were only four converts by 1948. However, in the years after the Cultural Revolution, many Han turned to the Christian churches; T'ien attributed this is to their dissatisfaction with the government's promises of improvements after 1949.[5]

While Protestant missionaries were working among the tribal peoples of southern China, European Roman Catholic missionaries were at work among both Han people and Mongols in northwest China. The Belgian order the Congregation of the Immaculate Heart of Mary (CICM), better known as the Scheut Fathers, from the location of their headquarters near Brussels, began work in the area within the bend in the Yellow River known as the Ordos[6] in 1874. The Scheut Fathers had many conflicts within their order among members who clung to the nationality and languages of their birth families; the disputes were usually among French, Flemish, and Dutch speakers.

The Ordos was a marginal desert in the late nineteenth century, with the desertification increasing year by year although some irrigation was possible in the areas immediately adjacent to the Yellow River. The early Schuet Fathers in the area had begun cultivating gardens for their own food, and

---

4. Readers will recall this same idea was common among early Roman Catholic missionaries in the Philippines. (See chapter 6.)
5. T'ien, *Peaks of Faith*, 24.
6. Patrick Taveirne, *Han-Mongol Encounters and Missionary Endeavors: A History of Schuet in Ordos (Hetao), 1874-1911* (Leuven: Leuven University Press, 2004), 120-21. The Mongol word *Ordos*, for this region, is the origin of the word *horde*.

gradually helped some of the local people with new farming techniques, although they recognized this was a secondary job to their main purpose—the conversion of the people. Soon the Fathers were renting out small plots of their land near their churches to local people, and in 1893 one priest defended this type of "colonization," arguing it would not produce "rice" or in this case "millet Christians."[7]

After the Boxer Uprising, the Scheut Fathers gained a lease on a large tract of land in the Ordos as part of the treaty settlement between the crumbling Qing government and the foreigners. The missionaries then rented out small portions of this land to both Han and Mongols who wanted to try farming in this very marginal area. (The Mongols were herders and hunters, but did sometimes till the soil in times of necessity.) Gradually, the Fathers required that those renting land from them attend religious instruction during the winter months. Apparently, the Fathers counted all those attending these classes as converts, which soon numbered in the thousands. When the missionaries' expenses in the Ordos grew beyond their meager budget, the Fathers invested in a house in Tianjin, the rents from which were used in the Ordos. At least some of the Fathers thought that this system of colonization around a church building, which had been used with success in the New World, would also work in the Ordos, totally ignoring the fact that the Han had a dynastic government that ruled the country and the Mongols had a long-established government to take care of their needs.

In addition to renting land, the Schuet Fathers had some other unusual methods of conversion. Many of them had learned to play musical instruments while studying for the priesthood, and in the Ordos at least one father advocated

---

7. Taveirne, *Han-Mongol Encounters and Missionary Endeavors*, 369–70.

using musical instruments to "lure the pagans, who are all big children, and, if God permits to convert them more easily."[8]

The Reverend Gilmour, who worked in eastern Mongolia during part of the time the Scheut Fathers were in the Ordos, mentioned several times in letters to his London board that he had heard of the Roman Catholics' great numbers of converts, but did not understand how they had done it. He likely would have been appalled at the colonization method, as Protestant board missionaries were forbidden by their boards to purchase land to rent out or to engage in any type of business.[9]

Statistics on China's Christians

Anyone who tries to estimate the number of Christians in China, at any time, is undertaking an uncertain task. Although the Chinese government had population statistics, they did not include anything about religion. The missionaries often tried to count how many converts they had made, but were reluctant to admit how many were backsliders.

Statistics about other aspects of the missions are also questionable. *The Christian Occupation of China*,[10] a 1922 compilation of information about China and, specifically, about Christian missions in the country, contains plenty of statistics. Published at the time of growing Chinese nationalism, the book's unfortunate title did nothing to win friends for the mission endeavor. The book is most interesting, as it gives much information not specifically related to missions. For instance, it details the amount of railroad track and which

---

8. Taveirne, *Han-Mongol Encounters and Missionary Endeavors*, 308.
9. Many early missionaries in China received requests from businessmen at home to purchase land or buildings or certain trade goods, instructing the missionaries to hold the items until the businessmen could get to China.
10. Milton Stauffer, ed., *The Christian Occupation of China* (Shanghai: China Continuation Committee, 1922).

places are served by trains throughout China. It also contains brief histories of the various provinces as well as each one's famous products, sights, and people. This book is likely the source of the statistic that Christians constituted less than one percent of China's population, for it gives the population of the country, around 1922, at slightly over 438 million and the number of Christians as 366,524. These figures would put the percentage at far, far less than one percent.

Although the *Christian Occupation of China* contained many charts listing the number of mission schools, doctors, stations, Chinese evangelists, Bible women, etc., its trouble is that perhaps 40 percent of the statistics contained on its many charts bear the caution "returns not complete." For example, it lists 675 Christian elementary, higher elementary, and middle schools which educated 19,057 thus giving each school an average of twenty-eight students, a number most scholars find hard to believe.

In other cases, the number of missionaries in a specific place are said to be only those directly working full-time on the evangelization of Chinese. Exactly what that meant is anyone's guess, but the author assumes any administrative people, from the mission agent to the director of the CIM, were not included since they are not working full-time on evangelism. As there were dozens, maybe hundreds, of missionaries who reported these numbers to the compilers of the book, one wonders how they counted the missionary wives, or ordained men who at the moment might be supervising the construction of new buildings for the station.

At the height of the mission movement on the eve of the 1927 violence, which caused many missionaries to flee, Kenneth Scott Latourette in his *History of Christian Missions in*

China[11] estimated there were eight thousand missionaries on the field, but does not explain how he arrived at that figure.

This author's own guess that fifty thousand different people were in China as missionaries between 1809 and 1949 is based on research for *The Chinese Recorder Index*. There are about ten thousand people in the published volumes that list individuals, with married women counted separately. For reasons of space, anyone with less than three references in the periodical was excluded and the author estimated these numbered thirty-five thousand. (Data on those not included may be found at the Yale Divinity School library.) The periodical used ships' passenger lists to publish the names of people arriving and departing from Shanghai. Thus any missionaries entering China at other ports were less likely to be included. Also, some missions, particularly the smaller ones, were less likely to have informed *The Chinese Recorder* of arrivals and departures, which was another way the editors gathered information. Some years after completing *The Chinese Recorder Index* when working on the APM on Hainan, this author discovered that only three of the eighty-seven people who served in that mission appeared in *The Chinese Recorder!* (Those serving that mission traditionally entered China by Hong Kong.)

Also based on the author's work on *The Chinese Recorder*, the author estimates there were nine hundred different mission groups operating in China between 1809 and 1949. There are about 825 agencies and quasi-mission agencies mentioned in the periodical. (Groups that were not missions, and would have not been in China if missions had not been there, the author called quasi-missions. These include the Red Cross, the Boy Scouts, the Women's Christian Temperance Union, and the

---

11. Kenneth S. Latourette, *A History of Christian Missions in China* (New York: Macmillan, 1929).

YMCA and the YWCA.) Also, there are relatively few Roman Catholic groups mentioned, as *The Chinese Recorder* was a Protestant periodical. *The Chinese Recorder* ceased operation with the December 1941 issue, so did not include mission work during the United States' involvement in World War II and in the years between 1945 and 1949. (In the 1980s at a professional meeting, a person who had been a missionary in Taiwan heard the author say she thought there had been about nine hundred agencies in China. He responded that there were then more than one hundred agencies at work on Taiwan, so he thought the nine hundred estimate was probably a good one.)

Statistics for the period since 1949 are equally difficult to determine. Some scholars think the Protestants, who went underground during the Cultural Revolution (1966–1978), experienced a huge growth in those years, when many Christians lived in rural areas. Over the centuries many villages in South China had developed as one-surname villages where everyone was a member of the same clan, while in North China it was more common for there to be two or three surnames in a village. During the heyday of the missionary century, some entire families converted to Christianity together, particularly if the patriarch decided to convert and brought all his relatives into the church with him. Thus over the years, some villages came to be known as Christian villages. Even in North China it was not uncommon for a several-surname village to be entirely Protestant or Roman Catholic, with the church becoming the village gathering point instead of the traditional clan temples. It might have been possible to proselytize in these villages, among people from nearby areas, even during the Cultural Revolution. The primary difficulty in ascribing the huge increase in the number of Protestants to this type of proselytizing is that these years were the ones of the collectivization of agriculture, with communal dining, when people were closely supervised by government cadres at all times.

Even given the repression of the Cultural Revolution and the collectivization policies, it does seem likely that Protestants were still able to evangelize among non-Christians with whom they had contact, as there is no other explanation for the huge increase in numbers. Of course, this does not explain why there was no corresponding increase in the number of Roman Catholics. Certainly, it was much easier for the Protestants to worship together than it was for the Roman Catholics, who needed a priest to conduct the mass, baptize, and confirm converts.

By whatever method one uses, in truth, accurate numbers about the China missionaries and the number of Chinese Christians at any given time do not exist, and any figure given, the author's included, was surely arrived at by voodoo statistics. The simple truth is no one knows.

Chinese Christians Today

During the heyday of the Protestant missionary endeavor in China the foreigners concentrated on converting people in small towns and rural areas. Of course, the missionaries worked in the big cities of China, such as Guangzhou, Shanghai, Beijing, Tianjin, etc., but proportionally there were more mission stations in the rural areas. In the years after the Cultural Revolution the population of China began moving from rural to urban areas. With China's increasing trade with the rest of the world, and the accompanying industrialization of China, cities grew quickly. As many of the migrants lacked permits to reside in the cities, their presence placed a burden on urban services ranging from housing to schooling for their children. Among the millions of migrants were, of course, Christians. Their movement to urban areas in recent years has increasingly meant the churches became more urbanized than in years past. Yet, in recent times, more and more Chinese factories are moving to China's interior to avoid the high costs of the coastal cities. As the population moves back to their home provinces, one can assume that their churches will go with them. Those minority groups, like the Lisu, the Miao, and the Yi who were converted to Christianity by missionaries, tend to continue to live in the rural areas they have traditionally called home.

Conclusion

China's high culture and long-established, highly-structured social order were problems that all missionaries—Roman Catholic and Protestant—had to deal with. Many missionaries, having discovered the dominant tradition of the Han Chinese elites was a significant roadblock in trying to convert people to Christianity, tried to convert marginalized peoples. Some of these minority peoples did become Christians, but, in many cases their own religions and beliefs hindered their conversion.

The vast numbers of people in China, all of whom were potential converts to the missionaries, complicated their work. No one, in China or in the Western countries, had any idea how many missionaries were at work in China and how many Chinese they had contact with and how many of those people became Christians. Missionaries liked to have statistics to report to mission boards at home and folks in the churches that supported them, with numbers for church attendance, students enrolled in mission schools, people baptized and confirmed, people given Christian burials, etc.; but there was never a set of criteria for counting these things. All missionaries knew there were backsliders among those they had converted, but aside from mentioning it, no one ever tried to determine how many Chinese fell into that category. The end result is that no one knows how many missionaries served in China or how many Christians there were at any time in China, today included.

5

Missionary and Chinese Christian Biographies

Whatever the number of missionaries who served in China, the number was high enough to make it dangerous to try to lump them together under any one category. In any group, there are always great individual differences, based on country of origin, denominational affiliation, evangelical fervor, professional qualifications, and personalities. Over the years the author has studied the Protestant mission movement in China, she has come up with some rough classifications for missionaries, determined by what their major contributions to the China mission efforts were. Missionary qualifications varied greatly as attitudes toward education differed in the United States and Britain, and in the other European countries, and mission qualifications changed over the years.

The author has never tried to put every missionary into one of these categories, and some individuals, such as James

Hudson Taylor, who founded and ran the China Inland Mission (CIM) until his death in 1905, defy categorization. Yet, despite any one person's contribution spilling out from one category to another, the author has grouped some of the Protestants who served in China as follows: Pioneers, Adventurers, Scholars, Teachers, Medical doctors, and Women.

Pioneers

Using these classifications, the Pioneers were the first missionaries to set up a station in a particular locale. These would, of course, include the Reverend Elijah Bridgman and his wife Eliza, both with the American Board of Commissioners for Foreign Missions (ABCFM). Other pioneers include the Reverend George L. MacKay (1844-1901), Canadian Presbyterian Mission (CPM), who first settled in Taiwan; and the Reverend Frank P. Gilman (1853-1918), American Presbyterian Mission (APM), who started mission work on Hainan.

The Reverend Bridgman was the first American missionary to arrive in China, in 1829, but he had been preceded by the Reverend Robert Morrison, London Mission Society (LMS), who had arrived in 1807. Mrs. Bridgman arrived in China in April 1845 as one of the first single women sent by her mission, and married her husband two months later.

Bridgman was restricted to the Guangzhou factory area with the foreign merchants, and had to retreat to Macau with them when the trading season ended each year. He was instrumental in the organization of the Medical Missionary Society and for establishing a China branch of the British Society for the Diffusion of Useful Knowledge. He also contributed many articles to the *Chinese Repository,* which he started, and the

North China Herald, which were the earliest English-language periodicals published on the China coast. After the signing of the first treaties between China and the Western countries, the Bridgmans moved to Shanghai, pioneering mission work in the city that was to become the center of all foreigners' activities in China.

MacKay was a Canadian and the first sent by his board to Taiwan, in 1872. He learned the local dialect by listening to young boys as they tended their animals. After years of working on the island he made a convert, who in turn brought him local scholars to debate religions. MacKay was not a trained doctor, but he learned some elementary first aid, which helped many of the local people. Tooth problems plagued many of them, and MacKay became quite skilled, through practice, at extracting teeth with forceps. MacKay was most unusual as a missionary in the nineteenth century as he married a Chinese Christian woman in 1878, who he said would be able to evangelize the local people better than any foreigner could. They had three children.

Gilman pioneered the mission on Hainan. A native New Yorker, he attended Princeton University with Woodrow Wilson, a fraternity brother. The two maintained their friendship throughout their lives. Gilman traveled to China by way of India where he married Marion MacNair, another New Yorker, who then was teaching at the missionary boarding school at Woodstock. Together they went to Hainan. Gilman was sometimes mistaken for a Frenchman, and on several occasions was attacked, as the French were then interested in colonizing the island and incorporating it into French Indochina, which the local people opposed. Gilman established mission stations at Jiaji, Nada, and Haikou, the island's port.

Adventurers

Adventurers among the missionaries were those who went to parts of China where few foreigners had ever been seen. Examples would be the Reverend James Gilmour (LMS), who from 1871 to 1892 worked among the Mongols in what is today Inner Mongolia, and parts of the country of Mongolia; and Evangeline and Francesca French and Mildred Cable of the CIM, who financed their own work in China's far western provinces in the 1920s and the 1930s.

Gilmour wrote the book *Among the Mongols*,[1] which was first published in 1883 and has never been out of print. The Japanese army translated it into Japanese for their World War II invasion of North China. When it was republished in the United States a century after it first appeared, Denis Sinor, longtime dean of the American Central Asian scholars, wrote a new Introduction in which he stated the book had "withstood the test of time," and called it one of the best books ever written about Mongolia.[2] This book alone would qualify Gilmour for the Scholars category, but the author has chosen to call him an Adventurer, because he worked in an area of north China and Mongolia where few other foreigners ever trod. His appreciation for the culture of the Mongols was unusual among nineteenth-century missionaries. After one of his early trips to his field, he wrote about a Mongol woman who had awakened him early, prepared his breakfast, and helped him load his camel for a dawn departure. He said that no one in so-called civilized Britain could have been kinder or more helpful.

Linda Benson has written a monograph, *Across China's Gobi*,

---

1. James Gilmour, *Among the Mongols* (London: Religious Tract Society, 1883).
2. Gilmour, *Among the Mongols*, 3.

on many aspects of the careers of Cable and the French sisters.³ The three served in a traditional mission station for twenty years before embarking on their personal mission to China's West.

China's Muslim minority, called *Hui*, mostly live in the extreme Western parts of the country and are linked to the Persians and the Turks. When Cable and the French sisters told the men of the CIM leadership in Shanghai they wanted to itinerate among the Muslims, the men hesitated. Reluctant to permit the women to go off to central Asia, the CIM leadership realized they could do little to stop them as the women financed their own work. Accompanied by their adopted deaf-mute daughter and a male servant, the women traveled by slow-moving donkey carts, which carried all their worldly possessions and Christian tracts for distribution. In each place they stopped the women asked what the conditions were in the area, and if they learned there were an army nearby or bandits had been particularly troublesome on a certain road, they simply left the next day in another direction!

On one occasion the women decided to take a furlough in Britain, so set off west until they reached the trans-Siberian railroad, which bore them to Moscow. When they reached London, they realized they had not told anyone of their arrival, so had to go to a hotel! The women wrote several books about Central Asia, which were published under Cable's name and made her a much-sought-after speaker on their visits to Britain. Perhaps the three should also be in the Scholar category because they certainly knew more about Central Asia of the 1930s than the vast majority of diplomats and scholars of the region.

3. Linda Benson, *Across China's Gobi: The Careers of Evangeline French, Mildred Cable, and Francesca French of the China Inland Mission* (Norwalk, CT: EastBridge, 2008).

Scholars

One of the first among the scholars was the Reverend James Legge (LMS) (1815–1897), who first translated the Chinese classics into English, as well as those like the Reverends Absalom Sydenstricker, American Southern Presbyterian Mission (ASPM) (1852–1931), and Samuel Schereschewsky, American Protestant Episcopal Mission (APEM) (1831–1906), who worked on the Bible translation. Also classified as Scholars are the many missionaries who compiled Chinese-English dictionaries, many in the dialects of the places they lived. In this latter category are two women, Adele Fielde, American Baptist Missionary Union (ABMU) (1839–1916), and Margaret Moninger (APM) (1891–1950).

Legge's monumental translation of the Chinese classics into English occupied most of his time in Hong Kong in the 1870s. After his return to Britain he became the first chair of Chinese at Oxford University. Legge's life and career are thoroughly dealt with in Norman Girardot's award-winning monograph, *The Victorian Translation of China: James Legge's Oriental Pilgrimage*.[4]

The Reverend Absalom Sydenstricker, father of Pearl Buck, was one of the first of the Southern Presbyterians to work in China, where he served for fifty-one years. He had a flair for Chinese and was appointed to work on the Bible translation the Protestants were anxious to complete. His colleague, the Reverend Samuel Schereschewsky, was quite unique among the foreigners in China. Schereschewsky had been born a Jew in Russia, migrated to the United States, converted to Christianity, and then was ordained in the Episcopal Church,

---

4. Norman Girardot, *The Victorian Translation of China: James Legge's Oriental Pilgrimage* (Berkeley: University of California Press, 2002).

which sent him to China where he served as its bishop of Shanghai from 1877 to 1884. He also founded St. John's University in that city. Alone among the China missionaries he had a vast command of Hebrew and other languages few of his colleagues were fluent in, making him a prime candidate for the work on Bible translation, which took most of his life.

Two of the missionary Scholars were women: Fielde and Moninger. Both compiled dictionaries of the local dialect, Chinese characters, and English: the Shantou dialect for Fielde and the Hainan dialect for Moninger. Both also published scientific articles on various subjects.

Teachers

The author categorizes as Teachers those China missionaries who devoted their years in the field to the education of young Chinese. Teachers organized and taught in elementary and secondary school, and later in universities that served Chinese. The Teachers include Eliza Bridgman and Dr. Claude Thomson (APM).

Shortly after marrying, the Bridgmans moved to Shanghai and Eliza began a school. She solicited funds from her friends in the United States, as both she and her husband were certain the ABCFM would not be willing to support a school. When the school began, she had about a dozen students enrolled.

Thomson taught at the University of Nanjing, beginning in 1918, educating generations of students in Western-style chemistry, and they, in turn, taught others. By the time Thomson arrived in China, the mission colleges were more interested in advanced academic degrees in specific subjects than they were in whether or not one was ordained. When the Thomsons' youngest son, James, came home to Nanjing for a summer, with a college friend, Thomson helped them do a survey of the living conditions in a neighborhood of Nanjing. Unfortunately, not far into their survey, the young men were detained by police who thought they were spies!

Medical Doctors

In a special category are the medical doctors who were China missionaries. American mission boards did not send missionaries anywhere overseas without an accompanying doctor, since the lands in which they served did not have Western-style medical facilities and personnel. In the nineteenth century, most mission boards required that medical doctors also be ordained. Such people were hard to find, and the mission boards also required that the men be married. Occasionally, if desperate, a mission board would dispatch a single, male medical doctor, if he were at least ordained.

Outstanding medical doctors include the Reverend Dr. Peter Parker, MD, (ABCFM) (1804–1888), the first Western doctor on the China coast, and the Reverend Dr. John Kerr, MD, (APM) (1824–1901), Guangzhou, who took over Parker's hospital at the latter's retirement.

Parker, who held his MD degree from Yale, was a skilled surgeon and specialized in ophthalmology. Some of his surgical feats were recorded by George Chinnery, an artist who was resident in Macau. Parker introduced Western anesthesia to China. Later he served the US government as an interpreter during the negotiations for the treaties ending the Opium War.

Several other mission medical doctors were as adventurous as Parker had been in their treatment of the Chinese. For example, Kerr, a graduate of Jefferson Medical School in

Philadelphia, established China's first hospital for the mentally ill in Guangzhou in 1898.

Other doctors developed a Braille system for the Chinese and taught the blind how to read it—no small feat considering the missionary first had to learn Chinese, then invent Chinese Braille. Most doctors also tried, unsuccessfully, to cure opium addiction.

Women

Essential to the China missionary effort were women, many of whom could also be listed in all the other categories, in addition to having specific roles in the mission determined by their gender. Single women filled every job at their stations, except, of course, that of ordained clergy, as none of the Protestant denominations permitted women to hold that position. Even so, when the missionaries held their English church services for themselves, many of them permitted their women colleagues to offer a Bible lesson or speak, if not actually preach, on their choice of text.

Women medical doctors particularly were sought for mission work as China, like many traditional societies, prohibited men, other than their husbands and close male relatives, from having any contact with women after puberty. Women medical doctors were still quite scarce in Western countries, particularly in the years after many American women's medical schools closed due to increasing accreditation standards. Few families were able to send their daughters to college, let alone on to medical school, and those who did likely expected the women to remain close to home upon graduation, in the hope that they might help to reimburse the family for the cost of their education.

Women's missionary societies solved this problem by recruiting bright, capable women who wanted a medical education, and who were willing to serve in their churches' overseas missions. The women's missionary societies financed the cost of medical school for these women, as they shared a goal, namely, to serve women in missionary countries, particularly China.

Immigrants as Missionaries

Another very interesting aspect of the China missions was that a relatively large number of missionaries from the United States and Canada were themselves immigrants to those countries. Even allowing for the large numbers of people flowing into both countries in the late nineteenth and early twentieth centuries, one cannot help but be surprised at how many of these folks then became China missionaries. As a whole, the immigrant missionaries the author has encountered in mission records do not seem to be people who just did not fit in to North American society, as all were church members and most were college graduates. The author can offer no explanation other than to state she has observed the situation. The Reverend Frank Rawlinson, editor of *The Chinese Recorder*, was British by birth, the Reverend Samuel Schereschewsky, mentioned above, was Russian by birth, and Dr. Nathaniel Bercovitz, MD, (APM), who worked on Hainan, had been born in a Presbyterian mission in Peru, to name just a few.

An excellent example of the immigrant missionary was Donaldina Cameron (1869-1968), whose Presbyterian family emigrated from Scotland to New Zealand, where she was born. Cameron then migrated to San Francisco and worked at a refuge mission, now called Cameron House, for abused Chinese women. She even managed to safely move her charges in the aftermath of the 1906 earthquake. The account of her life and activities, *China's Angry Angel*,[5] relates that she helped San Francisco's Irish policemen physically break up Chinese brothels and opium dens, vividly demonstrating the author's contention that missionaries were not timid, retiring people. In response to a request from a family in China, who asked for help in recovering their kidnapped daughter, Cameron once traveled to every Chinese brothel on the coast from San Francisco northward until she located the woman, then helped her return to her family.

Short Biographies of Some Chinese Christians and Some Missionaries

The missionaries, beginning with the Jesuits in the Ming dynasty (1368–1644), always hoped that a Chinese leader who was a practicing Christian would lead the entire country to his religion. Two of China's twentieth-century leaders, Sun Yixian (Sun Yat-sen) and Jiang Jishi (Chiang Kai-shek) were Christians, but the mass conversions so many missionaries sought never occurred. However, many of the Chinese Christians listed here were leaders among the Christian communities at various times.

The task of trying to decide who to include in a list of Chinese Christians and missionaries is daunting. The author includes here some individuals in each category listed above, trying to reach a balance among men and women, Protestants and Roman Catholics, and Chinese and Westerners. The list is by no means comprehensive. It is in alphabetical order, and the

---

5. Mildred C. Martin, *Chinatown's Angry Angel: The Story of Donaldina Cameron* (Palo Alto, CA: Pacific Books, 1977).

author make no claim to assessing each person's contribution to the overall mission in China.

Allen, Reverend Young J. (1836-1907), American Southern Methodist Mission (ASMM), Shanghai. Sailing for China a decade before the American Civil War, Allen established himself in Shanghai. Cut off from funds during the War, he engaged in business to support his missionary work. He had taken a printing press to China and published newspapers and tracts that introduced many Chinese to Western thought and ideas, influencing the late Qing reforms, in the years after the defeat of the Taiping Rebellion, and again after the Boxer Uprising. Allen was also interested in education, particularly of women, and was instrumental in the establishment of McTyeire School for Girls in Shanghai, which was headed by Laura Haygood, sister of one of his friends. The school is still in operation, but of course, not as a mission.

Bridgman, Reverend Elijah C. (1801-1861) and **Eliza Gillett Bridgman** (1805-1871) (both ABCFM), Shanghai. The first American missionary to reach China, in 1829, Bridgman was a graduate of Amherst College and Andover Theological Seminary. He traveled to China on a ship owned by David Olyphant, an American China trader, who transported many of the missionaries free of charge and supported their early efforts in Guangzhou and Macau and later in Hong Kong. Bridgman married Eliza Gillett shortly after she arrived in China. Elijah worked on translating the Bible into Chinese and also published *The Chinese Repository*, the first English-language periodical in China. He organized the Morrison Education Society, the Medical Missionary Society, and the organization that became the North China Branch of the Royal Asiatic Society. After the Treaties of Beijing of 1860 were signed, the

Bridgmans moved to Shanghai where Eliza organized schools for Chinese. Both died in Shanghai and are buried there.

Buck, Pearl Sydenstricker (Mrs. John Lossing Buck) (1892–1973) (APM), Nanjing. Buck is the best known of all the China missionary children, and was the first American woman to receive the Nobel Prize in Literature, in 1938; she remains the only noted American author who spent her entire formative years outside the United States. She was the daughter of the Reverend Sydenstricker and later served with her husband, John L. Buck, an agricultural specialist who did some of the first scientific studies of land use in China. The subject of an outstanding biography by Peter Conn, *Pearl S. Buck: A Cultural Biography*,[6] Buck's birth family was typical of many missionary families, with rare furloughs and the deaths of several babies. Buck's biographies of her parents, *Fighting Angel* and *The Exile*,[7] are among the best portraits of missionaries ever written. Buck, who admitted she wrote her first novel, *The Good Earth*,[8] to supplement her family's income, had grown up among the Chinese servants and had an understanding of their daily lives that far exceeded that of most other Westerners in China. Her books focused on the great problems of twentieth-century China: the status of women, the peasantry, and the warlords.

Cable, Mildred (1878–1952); **Evangeline French** (1869–1961); and **Francesca French** (1871–1961); (all CIM), Shanxi, later Western China. After twenty years working in a mission station in Shanxi, they decided to go to China's far West, a mostly Muslim area, to evangelize. Evangeline and

---

6. Peter Conn, *Pearl S. Buck: A Cultural Biography* (New York: Cambridge University Press, 1996).
7. Pearl Buck, *Fighting Angel* (New York: John Day, 1936), and *The Exile: Portrait of an American Mother* (New York: John Day, 1936).
8. Pearl Buck, *The Good Earth* (New York: John Day, 1931).

Francesca French were from a well-to-do family in Britain, but had been raised mostly on the Continent. Evangeline joined the mission in 1893, and met Cable shortly after she arrived in China in 1901. Francesca joined the mission in 1908 after the death of the sisters' mother. Francesca was thought too old to join a mission, but as she was paying her own expenses, the CIM took her. Although all three women contributed to their writings, most were published in Cable's name. Her book *The Gobi Desert*[9] was widely regarded as the best account of the region in the 1930s, and after its publication she became the first female member of the Royal Geographic Society. She was also vice president of the British and Foreign Bible Society from 1938 to 1952.

Castiglione, Giuseppe (1688–1766), Society of Jesus (SJ), Beijing. Italian by birth, Castiglione was a skilled painter in the style of Renaissance Italy. He was not ordained, but was a lay brother of the Jesuits. He became the official painter to the Qianlong emperor (1736–1796) and is famous for his portrait of the emperor, in golden clothing, on horseback, shooting an arrow. In old age the Qianlong emperor said he could recover his youth by looking at the portraits of him that Castiglione had painted. Another of Castiglione's well-known works depicts eight horses in different poses, clearly demonstrating his combination of Chinese and Western painting styles. Eight horses in different poses are a common, and very lucky, theme in Chinese art, but Castiglione painted his in the highly realistic, muscular style of Renaissance Europe, while omitting the chiaroscuro which the Chinese disliked.

Fielde, Adele (1839–1916) (ABMU), Siam, later Shantou, Guangzhou. Likely the first accidental missionary, Fielde was

---

9. Mildred Cable with Francesca French, *The Gobi Desert* (London: Hodder and Stoughton, 1943).

raised a Universalist, but agreed to become a Baptist and marry a missionary serving in Siam. Unfortunately, when she arrived there in 1865 she learned her beloved had died. She stayed on in Siam learning the Fujian dialect of the Chinese migrants who had been there for generations. She alienated many of her Baptist colleagues by socializing with the foreign business community, dancing, and playing cards. Finally, her colleagues tired of her and sent her home. When she stopped in China en route, the Baptist missionaries in Fujian begged the mission board to allow her to serve there, because she knew the local dialect. Fielde published several scientific articles and compiled a dictionary of the romanized Shantou dialect, Chinese characters, and English. She also published a book of Chinese fairy tales. At the time of her retirement she refused to accept a pension from the Baptists, stating she had never shared their beliefs! She returned to the Pacific Northwest and campaigned successfully for electoral reforms and women's suffrage.

French, Evangeline and **Francesca** (see **Cable, Mildred**).

Gilmour, Reverend James (1843–1891) (LMS), Beijing and Mongolia. Having decided he would become a missionary while at university, Gilmour applied to the LMS indicating he would go anywhere. Under the influence of Mrs. A. Stallybrass who with her husband and a few others pioneered a mission to the Mongols in Russian Siberia early in the nineteenth century, Gilmour was selected for Mongolia. (The earlier mission closed when the tsar withdrew permission for the missionaries to be in his territory.) The LMS decided to reopen the Mongolian mission and assigned Gilmour to do so, from a base in Beijing. He traveled almost annually to Mongolia for twenty years and found the people there as civilized as anyone in Britain, but he made no converts, for as he wrote to the LMS Board, the

Mongols had their own religion and could see no reason to change. In 1873 he published *Among the Mongols*, about the people, their customs, their religious practices, etc. It is still in print.

Gutzlaff, Karl (1803–1851), Chinese Evangelization Society (CES), Guangzhou. One of the earliest of the European missionaries in China, Gutzlaff was Pomeranian by birth. He arrived in China after some time in Southeast Asian ports, where he had become acquainted with overseas Chinese and learned enough of some of the coastal dialects to be able to communicate when he got to China. He organized the CES, the purpose of which was to distribute Christian tracts throughout China by means of local men. Others in the early mission community thought his plan unworkable, as his assistants knew little of the doctrines in the pamphlets they were employed to distribute. The system broke down and Gutzlaff's plan was discredited when it was discovered that the men he had employed took their pay and pamphlets, but did not distribute them.

Jiang Jishi (Chiang Kai-shek) (1897–1975). (See also **Song Family; Song, Meiling.**) A native of Zhejiang, Jiang gained power after the death of Sun Yixian. As leader of the Guomindang (GMD) (Kuo Ming Tang, KMT), he conducted the Northern Expedition in 1926–27 to consolidate his power, and then split with the Chinese Communist Party (CCP), massacring many of their members in Shanghai in 1927. He was president of the Republic of China from 1928 to 1975, having taken refuge on Taiwan after losing the Chinese Civil War in 1949. Astute at manipulating American politicians, Jiang's wife, Song Meiling, addressed the US Congress during World War II. Jiang's detractors nicknamed him Cash My-check, for his ability to gain financial aid from the US government and American church folk, who had long supported China missions. Jay Taylor's *The Generalissimo*[10] states that Jiang, under the influence of his wife and some of her missionary friends, agreed to become a Christian after reading the Bible through twice.

Jing Dianying (1893–1953?). He was the leader of the Jesus Family (*Yesu Jiating*), which began in Shandong in the late 1920s. The Christians in this group were Pentecostals and millenarianists, expecting the imminent return of Christ. They organized themselves into fictive families, each headed by a Chinese man, and the group spread primarily in rural areas. Its membership was thought to number several thousands at the time it was suppressed in 1953. There was a brief revival of the group in the post-Mao years, but it was suppressed again as it was not one of the government-sanctioned churches. The Jesus Family did influence some of the Chinese crypto-Christian cults of the late twentieth and early twentieth-first centuries.

Kang Cheng (Ida Kahn. See **Shi Meiyu**.)

Kerr, John, MD (1829–1901) (APM), Guangzhou. A pioneer of the Guangzhou mission, Kerr arrived in 1854 and took over the hospital established by Dr. Peter Parker, MD. During his career Kerr trained many Chinese to do simple medical tasks, a practice later adopted by the Chinese Communists to care for their people, in the absence of an adequate number of medical doctors. Chinese officials and the British in Hong Kong not only sent many patients to Kerr's hospital for the mentally ill, founded in 1898, they supported it with contributions. The hospital closed in 1937, as World War II began in China.

Kung, H. H. (1880–1976). (See also **Song Family; Song, Ailing.**) Kung became a Christian as a young man and survived

---

10. Jay Taylor, *Generalissimo: Chiang Kai-shek and the Struggle for Modern China* (Cambridge, MA: Belknap/Harvard University Press, 2009), 29.

the Boxer Uprising which took the lives of many of his friends. Kung was educated at Oberlin and Yale, along with T. V. Song, his brother-in-law. They came to dominate the financial side of the Republican government in China. He married Song Ailing in 1919. Kung was once known as the richest man in China and one of the richest in the world.

Legge, Reverend James (1815–1897) (LMS), Hong Kong. One of the earliest missionary scholars, Legge was the first to translate the Chinese classics into English, and became the first professor of Chinese at Oxford University. Done with the assistance of several Chinese literati, Legge's translations are still used.

Li Zhizao (also known as Leon Li) (1565–1630) (RC), Hangzhou. Li is one of the Three Great Pillars of the Catholic Church along with Xu Guangxi and Yang Tengyun. He was active in building the church in Hangzhou in the late Ming dynasty.

Liang, Reverend A-fa (1789–1855), Guangzhou. Long identified as the first convert to Protestantism, Liang is no longer thought to hold that distinction. He was employed as a woodblock carver and was hired by Robert Morrison to cut the blocks for the New Testament, although publishing Christian works was forbidden in China at the time they worked. Liang accompanied the early missionaries to Malacca, where he was baptized in 1816 by William Milne. Liang was later ordained by Morrison, and worked distributing tracts around Guangzhou. He is thought to have given one of these to Hong Xiuquan, leader of the Taiping Rebellion.

Martin, Reverend W. A. P. (1827–1916) (APM), Ningpo and Beijing. Arriving in China in 1849, Martin was stationed at Ningpo until 1857 when, because of his ability in Chinese, he was asked to work as an interpreter for the US legation. In 1863 he moved to Beijing where he organized the International Law and Language School. He survived the siege of the legations during the Boxer Uprising, and later held various posts with the government of the late Qing, trying to help Chinese officials modernize the country. He died in Beijing in 1916, having spent sixty-two years in China.

Moninger, Margaret (1892–1948) (APM), Hainan. A 1913 graduate of Grinnell College, Moninger had signed the Student Volunteer Movement for Foreign Missions (SVMFM) pledge. She arrived in China in 1915 and taught at all of her station's schools. She did itinerating through the remote mountains of the island to try to convert the aborigines, who were still living a Stone Age existence. She published several articles about these people, and compiled a dictionary of the romanized Hainan dialect, Chinese characters, and English. Along with her colleagues she lived under the Japanese occupation of the island from 1937 until she was repatriated on the *Gripsholm* in 1942.[11]

Moon, Charlotte Digges (Lottie) (1840–1912) (ASBM), Shandong. Moon's contributions to the American missionary effort changed America more than they changed China. She worked in Shandong by herself, but she altered the role of women in the Southern Baptist church at home. They raised money to send Moon to China and to support her there, and the Southern Baptist churches still annually collect mission funds in Moon's name at Christmas. Moon's career and the changes it brought in her church, namely giving women a greater voice in church matters, are the subject of Regina

---

11. Kathleen L. Lodwick, *Educating the Women of Hainan: The Career of Margaret Moninger in China, 1915-1942* (Lexington: University Press of Kentucky, 1995).

Sullivan's *Lottie Moon*;[12] and her career in China is dealt with in Irwin Hyatt's *Our Ordered Lives Confess*.[13]

Nevius, Reverend John L. (1829–1891) (APM), Shandong. A native of New York, Nevius developed what became known as the Nevius Plan for spreading Christianity in China and elsewhere. The Plan emphasized that converts remain in their homes and occupations and witness for Christ among those they met, rather than moving close to a mission outstation or being employed as a native assistant by the missionaries. Any programs and churches these Christians started needed to be those that could be sustained by the local church, without foreign funds. Nevius urged that church buildings should be built with local materials in the local style with funds and materials supplied by the church members. The national church needed to be responsible for calling pastors to staff these churches. The church leaders needed to have instruction in the Bible and the church's doctrines on a yearly basis. The Nevius Plan became the model for the Three-Self Patriotic Movement (TSPM) after 1949, and was followed with great success in Korea.

Ni Tuosheng (Watchman Nee) (1903–1972). Ni was the leader of the Assembly Hall (*Juhuichu*) or the Little Flock (*Xiaoqun*) from the 1920s to 1937. Influenced by the Holiness tradition's emphasis on the Holy Spirit as well as ideas of the Brethren tradition, Ni wrote many pamphlets, some of which were translated into English and circulated worldwide. He was a critic of the foreigners and the organized missions in China. His Little Flock was disbanded after 1949, and Ni was imprisoned, where he died in 1972.

12. Regina Sullivan, *Lottie Moon: A Southern Baptist Missionary to China in History and Legend* (Baton Rouge: Louisiana State University Press, 2011).
13. Irwin Hyatt, *Our Ordered Lives Confess: Three Nineteenth-Century Missionaries in East Shantung* (Cambridge, MA: Harvard University Press, 1976).

Parker, Reverend Peter, MD (1804–1888) (ABCFM), Guangzhou. The first Western medical doctor in China, Parker arrived in 1834. He held both theological and medical degrees from Yale. Parker quickly became known as a surgeon who could accomplish great feats with his knife and was highly skilled at the removal of cataracts. Parker joined Elijah Bridgman in assisting the Chinese to understand Western law at the time of the negotiations of the treaties ending the Opium Wars.

Rawlinson, Reverend Frank (1871–1937) (ASBM, later ABCFM), Shanghai. Born in England, he migrated to the United States and applied to the ASBM, because they were one of the few mission boards that accepted married men with children for service in China. Editor from 1914 to 1937 of *The Chinese Recorder*, an ecumenical publication for Protestant missionaries and supporters at home, Rawlinson was influential in championing liberal ideas and causes among the missionaries. As he became more liberal he parted with the ASBM and joined the ABCFM. Once called one of the one hundred most influential Americans in China, he greatly favored a Chinese indigenous church that would not need foreign involvement. He also favored Chinese nationalism. He was killed during the Japanese attack on Shanghai in 1937.

Ricci, Father Matteo (1552–1610) (SJ), Macau. Arriving at Macau at the end of the Ming dynasty, Ricci was not the first Jesuit in China, but was the first to survive long enough to learn the language, publish some pamphlets in Chinese explaining Christianity, and become friends with some members of China's literati. In his Christian explanations Ricci drew comparisons with traditional Chinese beliefs and practices. After careful study and asking questions of many literati, Ricci decided the Confucian ceremonies were not religious, and therefore could be practiced by Christian converts. Ricci published a book in Chinese, *The True Doctrine of God*, in which he set forth what a potential convert needed to know before conversion was possible. Topics included the existence and unity of God, reward or punishment in the afterlife, the immortality of the soul, and the creation. Before baptism, the convert needed to renounce the beliefs in the transmigration of the soul and the worship of idols.

Ricci also used the many items he had brought to China to interest the literati in Western culture. These included prisms, clocks, astronomical instruments, and musical instruments. Ricci's map of the world intrigued many literati because this document showed China as one of many countries in the world and not the center of the world, which was how the Chinese viewed their country. The Chinese had long considered themselves as the only civilized country, as all the surrounding countries had borrowed various aspects of Chinese culture for their own. Ricci eventually reached Beijing in 1601, having been summoned by the emperor. (See chapter 6 for a discussion of the Chinese Rites Controversy, which was the result of Ricci's accommodations to Chinese culture.)

Rong Hong (Yung Wing) (1828–1912). Sent by the Bridgmans to study in the United States, he enrolled at the Monson School in Connecticut and then at Yale in 1850. At Yale he became a college student in the tradition of the times: singing in the choir, rowing, and excelling academically—he won two prizes in English. It was his dream to lead a group of Chinese young men to study in the United States, which he finally succeeded in doing in 1872. Rong became an American citizen while at Yale. In China he worked for missionaries as a translator and later for the Qing government. Employed for a short time by Zeng Guofan, the Qing official who put down the Taiping

Rebellion, Rong purchased equipment in the United States to manufacture firearms in China. Rong married Mary Kellogg in 1875 at a Congregational Church in Connecticut where they were both members. They had two sons, Morrison Brown Rong (Yung) and Bartlett Golden Rong (Yung). Mary died in 1886. As a result of his involvement in the Reform Movement in 1898, which was crushed by the Empress Dowager Cixi, Rong fled to the United States, this time with the help of American friends, as his entry to the country was illegal; he had lost his citizenship under the Chinese Exclusion Act of 1882. He died in and is buried in Hartford, Connecticut.

Schall von Bell, Father Johann Adam (Adam Schall) (1591–1666) (SJ), Beijing. Schall arrived in China in 1619 in the midst of a persecution of Christians, which led to two of the four Jesuits resident in Beijing being ordered to Macau. Schall was in Macau until 1630 when he was summoned to Beijing to take over work on the Chinese calendar. China used a lunar calendar to calculate the dates for rites, ceremonies, and holidays. The methods the Chinese astronomers used had been introduced by Muslims during the Yuan (Mongol) dynasty (1271–1368), and by the late Ming the calendar was considerably compromised, with astronomers not even able to predict lunar eclipses. Schall's time in Beijing included the Manchu invasion of China which created the Qing dynasty. To help the Ming against the invaders, Schall cast cannon for their army. (These cannon were used in the mid-nineteenth century in warfare against the Westerners.) Schall was asked to become president of the Board of Mathematics, but declined on many occasions, because of the prohibition against priests holding secular offices. He eventually accepted and his action was approved by the pope. Christianity was permitted by the emperor, which the Jesuits attributed to their work in astronomy. In 1662, when the Kangxi emperor was still a child, the Jesuits were denounced by their enemies, the Muslim astronomers. Schall was sentenced to death, but an earthquake, then a meteor, hit the imperial palace. Schall's sentence was canceled and he lived four more years. His astronomical instruments are today on display on the roof of a small observatory on Changan Road to the east of Tiananmen Square in Beijing.

Shi Meiyu, MD (Mary Stone) (1873-1954) and **Kang Cheng, MD** (Ida Kahn) (1873-1930) (both AMEM), Jiujiang. Shi and Kang were the first Chinese women to receive American medical degrees, both graduating from the University of Michigan in 1896. Shi was the daughter of an ordained Methodist minister and her mother taught at the mission school. Kang was raised, in part, by the AMEM missionary Gertrude Howe, spending some of her childhood in the United States. As medical doctors both Shi and Kang returned to China and worked with the AMEM to establish hospitals, which also did nurses' training. Shi did graduate work at Johns Hopkins on a scholarship from the Rockefeller Foundation. She left the Methodists to start the Bethel Band. She also founded the Women's Christian Temperance Union in China. The careers of Shi and Kang are dealt with in Connie Shemo's *The Chinese Medical Ministries of Kang Cheng and Shi Meiyu, 1872-1937*.[14]

Song Family: Charlie Jones (1866?-1918); a son, **T. V.** (1894-1971); and daughters **Ailing** (Mrs. H. H. Kung, m. 1919) (1888-1973); **Qingling** (Mrs. Sun Yixian, m. 1915) (1893-1981); and **Meiling** (Mrs. Jiang Jishi, m. 1927) (1897-2003); and two other sons. (See also **Jiang Jishi, Kung, H. H.,** and **Sun Yixian**.)

---

14. Connie Shemo, *The Chinese Medical Ministries of Kang Cheng and Shi Meiyu, 1872-1937: On a Cross-Cultural Frontier of Gender, Race and Nation* (Bethlehem, PA: Lehigh University Press, 2011).

Charlie Jones Song, father of the famous Song sisters of twentieth-century China, traveled to the United States in 1878. He spent eight years in the South, converting to Christianity in 1880 in a Methodist church in Wilmington, North Carolina. He attended Trinity College (later Duke University), but transferred to Vanderbilt University after he fell in love with an American girl whose family disapproved of him. He received a divinity degree from Vanderbilt in 1885, and later married a Chinese Christian. His children, three sons and three daughters, constituted one of the strongest political dynasties in early twentieth-century China.

In China in the late 1880s, Song worked briefly for the Methodists, but they paid him only the salary of a native preacher, not one equal to a Westerner with an education similar to his, so he left their employ. He became a publisher, specializing in Bibles and religious literature. All three of the daughters were educated at Wesleyan College in Macon, Georgia, while their brother, T. V., attended Harvard. T. V. and his brother-in-law, H. H. Kung, controlled the banks and the government treasury while their other brothers-in-law, Sun Yixian and Jiang Jishi, controlled China's government from the overthrow of the Qing dynasty until their defeat in 1949. Of the Song sisters it was said that one loved money, one loved China, and one loved power. Qingling died in Beijing, while Ailing, Meiling, and Kung all died in New York. T. V. died in a San Francisco restaurant, choking on a fish bone.

Song, John (1904–1944). A second-generation Christian from Fujian, Song studied in the United States from 1919 to 1927 and received a PhD in chemistry from Ohio State University before moving on to Union Theological Seminary (UTS) in New York for a year. While in New York he had a conversion experience after a revival, then an emotional crisis, and spent six months in a mental hospital. Returning to China, Song associated himself with the Bethel Mission, and later with four other men, formed the Bethel Worldwide Evangelist Band and began his career as an evangelist. He was noted for his emotionalism and his denunciation of those with whom he disagreed, including many foreign missionaries. His autobiography was revised several times after his death to strengthen the Fundamentalist faction in the Chinese Christian community.[15]

Sun Yixian (Sun Yatsen) (1866–1925) (see also **Song Family, Qingling**). A native of Guangdong, Sun's older brother had migrated to Honolulu, and subsequently placed his younger brother in Iolani School, a mission institution in that city. There Sun came into contact with Christianity and he formally adopted the religion in 1884 after he returned to China. After medical school in Hong Kong, Sun became involved with anti-Manchu organizations that were seeking to overthrow the Qing dynasty. Forced to leave Hong Kong because of his activities, he settled for a while in Japan but was soon asked to leave that country. The success of the revolution in October 1911 found Sun in the United States on a fundraising tour, but he soon returned to China, and became president of the republic. He married Song Qingling in Japan in 1915. He was twenty-six years older than his bride, and her father, Charlie Jones Song, a Christian, was outraged at the marriage, since Sun had been married twice before.

Taylor, Reverend James Hudson (1832–1905) (CIM), Shanghai. Among the many eccentrics who went to China as missionaries, Taylor, the founder and head of the CIM, was one of the most unusual. Extremely secretive, he permitted only positive news be released to his supporters at home. Like

---

15. Daryl Ireland, "John Sung's Malleable Conversion Narrative," *Fides et Historia* 45, no. 1 (Winter/Spring 2013): 48–75.

many other nineteenth-century missionaries, Taylor felt he had been called to labor in the China mission. So great was his belief in the correctness of what he did, that he relied only on God to supply the earthly needs of his missionaries, paying them no regular salaries. Destined to be the largest of all the missions that worked in China, the CIM also had many resignations and dismissals, which were usually the result of doctrinal differences, but sometimes stemmed from the lack of financial support.

Taylor ran the mission single-handedly, and had the most ecumenical of all mission bodies in China. Denominationalism meant little, if anything, to Taylor, although he did subscribe to a Fundamentalist view of Christianity and eventually withdrew from the Church of Christ in China, the all-China mission body that had formed out of the mission conferences. Following an attack upon CIM missionaries in Yangzhou in 1867, Taylor vowed never to appeal to diplomats again, even in the event of the death of his personnel.

Vautrin, Wilhelmina (Minnie) (1886–1941), United Christian Missionary Society (UCMS), Nanjing. A native of Illinois with a teaching degree from the University of Illinois, she taught at Ginling, the Protestant women's college in Nanjing. She did not evacuate the city when consular officials ordered Americans out in December 1937, staying behind even though the Japanese army was approaching. During the Rape of Nanjing in December, she protected many of Ginling's women as well as many others by hiding them wherever she could on the campus. (She was likely the only foreign woman in the city during the Rape.) Vautrin is an example of a single woman missionary who went to China, and after the death of her parents, had no home in America. She had a brother who had a family of his own, but he disapproved of her career choice. Thus when she returned to the United States in the midst of World War II, she shuffled from one house to another, always as someone's guest. Clearly suffering from post-traumatic stress syndrome, known since World War I as shell-shock, Vautrin's increasingly fragile psychological state caused her to commit suicide in May 1941. Vautrin's career needs to be thoroughly researched, although an account of her activities during the Rape of Nanjing was the subject of a non-scholarly, poorly researched book several years ago.

Verbiest, Father Ferdinand (1623–1688) (SJ), Beijing. Arriving in China after the pope, in the first round in the Chinese Rites Controversy, sided with Matteo Ricci and his accommodation with Chinese customs, Verbiest was in Beijing assisting Adam Schall when the persecution of Christians began in the mid-1660s over a controversy between the Jesuits and the Chinese astronomers about eclipses. In 1668 Verbiest successfully predicted the length of a shadow at a certain time as well as the time of an eclipse. His success convinced the Kangxi emperor to make the Jesuits the official court astronomers and to allow their brethren to continue their work in the provinces.

Wang Mingdao (1900–1991). Wang was born in the Legation Quarter during the Boxer Uprising, to parents who worked for the LMS, which educated him in their schools. He later taught at a Presbyterian school in Baoding, but left over the issue of arming the students and faculty to oppose the troops who had invaded the area in 1920. He became the best known of China's self-taught evangelists. Wang spent most of the years between 1955 and 1980 in prison for opposing the Communists and the TSPM.

Wu Yaozong (Y. T. Wu) (1893–1979). Wu became a Christian in 1918, having been influenced by the rallies of John R. Mott and Sherwood Eddy. Wu joined a Congregational Church and worked as Student Secretary of the YMCA. He studied at UTS and Columbia University in New York, receiving an MA in philosophy. Wu was a pacifist during the 1920s and organized the Chinese branch of the Fellowship for Reconciliation, seeking a measure of union between the Communists and the Christians. Criticized by many for his work with the Communists, he was instrumental in publishing the Christian Manifesto in 1950, which some see as the beginning of the TSPM, which he eventually led. He was denounced during the Cultural Revolution and sent to a labor camp.

Xu, Candida (1607–1680) (RC), Shanghai. The granddaughter of Xu Guangxi, Candida was a dedicated Christian. After she was widowed she spent some forty years helping Christian communities and building churches with the help of her son, Basil.

Xu Guangxi (Paul Hsu) (1565–1633) (RC), Shanghai. A Confucian official with expertise in agriculture, astronomy, and mathematics, Xu served the Ming dynasty. He studied with Ricci and adopted Ricci's Western mathematics and published the first book in Chinese on the subject. Xu took the name Paul when he was baptized. Considered the first Chinese Catholic, Xu gave his family lands in Shanghai to the church, which today house a Catholic church, the library at Xujiahui (*Zikawei*), and Xu's tomb. He is one of the Three Great Pillars of Chinese Catholicism, along with Yang Tengyun and Li Zhizao. Xu has the status, Servant of God, the first stage to canonization.

Yang Tengyun (Michael Yang) (1557–1627) (RC), Hangzhou. The Catholic Church designated Yang one of the Three Great Pillars of the Faith in China, along with Xu Guangxi and Li Zhizao. Yang took the name Michael at his baptism. He is one of the prominent leaders responsible for the growth of the church in Hangzhou during the late Ming dynasty.

Yen, James (1893–1990) (YMCA). One of the young educated Chinese who took Christian teachings to a new level, Yen was a graduate of Yale and went to Europe during World War I, under the auspices of the International YMCA, to work with Chinese who had been recruited as laborers to unload ships and to dig trenches and graves. Yen spent a great deal of time writing letters home for the workers, who were mostly illiterate. Yen, the subject of Charles W. Hayford's *To the People: James Yen and Village China*,[16] returned to China and worked for the uplift of China's poorest. After 1949 Yen took his ideas for rural reconstruction to the Philippines.

Yung Wing (see **Rong Hong**).

---

16. Charles W. Hayford, *To the People: James Yen and Village China* (New York: Columbia University Press, 1997).

6

Four Theological Issues in the China Missions

Four major theological issues arose among the China missionaries and their converts, each of which had major consequences for the Christian church in China, the wider Christian community, and the church folks at home who supported the missionaries. The four are: the Roman Catholic Chinese Rites Controversy, the Protestant Fundamentalist-Modernist controversy, the Protestant ecumenical movement, and the feminization of Protestant Christianity.

Two of these—the ecumenical movement and the feminization of Christianity, specifically, the education and ordination of women and women's roles in the home churches began in the China missions in the nineteenth century and spread to the home churches. Ecumenism was the watchword for the early missionaries to China: the task of converting the Chinese, thought to number about four hundred million in

203

the early nineteenth century, was simply too immense for the missionaries to argue about the doctrinal differences that had split the churches into many denominations in the West. The feminization of Protestantism, which some see as significant as the Reformation, changed women's role in the home churches, and saw the ordination of women increase, spectacularly, in both the home countries and in China. Both of these enormous changes in Protestantism occurred in the China missions in the nineteenth century and spread to the home countries. Few in the Western churches even know that these two features of twentieth-century Christianity began among the missionaries and Chinese Christians, but the author believes there is adequate evidence to support this contention.

The four controversies are discussed in chronological order.

The Chinese Rites Controversy in the Roman Catholic Church

How to transmit Christianity to people who have never before heard of the religion is a difficult problem any pioneer in a mission field must face. Where does one begin and, perhaps, more important, how does one translate concepts that are specific to Christianity into a language that previously had no words for these ideas?

Father Matteo Ricci, Society of Jesus (SJ), arriving in China during the late Ming dynasty (the Renaissance/Reformation era in Europe), tried to determine who the leaders of the local communities were, but as he spoke no Chinese this was not an easy task. Initially, he dressed himself in the garb of Daoist monks, until he realized that they were not the leaders of the society and were, in fact, marginalized by the elites. When Ricci learned that the Confucian bureaucracy, who spent their lives in study for the all-important government examinations, and were part of the scholar-official-gentry class, were society's elite, he adopted their manner of dress.

The Confucian literati, who were skilled in the Chinese classics, which they revered as models for human interaction, considered both Buddhism, a belief largely for women, and Daoism, a folk religion, beneath their concern. Consequently, the literati had little interest in Ricci and his beliefs. However, having come from Renaissance Italy, Ricci was skilled in the mnemonic techniques of his day, and, applying them to memorizing Chinese characters, dazzled many a literatus. As the Confucian examinations were based totally on memorization, anything that could improve one's memory was extremely valuable, and some scholars wanted to learn Ricci's techniques. Jonathan Spence's *The Memory Palace of Matteo Ricci*[1] is the most outstanding account of Ricci and the European and Chinese worlds he inhabited. Through his contacts with literati, Ricci gradually gained a knowledge both of Chinese and of Chinese culture.

Ricci looked for similarities between the Chinese classics and Christian teachings. For instance, Chinese tradition taught one to honor one's parents and contained a version of the Golden Rule. Ricci also carefully studied the rituals that the literati and the common folk practiced. All Chinese honored their living parents and grandparents and extended that honor to their long-dead ancestors, thus emphasizing the continuity of the family. Part of this ritual involved putting food in front of the names of one's ancestors, inscribed on small pieces of wood or paper on the family shrine, which each home had.

The early Jesuits in China discussed these practices at length and finally decided, at meetings in 1603 and 1605, that Chinese

---

1. Jonathan Spence, *The Memory Palace of Matteo Ricci* (New York: Viking Penguin, 1984).

converts could keep the tablets with the ancestors' names on them and decorate the shrines with flowers and candles. However, converts were not permitted to pray to their ancestors, or to believe that ancestors would return and eat the food left as offerings. The Jesuits also decided that the Confucian ceremonies, conducted on the first and fifteenth of each month by scholars to honor the Sage, were civil rituals, similar to venerating one's ancestors, and thus these practices were permitted to converts.

A more complicated problem for Ricci and his fellow Jesuits was how to translate Christian teachings into Chinese. Chinese folk religion had a concept of heaven, that is, the place one's spirit went after death. They traditionally burned paper money and paper pictures of everyday objects at funerals and at Chinese New Year, so that the smoke would transport these items to wherever the deceased's soul had come to rest. The Chinese character for heaven, *tian*, is that of a man with outstretched arms with a horizontal line at the top—clearly an indication of something big and higher than man. The Jesuits decided this word for heaven could be used to indicate the Christian version of heaven.

More difficult was which Chinese characters were appropriate to use for the words for God, Heavenly Father, Jesus Christ, etc. The Jesuits decided that both *Tianxu* (Lord of Heaven) and *Shangdi* (Lord Above or Supreme Lord) were acceptable for God. All of this was complicated by the Chinese use of *Tianzi* (Son of Heaven) for the emperor, who was said to rule by heaven's mandate. If the emperor were the son of heaven, then who was Jesus? Furthermore, the Chinese knew that emperors were mere mortals like everyone else, and that strong families from time to time overthrew a dynasty to establish another one. The transitory nature of the imperial throne was simply accepted as part of how China functioned. Indeed, at least one beggar had become emperor, and the Chinese have a saying: Even the emperor has straw-sandaled relatives.

In Europe the Jesuits had ingratiated themselves into the power elites of the Catholic countries, and had become the confessors of various Catholic monarchs. In China they sought to do the same, believing that if the emperor were converted to Christianity, the entire country would follow his lead. Such a thought indicates how little of the Confucian tradition the Jesuits actually understood. The entire literate class of China based its hopes for a government job, and status as a member of an elite group, on memorizing the Confucian classics and passing the government examinations, which were based on Confucius's teachings. To change the system was to destroy the entire social and governmental structure of the country.

Once the Jesuits decided which aspects of Confucian society they would accept among their converts, they might have made more progress in transmitting their beliefs to the Chinese had it not been for other European religious orders. The Jesuits were not alone in doing missionary work in China; they were joined by Dominicans, Franciscans, Augustinians, and secular orders, which were all from Europe. Some of these men had sojourned in Southeast Asia, especially in the Philippines, before arriving in China.

(The story of these orders in the Philippines is likewise one of great cultural misunderstandings. The European priests were shocked that the Filipinos bathed naked together in the ocean on a daily basis, and did not live in what the foreigners considered to be towns. Forcing the Filipinos to live more closely together to make it easier for priests to visit them, and halting the daily bathing that the priests considered immoral, resulted in the spread of diseases, which had never before been a problem. Furthermore, as the priests refused to translate certain key Christian words, namely, God, Jesus Christ, Virgin Mary, etc. into the local languages, whenever revolts began against the Westerners, and the ringleaders were arrested, the authorities were shocked to discover they had several God Almightys, a number of Virgin Marys, and even some Jesus Christs in jail, as the leaders of the revolts had taken these powerful names to ensure their success!)

The Dominicans, Franciscans, and Augustinians, as well as other orders, had worked with aboriginal people in the New World, many of whom lacked written languages, but these orders were unprepared to work in China, with its high culture. They were determined to convert the Chinese from the grass roots, or rather the rice paddies, up. They also made no accommodations to living in China, deciding instead to live and dress as they had in Europe. The mere fact that many of these newly arrived priests wore sandals convinced many of China's elites that the priests were poor beggars and thus beneath their notice, as, in their view, no one who could afford shoes would willingly wear sandals.

Also, the newly-arrived Catholic orders maintained an antagonism toward the Jesuits, because of the latter's successes in Europe. The newcomers immediately seized upon the Jesuits' ideas of accommodating Christianity to Chinese culture as a point to dispute. Antagonisms between the orders—Jesuits on one side and the Dominicans, Franciscans, and Augustinians on the other, kept these disputes over the Chinese Rites raging at the Holy See for over a century, and beyond. Known as the infamous Chinese Rites Controversy, it caused the Catholic missionaries to be expelled from China, ending the mission.

The issues were last discussed by the Catholic Church at Vatican II in the 1960s.

Briefly, the Chinese Rites Controversy was mainly a struggle between Roman Catholic holy orders to determine who had the greatest influence at the Vatican. In 1631 two Dominicans arrived in China, followed two years later by two Franciscans; all were Spanish by nationality. Without much study of the Jesuits' accommodation policies, both groups denounced the Jesuits to the bishops who were resident in the Philippines, and had never been to China. The bishops, in turn, informed Pope Urban VIII (1635) about the matter. Missionaries in the Philippines then began to argue one side or the other in the dispute and in 1643 one Dominican from the Philippines traveled to Rome to present the arguments to the Holy See.

The series of issues submitted included the charge that the Jesuits had permitted their converts to take part in the Confucian rites. When the Jesuits learned of this they immediately denounced the charge. Without hearing the Jesuits' side of the dispute, Pope Innocent X ruled against the Jesuits in 1645.

When the Jesuit representative from China arrived in Rome in 1651, he presented the Jesuits' view of the matter and in 1656, Pope Alexander VII ruled in favor of the Jesuits, noting that the Confucian ceremonies seemed to be purely civil and political.

Meanwhile, a persecution of the missionaries began as the Qing dynasty (1644-1911) was consolidating its power. Accordingly, all the missionaries were required to retreat to Guangzhou, where they lived in the same house. In such close proximity, and unable to do any mission work, the Jesuits, Dominicans, and one Franciscan discussed the matter at length and agreed, with one dissension, to adopt a common approach

209

to conversion, and to permit converts to engage in Confucian ceremonies.

Only the Dominican superior dissented, but by late 1669 he, too, agreed. Then he secretly left Guangzhou for Macau and a ship to Rome, where in 1673 he denounced the agreements reached at Guangzhou. At that moment, the Holy See did not wish to revisit the issue, but they were forced to do so in 1693, after the superior of the Mission Étrangère, then serving as Vicar Apostolic of Fujian, forbade the China missionaries to use the words *Tian* and *Shangdi* for Christian concepts and prohibited converts from participating in Confucian ceremonies.

The Holy See resumed studying the questions in 1697, by which time many of the non-Jesuit missionaries in China had decided to use the Jesuit interpretations of the Confucian Rites and the Jesuits' use of *Tian, Tianxu,* and *Shangdi*. A decision was reached in 1704 and Pope Clement XI sent a personal representative, appointed Patriarch of Antioch, to China to ensure that converts did not participate in the Confucian Rites. Arriving at the court of the Kangxi emperor, the papal legate revealed to the emperor that his mission to China was to ensure that converts did not practice the Confucian Rites. Learning this, the emperor ordered the Legate out of Beijing and required that all missionaries who wanted to work in China have a ticket from the emperor, which would be given only to those who guaranteed they would not oppose the Confucian Rites and would follow the guidelines of Ricci.

In his edict, the Kangxi emperor pointed out that he believed the Westerners were petty, and did not understand large issues as the Chinese did. He stated that no Westerner was well versed in the Chinese classics and as a result they made incredible and ridiculous remarks. He denounced Christianity as "no different from other small, bigoted sects of Buddhism or Daoism" and stated that the papal degree was "nonsense." He then ordered all Westerners not to preach in China, lest they cause further trouble. (Those Jesuits directly serving at the court were exempted.)[2]

Once the emperor's edict was made public, in 1707, the papal legate revealed that the Holy See had two years earlier issued a decision against converts participating in the Confucian Rites, but had not announced it in Europe, so that it could be first revealed in China. The announcement clearly stated that any missionary violating the order would be excommunicated.[3] The Catholic Church issued more orders concerning the controversy, but in China, what mattered was the Kangxi emperor had acted, and his order had to be obeyed.

The Kangxi emperor's grandson, the Qianlong emperor, greatly admired the works of some of the Jesuits, particularly those of the lay member, Giuseppe Castiglione, a talented artist trained in the techniques of the Italian Renaissance, who was appointed a court painter. Despite the emperor's admiration for Castiglione, in 1737 the Qianlong emperor reinforced his grandfather's edict against Christianity. Castiglione and other Jesuits also worked on creating many of the Qianlong's imperial gardens in Beijing, which survive to this day.

The Chinese Rites Controversy went dormant with the dissolution of the Society of Jesus by Pope Clement XIV in 1773. However, events in Japan in the 1930s brought the Chinese Rites Controversy to the fore once more. In 1932 students at Sophia University, run by the Jesuits, refused to pay homage to the war dead at the Yasukuni shrine, but later the bishop

---

2. Michael Collins, *The Fisherman's Net: The Influence of the Popes on History* (Mahwah, NJ: Hidden Springs, 2003), 185.
3. "Matteo Ricci" www.newadvent.org/cathen.

of Tokyo permitted the practice for Roman Catholics, after he received a letter from the Japanese government telling him that the ceremonies were patriotic and expressed loyalty.[4]

Also in 1932, the Japanese required everyone bow before a picture of Confucius in their newly-created state of Manchukuo, in Manchuria. This too was permitted to church members after the local Roman Catholic bishop obtained a letter from the new government stating that the ceremonies were to "show the spirit of patriotism" and were not religious.[5]

By 1935 the issue was again being discussed at the Holy See, and in 1939, a directive was issued stating that Catholics could participate in Confucian ceremonies as they were not religious. (The reader is reminded that this is exactly what Ricci had decided centuries earlier.) In 1941 the Catholic Church took the position that practicing Japanese Catholics needed to follow their own consciences in deciding what was proper regarding ceremonies that honored the Japanese emperor.[6]

Yet even that ruling did not end the Chinese Rites Controversy, as it was discussed at Vatican II (1962–65) when the Church leaders decided Catholics should incorporate local beliefs into their masses whenever possible.[7] The Chinese Rites Controversy is the reason the early Jesuits in China—Ricci, Schall, and Verbiest—were never canonized, although Chinese Catholics acknowledge their contributions to their church.

However, the biggest problem all the missionaries in China faced was the concept that everyone is equal in the eyes of God. This directly challenged the Chinese traditional social order, in which everyone's place was determined by their gender and birth order in a series of unequal relationships, some of

---

4. "Japan" www.newadvent.org/cathen.
5. Ibid.
6. Ibid.
7. "Vatican II" www.newadvent.org/cathen.

which changed as one aged and married. No missionary ever succeeded in altering this system.

Fundamentalist-Modernist Controversy

The Fundamentalist-Modernist controversy, a very different kind of dispute, had been going on for decades in American churches when it erupted in China, spectacularly, in the 1920s. The controversy had a lasting impact on the China missionaries and their converts, as well as the churches at home. The dispute began in the Presbyterian Church, then the fourth-largest denomination in the United States. Although the issues became quite complicated, the controversy essentially entailed a literal, conservative reading of the Bible on one side and a liberal interpretation of Christianity that allowed shaping the religion to fit new scientific and literary ideas, on the other. The dispute involved splits in the Protestant churches, Darwin's theory of evolution, the Scopes' Trial, attitudes toward Germany after World War I, as well as more narrow theological issues, such as the Virgin Birth, the divinity of Christ, etc. The result was American churches divided into the mainline denominations, those accepting the modern, liberal interpretation of Christianity; and those that hold to a more traditional, conservative interpretation of the religion.

The issue reached China, shattering the ecumenical tradition that had existed among the Protestant missionaries since the beginning of their work in 1809. Up to that point, the unity of Protestants in China had long been emphasized, and the three all-China mission conferences reinforced this idea. The Church of Christ in China was created in 1927 to further emphasize the unity of Christians in the country, even though it weakened itself by excluding the indigenous churches.

This dispute spread to China just as the indigenous Christian churches were exerting more influence in the country. Many of the leaders of these churches were vocally opposed to the foreign missionaries, particularly the manner in which the foreigners controlled the funds available to the Chinese churches, decided issues of faith without consulting Chinese Christians, and ran the mission schools with Chinese input only when required by the government.

In China the controversy began at the North China Theological Seminary, where the faculty debated the same issues that were discussed in the United States. Issues of faculty governance of the institution, funding organizations having voting rights over the institution, and the ownership of the property of the seminary all became matters of dispute. While the China missionaries had always prided themselves on their ecumenical outlook, when the Fundamentalist-Modernist controversy erupted, the China Inland Mission (CIM) withdrew from the Church of Christ in China, shattering any sense of Christian unity.

John Song, one of China's most popular evangelists, became a player in the controversy, but only after his death, when others altered his autobiography. (See chapter 5 for a brief biography of Song.) In the altered version of Song's life story, he supposedly had a sudden conversion to a literal Bible belief while at Union Theological Seminary (UTS) in New York. The story related is that Song attended a revival at which a sixteen-year-old girl evangelist spoke, an event that brought on his conversion.

Song's personal turmoil, which had plagued him since his days at Ohio Wesleyan University, increased after the revival.

At one point he reported that Jesus had found him in his dormitory room. Song's official autobiography, altered several times after his death, reported he then burned his theology books and confronted and denounced Harry Emerson Fosdick, one of the leading liberal theologians, as the Devil. Shortly thereafter, UTS officials had Song committed to a mental hospital as many of the faculty thought he had gone insane. He was released, after six and a half months, only with the intervention of Chinese diplomatic officials.

As Song was an informal student who spent only a year at UTS, there are no records of his academic work. However, recent research by Daryl Ireland reported in *Fides et Historia*[8] states he discovered some incidental papers at the UTS archives that indicate Song and Fosdick likely never even met, as Fosdick was away during Song's time at the seminary! Ireland concludes that the story was fabricated to make it appear as though Song was firmly in the Fundamentalist camp while still at the seminary.

Song was not alone in his turn toward the Fundamentalist faction in the dispute with the Modernists. Almost all the indigenous Chinese churches today hold to Fundamentalism, although some of the larger, mission-founded churches, such as Moore Memorial in Shanghai, still run many social welfare programs for their members and the surrounding community. In time the fundamentalism of the indigenous Chinese churches extended to the churches in overseas Chinese communities, particularly, in the United States.

---

8. Daryl Ireland, "John Sung's Malleable Conversion Narrative," *Fides et Historia* 45, no. 1 (Winter/Spring 2013): 48–75.

Ecumenism in the China Missions

The ecumenical movement of the second half of the twentieth century is another great change in Christianity that can trace its origins to the China missions, but it happened more by default than by anyone's plan.

The ecumenical nature of the Protestant missionary movement in China was evident on American college campuses with the creation of the Student Volunteer Movement for Foreign Missions (SVMFM) in 1888. (Although the SVMFM recruited for all parts of the world, the China field was by far the largest for all the mainline churches.) Most clergymen in the English-speaking countries were college graduates, and many missionary women had some postsecondary education, if not a degree, as education became more important for women, particularly in the United States. Denominational colleges were fertile recruiting points for mission boards.

The SVMFM was first suggested at a YMCA meeting in 1886, but was formally organized two years later, with John R. Mott as its first secretary. Often closely associated with the YMCA and the YWCA, the SVMFM had chapters on numerous American campuses and yearly held summer camp meetings. The SVMFM encouraged those who volunteered for church or outreach programs to consider foreign missions. The group's motto, "The Evangelization of the World in This Generation," was an ambitious one, resulting in many college students, particularly at summer meetings, signing the pledge "God willing, I will become a foreign missionary." This was a powerful commitment, particularly for those college students whose first journey away from home was to attend a nearby Protestant-affiliated college.

Missionaries home on leave were featured speakers at the

camp meetings and sometimes on college campuses. It was not uncommon for future missionaries to be inspired by someone from a denomination the students did not belong to or from a country the students were not interested in as a mission field. Once the SVMFM pledge was signed, it was sent to the mission board of the church the applicant indicated was his or hers. The SVMFM was itself an ecumenical movement; it sent no missionaries out, but rather served as a recruiter for Protestant church mission boards.

The Journey to China

Sailing to China, after the advent of the steamship, meant one met missionaries of other denominations who were bound for China, either to take up new work or to return to their stations after furloughs. Few mission boards ever sent single women to China alone, but if a woman were the only single woman in a group of couples or families, the single woman was assigned a cabin to share by the steamship company. (The shipping firms were quite aware they were taking to China two distinct groups of passengers—the missionaries who needed the salon for church services on Sundays and prayer meetings on other days; and the businessmen/globetrotters, whom the missionaries termed "the fast crowd," who used the salon nightly for dances and gambling. Obviously, the two groups did not dine at the same tables. Those shipping company employees responsible for assigning cabin space to single travelers tended to pair missionaries with missionaries and businessmen/globetrotters with those who, it was hoped, shared similar interests.)

Those missionaries who were returning after furloughs frequently gave those making their first trips to the field some information about their lifestyle and the work they did at their various stations. As a result, the month-long Pacific crossing, with its forced camaraderie and close quarters, meant that the missionaries got to know one another quite well. Onboard missionaries of all denominations formed into a group, sharing religious services, and passing the long hours talking with one another. If one formed a particularly close friendship on board, as many single women did, it might continue for many years in China with correspondence, visits to one another's mission stations, summering together at the missionary resorts of Guling, in the mountains of Jiangxi, or at the beach retreat at Beidaho, Shandong, and meeting one another at various all-church gatherings.

Each shipboard group arrived at its own decision concerning what type of Sunday service and communion they would have, but letters home clearly indicate that the Protestants held one ecumenical service, not different ones for each denomination represented. It was not unusual for only two or three people of a given mission to be aboard one ship, and the total number of Protestant missionaries on any ship might only be a dozen or so, although there were exceptions.

Many China missionaries were from small towns and had attended church-related colleges, so it is quite likely that it was aboard ship that they first met people from Protestant denominations that had not been represented in their previous, rather narrow, social circles. Whatever differences, say, Lutherans and Presbyterians had found important at home, these began to fade as they all made their ways westward to save China.

Immediately upon arrival, the vast nature of the country and its population overwhelmed many a Westerner. If the missionary thought one could win the Chinese for Christ, the sheer magnitude of the population quickly squashed that idea. Hardly a letter was written to a mission board at home that did not beg for more workers and more money to tackle the task.

Mission boards, of course, did not have unlimited amounts of money, so resources had to be distributed fairly throughout the world. The goal of converting the heathen was never financed to the fullest. Given the vast size of the task they faced, most missionaries readily accepted that China would never be "Lutheran," or "Methodist," or "Anglican," and if there were any hope that it would ever be Christian, the missionaries were going to have to cooperate. That meant putting aside most of the quarrels in which they had engaged, in their home countries.

In response to the immensity of their task, many missionaries went through a reassessment of exactly what made one a Christian and, precisely, what of Christianity did Chinese need to understand to become members of God's church. Issues that had divided the churches at home, like infant baptism, adherence to a particular form of church governance, whether one used wine or grape juice for communion, etc., were quickly relegated to the sidelines in China.

Gradually, the Protestants developed the custom that if a clergyman were visiting a mission station on a Sunday, the guest would preach and offer communion, according to his belief, in the local church. If the guest were still there the second Sunday, then the host was free to preach and offer communion, according to his belief.

(Most visitors to mission stations were missionaries, but they were certainly not the only ones to make use of mission hospitality, as employees of the China Imperial Maritime Customs Service are often mentioned as guests by missionaries who lived in the treaty ports. Globetrotters also made use of mission hospitality and it was not unheard of for some women globetrotters to lend their hands to the mission work, staying at their own expense for months or even a year or more at a single station. In the twentieth century it was increasingly common for journalists and scientists doing research to be guests at mission homes. Missionaries who lived in remote areas tended to have many guests, as there were usually no Western-style hotels in the areas where they lived.)

Mission Conferences

By the 1870s some missionaries thought there were enough of them in China to constitute the need for an all-China conference to review their work and chart out plans for the future. The meeting was planned for Shanghai, and convened for two weeks in the spring of 1877. The evangelical flames that had started the China missions were still quite evident in this gathering, as among the largest issues discussed were whether or not missions should sponsor schools and hospitals. Some missionaries argued that both schools and hospitals detracted from the true work of the missions, which was to win the Chinese to Christ, while others emphasized the need for converts to read the Bible and the Bible's teaching that one needed to care for the sick.

It is significant that the subject of ecumenism was a topic at the conference, although it was not called that. Rather, the Reverend Alexander Williamson, Scottish United Presbyterian Mission (SUPM), spoke about the vast task of converting China: "No one can be a strict denominationalist in this heathen land ... we may have different 'forms' and 'practices' but substantial unity. I believe therefore that denominationalism as far as possible, should go to the winds . . . let nationality go to the winds." He also stated that he would "never consent to aid transplanting the sects and sectarianism of the West into this country." Most of the speeches given at the Conference were followed by a discussion period when dissenting views were presented. However, the Records of the Conference contain no mention of a discussion after Williamson's talk, so presumably no one disagreed with his views.[9] Also discussed at this conference was the possibility of creating uniform marriage and funeral ceremonies for use in all the churches in China.[10]

Other all-China missionary conferences were held, again in Shanghai, in 1890 and in 1907, the latter having been postponed by the Boxer Uprising. Again, ecumenism was a theme of these conferences. Not only did missionaries of all the denominations meet for these gatherings, but they also shared housing and dining accommodations, which offered great opportunities for the exchange of ideas. One finds many letters missionaries wrote home, either to their sending boards or to family members, relating how a visit to another denomination's mission compound offered new insight as to how to solve problems common to all the missionaries. (It was years after these all-Protestant missionary conferences in China had begun that the Protestants convened the Edinburgh Conference of 1910, which brought together missionaries from all parts of the world.) Out of these conferences in China eventually emerged the Church of Christ in China, a union of the mission churches, which brought them even closer together.

---

9. Alexander Williamson, "Speech," May 11, Records of the General Conference of the Protestant Missionaries in China held at Shanghai, May 10–27, 1877, (Shanghai: Presbyterian Mission Press), 61–62.
10. Records of the General Conference, 1877, 393–406.

Nondenominational Colleges

It was also the extremely high cost of university and medical school education that forced the Protestant missions into cooperation in the area of higher education. No one mission board ever had enough money to fund what its current missionaries thought they needed, and funding an entire institution of postsecondary education was simply beyond one church's abilities. If there were to be Christian institutions of higher education in China, they had to be ecumenical. This meant that no longer could, say, the Methodist church only give money to Methodist missions in the hope of making Methodist converts—the reality of the cost of institutions of higher education was so great that the churches at home, along with their mission boards, had to reconcile themselves to these new ideas of Protestant cooperation. Once the institutions were created, the various churches then undertook to support missionaries who taught at these institutions and to provide scholarships for worthy students, in addition to contributing their church's share of the overall cost of running the colleges. Eventually, there were thirteen church-related universities in China—the first institutions in that country to teach the same curricula as did institutions in the West.[11] The thirteen were united under the Christian Board for Higher Education in Asia in 1922. Although most of the mission schools went through various organizational and name changes over the years, many still exist in some form, and although they are all run by the government, students know of their schools' origins.

---

11. Contemporary names for the thirteen are: Fujian Christian University, Ginling College, Huajung University, Hangzhou University, Huanan College, Lingnan University, University of Nanjing, St. John's University, University of Shanghai, Shandong Christian University, Suzhou University, West China Union University, and Yenjing University.

When the China missions faced the even larger problem of creating a Western medical school in China, they quickly realized that it, too, was beyond their abilities to finance and turned to the Rockefeller Foundation. The Rockefeller family had long contributed to mission work, and now their Foundation undertook the creation of Peking [Beijing] Union Medical College (PUMC) and its related hospital, which trained both medical doctors and nurses, as well as people in various support occupations, in Western medicine. Of course, as the school was sponsored by the Rockefeller Foundation, some nonmissionary doctors worked there, but the overwhelming atmosphere of the place was mission related. Called Peking [Beijing] Number One hospital for several decades after 1949, the institution recovered its original name in 1985, and remains the premier Western medical facility in China. All of China's Western-style medical doctors today are in some way descendants of earlier generations of medical personnel educated at PUMC. Thus another building block of the ecumenical movement was laid in China.

The idea that visits and friendships with missionaries from other denominations and cooperation in the area of higher education was laying the foundation for the ecumenical movement in the West probably never occurred to any of these missionaries, yet they were cooperating, a century ago, at a level still considered unusual in their home countries.

The Feminization of Christianity

There were two sides to Christianity's feminization in China: 1) Western women who went to China as missionaries, and their supporters at home, who achieved a greater say in their churches through mission societies, and 2) the Chinese women whose lives were changed as a result of contact with the missionary women, many of whom sought theological education before it was common for women to do so in the West.

The feminization of Protestantism in the West in the twentieth century clearly began in China decades earlier. One might argue that women are generally more interested in Christianity than are men, and in the China missions, except for the earliest years, women outnumbered men quite substantially—perhaps as many as two-thirds of the missionaries were women, after about 1890.

Protestant boards were always reluctant to send single men to the mission field, believing that men would soon take up with, or even marry, local women. The boards, many composed totally of males or perhaps with a single token female, also believed that women could more easily resist romantic encounters and certainly would never marry a local convert. One should note that the few women who did marry Chinese quickly left their mission jobs and either established their own mission work, as did Anne Chang, or left church work entirely.

Turning to the field of literature, two of the most popular authors of the China missions were women. Of course, Pearl Buck, who was both a China mission child and a missionary wife, ranks at the top as the first American woman to have won the Nobel Prize in Literature. Her best-known work, *The Good Earth*,[12] published in 1931, continues to find new readers. Walter White, head of the National Association for the Advancement of Colored People (NAACP), said Buck was only one of the two people (both women) in America who understood the plight of the Negro in the 1940s; the other was Eleanor Roosevelt.[13]

---

12. Buck, *Good Earth*.

The other writer is Lotta Hume, whose *Favorite Children's Stories of China and Tibet* has sold over a quarter-million copies according to its publisher, Tuttle.[14] It was the first in their series of books on fairy tales from various Asian countries as well as other Asian-centered children's stories and language learning books.

Some women who grew up in the China missions returned to the United States in adulthood to implement changes in the home societies. Molly Yard, child of AMEM missionaries in Sichuan, was the president of the National Organization for Women, and campaigned for women's rights and many liberal causes in the United States.[15]

What the Protestant missionaries reported home about their efforts in China was widely spread among many women's missionary societies, and was destined to have an overwhelming role in shaping what churchgoers thought about China (so essential during World War II and in the years between 1945 and 1949).

Regina Sullivan's study, *Lottie Moon: A Southern Baptist Missionary to China in History and Legend,* is not so much about Moon's career as it is about how the Southern Baptist women in the United States gained control of the mission monies they raised and obtained for themselves places to speak in churches of their denomination. On one occasion when the male leaders forbade the women to speak at one of their conferences, the women retreated to a nearby church of a different denomination and held their own meeting! Relatively little has been written by scholars on the women at home who

---

13. Conn, *Pearl S. Buck,* xvi.
14. Lotta Hume, *Favorite Children's Stories of China and Tibet* (Rutland, VT: Tuttle, 1962).
15. Service, *Golden Inches,* 106–7.

supported the missions in general, and in China in particular, so this study is welcome as a well-researched monograph.[16]

Additionally, if one wanted to travel, joining a mission meant one could see the world at someone else's expense. It was not uncommon for American missionaries in China to return to the United States via Europe, seeing the sites along the way. Prior to the advent of the commercial jet passenger plane in 1960, it was rare for ordinary folk to travel abroad, but all foreign missionaries did, making them exotic speakers and fundraisers at church gatherings when they were home on furlough.

If a woman were a teacher or a medical doctor, at home she could never dream of heading up a school or a hospital, but such a job was common for women in the mission field. Single women on the mission field had their own homes, even if they shared with other single women. They hired the servants, arranged the décor, and decided on their menus, something they rarely would have had the opportunity to do if they were living in a brother's or sister's home.

Many single women in missions in China also took their turns serving as mission agents, responsible for all mission funds, hardly a job a woman would have held in a home church. Additionally, for those missions that had annual meetings for representatives of each station, usually in Shanghai, by the early twentieth century many required that both a man and a woman, usually a single one, be sent to the meetings.

The obverse of the feminization issue was the attraction of Chinese women to Christianity, usually through mission boarding schools, including at the university level, or through opportunities the missions offered to teach or to do medical work among their sisters. Many Protestants were also

---

16. Sullivan, *Lottie Moon*.

concerned about rescuing Chinese women from lives as concubines, slaves, or sex workers, the latter particularly in Shanghai, which was known as the world's capital of sin to many missionaries.

Rescuing women from lives of degradation was the aim of many missions in China, and foreigners at every mission station could point to some Chinese women residing and working for them who had been saved from a cruel fate.

On an institutional scale, the best known of the missions working to rescue women was that of the Door of Hope in Shanghai. Sue Gronewold, in her dissertation *Encountering Hope: The Door of Hope in Shanghai and Taipei, 1900-1976*,[17] traced the history of this institution. The Mixed Court in Shanghai, through an agreement with the police of the International Settlement and the French Concession, both foreign-governed areas of Shanghai under extraterritorial treaties, agreed to send any Chinese prostitutes who were arrested to the Door of Hope for rehabilitation.

The most beneficial, and astounding, part of Gronewold's work comes from the fact that she actually met some of the women who had been Door of Hope inmates in the 1940s. Gronewold admitted to scholars at several conferences that she had always thought the women assigned to the Door of Hope by courts might have been very resentful of their situation, but when she talked to the women, all in their eighties and nineties, she found the opposite to be true. The women told Gronewold things she said she would never have thought of.

One woman recalled that her first memory of the Door of Hope was that in the morning, having arrived late at night, she

---

17. Sue Gronewold, *Encountering Hope: The Door of Hope in Shanghai and Taipei, 1900-1976*. PhD diss., Columbia University, 1996.

was awakened by one of the foreign missionaries carrying a charcoal brazier which she waved back and forth to warm the girls' room before they got up. The Chinese woman remarked that no one had ever done such a thing for her before in her life.

Another woman wanted to be sure that whatever Gronewold wrote about the Door of Hope, she would be sure to state that every day the woman had been there, she was fed three times a day, and every meal had rice and vegetables and at least several times a week they had meat! To that woman, the Door of Hope had been life itself.

Greater Opportunities for Women

Variations on the issue of women medical doctors can be cited in the cases of Shi Meiyu and Kang Cheng, both of whom were born into Chinese Christian families. (See chapter 5 for short biographies of Shi and Kang.)

The establishment of schools for women by the missionaries contributed to the feminization of Christianity in China. It was more likely that students who attended mission schools would become Christians and church members, and it was in the mission schools that young Chinese women saw opportunities for themselves in the wider world, which had previously not been available to them.

For example, Judith Liu found that two of her mother's classmates from the 1930s had decided for themselves not to marry and to become social workers and spend their lives improving the lots of other Chinese women. They had successful careers until the insanity of the Cultural Revolution caused the radicals to attack them for being unmarried. The network of the mission girls' school students, then in their fifties and sixties, went to work and found the two women men who would marry them so that they would fit into the traditional Chinese role for women. Qualifications for these men included that they be practicing Christians who would not object to the women continuing their professions. The sisterhood of the former students quickly found the two men needed and they wed the women! Harassment from the Red Guards ceased once the women were married.

When World War II, which began in China in 1937, caused the Nationalist government to flee to the southwestern city of Chongjing, many of the Christian schools and universities went along in the attempt to avoid hostilities. Among those fleeing was the ecumenical Protestant Nanjing Theological Seminary. The seminary had received a large and unexpected legacy during the 1930s that allowed it to continue its work and support its faculty and many of its students. During their time in Chongqing, letters sent to members of the theological seminary's board in the United States indicate that the faculty, composed of Chinese and Western men, was becoming increasingly concerned that too many women were applying to become students at the seminary. They wanted to put a quota on women applicants, who were then amounting to nearly 40 percent of those applying. The faculty were concerned that the women would use too much of the recent legacy! Little did they know that a few years later, even more women applied to the seminary, obviously hoping to find a position where they could work after the Communists took control of the country. Women continued in leadership, some as clergy, in the Chinese church after 1949.

Examples of the feminization of Christianity in the China missions were numerous. Western women found new roles for themselves in their churches by working to support their sisters in China, while Chinese Christian women found jobs for themselves within the many churches and their educational, medical, and social programs.

Conclusion

The four major theological issues that concerned the China missionaries and the Chinese church were each destined to have long-range consequences for the home countries of the missionaries. One might argue that in at least three of these areas, excluding the Fundamentalist-Modernist controversy, the China missionaries were simply responding to the situations they found themselves in and not planning any huge changes in their churches at home or in the mission field. The great changes, like most such changes, were the result of unintended consequences.

Conclusion

Western Christians have long accepted that great variations exist in Christianity. The division of the church in 1054 into the Roman Catholic sect in the West and the Orthodox sect in the East has continued to exist for nearly a thousand years. It seems no one in the Western church criticizes the Coptic version of Christianity, practiced mostly in Africa, or wants to change it into something else. Latin Rite sects have existed for centuries without other Christians demanding they change. Syrian Christians are much in the news and are recognized as followers of Jesus, without question. The Filipinization of Christianity, the subject of a monograph by that name, exists as a version of Catholicism, as does another version among the Padaung tribe in Burma. Korean Christians have sculpted their own rendition of the religion.

And then there is China. Matteo Ricci wanted to accommodate Christianity to Chinese culture, but his methods were discredited by his church's leadership. Later missionaries wanted to change China and the Chinese to give up all their traditional beliefs and practices when they became Christians, even though the Chinese had been incorporating ideas from many religious traditions into their belief systems for centuries. Many missionaries thought Western clothing and a Western education would automatically make the Chinese Christians, and were aghast when they did not. If one may paraphrase André Malraux: "Westerners never understand anything of Chinese Christianity that does not resemble their version of the religion."

Perhaps Westerners will one day stop trying to fashion Chinese Christianity to mirror their own version of the belief. Here, one should note that in recent years some Chinese Christian churches in China have sent missionaries to the United States for the purpose of spreading the gospel among Americans.

Perhaps if foreigners would stop trying to reshape Chinese Christianity into their image, then the Chinese government would recognize that being Christian is not, in and of itself, a bad thing, and that there are numerous versions of the religion in the world—the Chinese is only one of many. More than seventy years after the Chinese body politic threw off the political privileges of the Westerners in China, it is time for Western Christians to realize Christianity does exist in China, and, although it might not be as those Westerners wish, it is a belief that a small minority of Chinese follow, and that small minority outnumbers the Christians in many other countries. If Westerners need to understand how Chinese Christians practice their faith, they must first be willing to hear, to understand, and to accept what the Chinese believers see in the faith and how they practice it. It is not necessary, and never was, to change China, but rather to accept it as it is, in all its glory.

Bibliography

Many books have been written on the Christian missions in China, but generally, they can be divided into two distinct groups: 1) scholarly studies, mostly histories, which seek to relate in thoughtful, carefully considered prose the cross-cultural interchanges between the missionaries who went to China and those folks they encountered there, drawing conclusions based on the evidence the authors uncovered; and 2) those works that detail the more emotional, usually personal, experiences of missionaries and/or their converts, and some advise readers on how to evangelize China today. Below is a short list of scholarly monographs, along with a few periodicals and websites on the missionary enterprise. Other works are listed in the narrative with author and title, to enable readers to locate them. The list is by no means inclusive of all the fine books on this topic.

Aikman, David. *Jesus in Beijing: How Christianity Is Transforming China and Changing the Global Balance of Power.* Washington, DC: Regnery, 2003.

Austin, Alvyn J. *China's Millions: The China Inland Mission and Late Qing Society, 1832-1905.* Grand Rapids, MI: Eerdmans, 2007.

Bays, Daniel H. *A New History of Christianity in China*. West Sussex, UK: Wiley-Blackwell, 2012.
Benson, Linda. *Across China's Gobi: The Careers of Evangeline French, Mildred Cable, and Francesca French of the China Inland Mission*. Norwalk, CT: EastBridge, 2008.
Brockey, Liam Matthew. *Journey to the East: The Jesuit Mission to China, 1579-1724*. Cambridge, MA: Harvard University Press, 2007.
Buck, Pearl S. *Fighting Angel: Portrait of a Soul and The Exile: Portrait of an American Mother*. New York: John Day, 1936.
———. *The Good Earth*. New York: John Day, 1931.
Cable, Mildred. *The Fulfillment of a Dream of Pastor Hsi and the story of the work in Hwochow*. London: Morgan and Scott, China Inland Mission, 1917.
———, with Francesca French. *The Gobi Desert*. London: Hodder and Stoughton, 1943.
Cao Nanlai. *Constructing China's Jerusalem: Christians, Power, and Place in Contemporary Wenzhou*. Stanford, CA: Stanford University Press, 2011.
Cao Shuji. "Qing Dynasty," vol. 5. In *History of China's Population (Zhongguo Renkou Shi)*. 6 vols. Edited by Ge Jian-Xiong. Shanghai: Fudan University Press, 2001.
Carbonneau, Robert. *Life, Death and Memory: Three Passionists in Hunan, China, and the Shaping of an American Mission Perspective in the 1920s*. PhD diss. Georgetown University, 1992.
Caulfield, Caspar. *Only a Beginning: The Passionists in China, 1921-1931*. Union City, NJ: Passionist Press, 1990.
Chen Da. *Colors of the Mountain*. New York: Random House, 1999.
———. *Sounds of the River*. New York: Harper Perennial, 2003.
Chinese Recorder. Shanghai, 1867–1941.

Collingham, Lizzie. *Curry: A Tale of Cooks and Conquerors.* Oxford: Oxford University Press, 2007.

Collins, Michael. *The Fisherman's Net: The Influence of the Popes on History.* Mahwah, NJ: Hidden Springs, 2003.

Conn, Peter. *Pearl S. Buck: A Cultural Biography.* New York: Cambridge University Press, 1996.

Crane, George. *Bones of the Master: A Journey to Secret Mongolia.* New York: Random House, 2001.

Crossley, Pamela Kyle. *The Wobbling Pivot: China since 1800: An Interpretative History.* New York: Wiley-Blackwell, 2010.

Elman, Benjamin A. "Changes in Confucian Civil Service Examinations from the Ming to the Ch'ing Dynasty." In *Education and Society in Late Ming Imperial China, 1600-1900.* Edited by Benjamin A. Elman and Alexander Woodside. Berkeley: University of California Press, 1994.

Entenmann, Robert. "Christian Virgins in Eighteenth Century Sichuan." In *Christianity in China from the Eighteenth Century to the Present.* Edited by Daniel H. Bays. Stanford, CA: Stanford University Press, 1996.

Esherick, Joseph W. *The Origins of the Boxer Uprising.* Berkeley: University of California Press, 1987.

Espey, John. *Minor Heresies, Major Departures: A China Mission Boyhood.* Berkeley: University of California Press, 1994.

Fairbank, John K. *Chinabound: A Fifty-year Memoir.* New York: Harper and Row, 1982.

Garrett, Shirley. *Social Reformers in Urban China: The Chinese Y.M.C.A., 1895-1926.* Cambridge, MA: Harvard University Press, 1970.

Gilmour, James. *Among the Mongols.* London: Religious Tract Society, 1883.

Girardot, Norman. *The Victorian Translation of China: James

Legge's Oriental Pilgrimage. Berkeley: University of California Press, 2002.

Gronewold, Sue. *Encountering Hope: The Door of Hope in Shanghai and Taipei, 1900-1976*. PhD diss. Columbia University, 1996.

Hayford, Charles W. *To the People: James Yen and Village China*. New York: Columbia University Press, 1997.

Hyatt, Irwin. *Our Ordered Lives Confess: Three Nineteenth-Century Missionaries in East Shantung*. Cambridge, MA: Harvard University Press, 1976.

Ireland, Daryl. "John Sung's Malleable Conversion Narrative," *Fides et Historia* 45, no. 1 (Winter/Spring 2013): 48–75.

Joiner, Lynne. *Honorable Survivor: Mao's China, McCarthy's America and the Persecution of John S. Service*. Annapolis, MD: Naval Institute Press, 2009.

Keating, John Craig William. *A Protestant Church in Communist China: Moore Memorial Church, Shanghai, 1949-1989*. Bethlehem, PA: Lehigh University Press, 2012.

Latourette, Kenneth S. *A History of Christian Missions in China*. New York: Macmillan, 1929.

Lian Xi. *Redeemed by Fire: The Rise of Popular Christianity in Modern China*. New Haven, CT: Yale University Press, 2010.

Liao Yiwu. *God Is Red: The Secret Story of How Christianity Survived and Flourished in Communist China*. Translated by Wenguang Huang. New York: HarperCollins, 2001.

Liu, Judith. *Foreign Exchange: Counterculture Behind the Walls of St. Hilda's School for Girls, 1929-1937*. Bethlehem, PA: Lehigh University Press, 2011.

Lodwick, Kathleen. *The Chinese Recorder Index: A Guide to Christian Missions in Asia, 1869-1941*. 2 vols. Wilmington, DE: Scholarly Resources, 1986.

_____. *Crusaders Against Opium: Protestant Missionaries in China,*

1874-1917. Lexington: University Press of Kentucky, 1996, reprint 2009.

———. *Educating the Women of Hainan: The Career of Margaret Moninger in China, 1915-1942*. Lexington: University Press of Kentucky, 1995.

———. *The Widow's Quest: The Byers Extraterritorial Case in Hainan, China, 1924-1925*. Bethlehem, PA: Lehigh University Press, 2003.

———. "Women at the Hainan Presbyterian Mission," *American Presbyterians*, 65, no. 1 (Spring 1987): 19–28.

———, and W. K. Chen, eds. *The Missionary Kaleidoscope: Portraits of Six China Missionaries*. Norwalk, CT: EastBridge, 2005.

Lutz, Jessie G. *Opening China: Karl F.A. Gutzlaff and Sino-Western Relations, 1827-1852*. Grand Rapids, MI: Eerdmans, 2008.

———, ed. *Pioneer Chinese Christian Women: Gender, Christianity, and Social Mobility*. Bethlehem, PA: Lehigh University Press, 2010.

——— and Rolland Ray Lutz. *Hakka Chinese Confront Protestant Christianity, 1850-1900 with the Autobiographies of Eight Hakka Christians, and Commentary*. Armonk, NY: EastBridge, 1998.

Martin, Mildred C. *Chinatown's Angry Angel: The Story of Donaldina Cameron*. Palo Alto, CA: Pacific Books, 1977.

McCunn, Ruthanne Lum. *Thousand Pieces of Gold*. San Francisco: Design Enterprises of San Francisco, 1981.

Michaud, Jean. *"Incidental" Ethnographers: French Catholic Missionaries on the Tonkin-Yunnan Frontier, 1880-1930*. Leiden: Brill, 2007.

Moninger, Margaret. *Papers*. Record Group 59. Presbyterian Historical Society, Philadelphia, PA.

Morse, Hosea Ballou. *International Relations of the Chinese Empire.* 3 vols. London: Longmans, Green, 1910–1918.

Mungello, D. E. *The Forgotten Christians of Hangzhou.* Honolulu: University of Hawaii Press, 1994.

_____. *The Spirit and the Flesh in Shandong, 1650-1785.* Lanham, MD: Rowman and Littlefield, 2001.

National Archives. "George D. Byers" and "Walter Coveyou." File 393.1123, RG59. *Papers Relating to the Foreign Relations of the United States, China.* Washington, DC.

Park, William H., MD compiler. *Opinions of Over 100 Physicians on the Use of Opium in China.* Shanghai: American Presbyterian Mission Press, 1899.

Price, Eva Jane. *China Journal, 1889-1900: An American Missionary Family during the Boxer Rebellion with the Letters and Diaries of Eva Jane Price and Her Family.* New York: Collier Books, 1990.

Rabe, John. *The Good Man of Nanjing: The Diaries of John Rabe.* New York: Knopf Doubleday, 2007.

Rossabi, Morris. *Voyager to Xanadu: Rabban Sauma and the First Journey from China to the West.* Berkeley: University of California Press, 2010.

Service, John S. *Golden Inches: The China Memoir of Grace Service.* Berkeley: University of California Press, 1991.

Shemo, Connie. *The Chinese Medical Ministries of Kang Cheng and Shi Meiyu, 1872-1937: On the Cross-Cultural Frontier of Gender, Race and Nation.* Bethlehem, PA: Lehigh University Press, 2011.

Spence, Jonathan. *God's Chinese Son: The Taiping Heavenly Kingdom of Hong Xiuquan.* New York: Norton, 1996.

_____. *The Memory Palace of Matteo Ricci.* New York: Penguin, 1984.

_____. *The Search for Modern China.* New York: Norton, 1990.

———. *To Change China: Western Advisers in China, 1620-1960*. New York: Penguin Books, 1980.

Stauffer, Milton, ed. *The Christian Occupation of China*. Shanghai: China Continuation Committee, 1922.

Sullivan, Regina. *Lottie Moon: A Southern Baptist Missionary to China in History and Legend*. Baton Rouge: Louisiana State University Press, 2011.

Taveirne, Patrick. *Han-Mongol Encounters and Missionary Endeavors: A History of Schuet in Ordos (Hetan), 1874-1911*. Leuven: Leuven University Press, 2004.

Taylor, Jay. *Generalissimo Chiang Kai-shek and the Struggle for Modern China*. Cambridge, MA: Belknap/Harvard University Press, 2009.

Ti'en Ju-K'ang. *Peaks of Faith: Protestant Missions in Revolutionary China*. Leiden: Brill, 1993.

Waley-Cohen, Joanna. *The Sextants of Beijing: Global Currents in Chinese History*. New York: Norton, 1999.

Weatherford, Jack. *The Secret History of the Mongol Queens: How the Daughters of Genghis Khan Rescued His Empire*. New York: Crown Publishers, 2010.

Williamson, Alexander. "*Speech*," May 11. Records of the General Conference of the Protestant Missionaries in China held at Shanghai, May 10-27, 1877. Shanghai: Presbyterian Mission Press, 1878.

Women's Occidental Board of Foreign Missions, San Francisco, *Annual Report*, 1908–9.

Wu, Judy Tzu-chun. *Doctor Mom Chung and the Fair-Haired Bastards*. Berkeley: University of California Press, 2005.

Yang, Fenggang. *Religion in China: Survival and Revival Under Communist Rule*. New York: Oxford University Press, 2012.

Yellow Emperor's Classic on Internal Medicine. Translated by Ilza Veith. Berkeley: University of California Press, 2002.

Websites

www.newadvent.org/cathen/.

www.pewresearch.org/2011/12/19/global-christian-exe/.

Index

Allen, Young J., 184
American Board of Commissioners for Foreign Missions (ABCFM), 158
American Presbyterian Mission (APM), xvii–xviii, 33, 54, 56, 65, 79–80, 101, 113, 139, 142, 145, 147, 162, 174, 182, 200, 213. *See also* American Southern Presbyterian Mission; Canadian Presbyterian Mission
American Southern Presbyterian Mission (ASPM), 178
Anti-Chinese violence in U.S., 142
Anti-Opium League. *See* opium
Assembly Hall. *See* Chinese Christians, churches, Protestant
Augustinans, 207, 208. *See also* Chinese Rites Controversy; Roman Catholics
Austin, Alvyn, 101, 104–12. *See also* China Inland Mission
Aylwald, Gladys, 35, 73

Baller, F. W., 113
Banditry, xiii, 136–38, 143
Basel Mission Society (BMS), 18
Bemis, Polly, 121
Bercovitz, Nathaniel, 182

Bethel Band, 44, 196, 198
Bible, 17, 19, 52, 59, 60, 68, 69, 96, 110, 117, 124, 167, 178, 179, 181, 184, 186, 189, 192, 197, 213, 214, 220. *See also* Chinese Rites Controversy
Bible Women, 114, 121–22
Borodin, Mikhail, 100–101, 102. *See also* Chinese Communists
Boxer Uprising (1900), xvii, 17, 23–26, 35, 73, 109, 139, 165, 184, 190, 191, 193, 200, 221
Bridgman, Elijah/Eliza (Mrs. Elijah), 124, 132, 174, 175, 179, 184–85, 193–94
Buck, Pearl S., 33, 40, 71, 91, 99, 178, 185, 224. *See also* Sydenstricker, Absalom
Buddhism, xix, 5, 8–10, 33, 48, 50, 69, 95, 96, 113, 161, 205, 211
Byers, George, 138–43, 147

Cable, A. Mildred, xx, 108, 176–77, 185–86. *See also* French, Evangeline/Francesca
Cameron, Donaldina, 182–83
Canadian Presbyterian Mission (CPM), 174
Castiglione, Giuseppe, 186, 211. *See also* Jesuits; Roman Catholics
Catholic Foreign Missionary Society of America (Maryknoll), 70, 144. *See also* Roman Catholics
Chen Da, 58, 60, 122–23
China Inland Mission (CIM), xx, 16, 30, 35, 38, 67, 73, 89, 92, 93, 98, 101–13, 163–64, 174, 176, 177, 185–86, 198–99, 214. *See also* Taylor, James Hudson
    conflicts with non-CIM missionaries, 105, 107
    conflicts within, 104, 105, 109
    fundamentalist, 106. *See also* Fundamentalist-Modernist Controversy
    principles, 103–4

INDEX

    recruits, 113
    relations with diplomats, 104, 105–8, 199. *See also* missionaries, relations with diplomats
    school, Zhifu. *See* missionaries, children, schooling, CIM school, Zhifu
    Yangzhou attack, 107–8, 199
Chinese attitudes toward Christianity, xiii, 11, 22, 28, 50, 58–61, 128, 129, 161. *See also* Chinese government attitudes toward Christians; Three-Self Patriotic Movement
    toward foreigners, 14–17, 23, 227
Chinese Christians, xxi, 12, 15, 24, 25, 41–48, 53–54, 60–61, 110, 170–71, 183, 201
    attitudes toward missionaries, 213
    baptism, 9, 89–90
    Church of Christ in China, 107, 199, 213, 214, 221
    churches, Protestant, xx–xxi, 41–44, 45, 47, 232; Jesus Family, 189; Little Flock, 44 (*see also* Ni Tuosheng); Moore Memorial Church, Shanghai, 47, 215
    clergy: Protestant, 41–48 (*see also* individual names); Roman Catholics, 145
    converts, 10, 12, 15, 17–18, 41, 58, 89–90, 95, 110–11, 114, 117, 121, 123–25, 128, 135–36, 143, 146, 158–59, 161, 163, 164–66, 169, 170–72, 175, 178, 183, 190–91, 194, 197, 203, 206–11, 213, 220, 224, 233
    evangelists, 44–48, 120, 122
    inquirers, 9
    legal disputes of, 15–16
    Manifesto (1950), 45–46, 201
    underground churches, 45, 57
    understanding of Christianity, 90–91
    Wenzhou, Zhejiang, 47–48, 60–61
    women, 114, 226–29. *See also* women, Chinese

Chinese Communists, xv–xvii, 25, 32, 45–47, 52, 55, 59, 61, 90, 95, 125, 144, 153, 188–89, 200, 201, 229. *See also* Borodin, Mikhail; Chinese government attitudes toward Christians; Patriotic Association (PA); Religious Affairs Bureau (RAB); State Administration of Religious Affairs (SARA); Three Self Patriotic Movement (TSPM)
Chinese culture, 8–10, 11, 13, 112, 114, 126, 150–58, 162, 169, 171–72, 204–12
Chinese elites, 17, 118, 120, 129, 208
Chinese Evangelization Society (CES), 102–3, 188
Chinese Exclusion Act (US), 195
Chinese government attitude toward Christians, xxi, 20, 45, 52–53, 55–57, 59–60, 90–91. *See also* Chinese Communists; Patriotic Association (PA); Religious Affairs Bureau (RAB); Three-Self Patriotic Movement (TSPM); State Administration of Religious Affairs (SARA)
Chinese Imperial Maritime Customs Service, 81, 219
Chinese language
    Christian terms in, 10–11, 25, 125, 204–12. *See also* Bible; Chinese Rites Controversy
    romanization of, 68–69
Chinese non-Christians views of Chinese Christians, 58–60
Chinese population, 66
Chinese Recorder, 24, 38, 86, 125, 127, 168, 169, 182, 193
Chinese Repository, 174, 184
Chinese Rites Controversy, 2, 11–12, 194, 200, 203, 204–13. *See also* Augustinians; Bible; Chinese language, Christian terms; Dominicans; Franciscans; Jesuits; Ricci, Matteo; Roman Catholics; Schall von Bell, Johann Adam; Verbiest, Ferdinand
Chinggis Khan, 3
Chinnery, George, 180
Christianity, beliefs and teachings, 9–10

Christianity in China, history of, 1-3
Chung, Margaret, 79-80
Church of Christ in China. *See* Chinese Christians, Church of Christ in China
Concubines, 40, 107, 114, 121, 136, 156, 227
Confucianism, xix, 8, 18, 19, 47, 95, 111, 150, 153-57, 162, 193, 201, 204-7, 209-12
 examination system, 17, 118-19, 123, 127-28, 153, 201. *See also* education, Chinese traditional
Confucius, 96, 155, 157, 212
Congregation of the Immaculate Heart of Mary, 164-66. *See also* Roman Catholics
Coveyou, Walter, 139, 142-45. *See also* Passionists; Roman Catholics
cults, xxi, 112, 189
cultural Christians, xxii, 90
Cultural Revolution, x, 16, 48-51, 54-55, 59, 60, 122, 164, 169, 170, 201, 228. *See also* Red Guards

Daoism, xix, 10, 50, 96, 161, 204-5, 211
Davies, John Paton, 99
Delano, Warren, 27. *See also* Roosevelt, Franklin Delano
demons, 111-12
Deng Xiaoping, 25-26
Depression (1930s), 41
Ding Guangxun, 45, 54-55
Dominicans, 11, 70, 207-9. *See also* Chinese Rites Controversy; Roman Catholics
Door of Hope, Shanghai. *See* women, Chinese, Door of Hope, Shanghai
Dudgeon, John, 30, 39
Dyer, Maria. *See* Taylor, Maria Dyer (Mrs. James Hudson)

ecumenism, Protestant, xix, 63–64, 132, 158, 203, 213, 216–23
Eddy, Sherwood, 201
Edkins, Joseph, 39
education, Chinese. *See also* missions, colleges; missions, schools
    traditional, 118–19. *See also* Confucianism, examination system
    women, 119. *See also* missions, schools, women
Espey, John, 99–101, 136
ethnic minorities, 58, 162–63, 171. *See also* Mongols; Muslims
    Liao, 58
    Lisu, 171
    Miao, 59, 171
    Yi, 58, 163, 171
exorcism. *See* demons
extraterritoriality, 14–16, 107, 138–45, 147, 160, 227. *See also* Westerners attitudes toward Chinese; missionaries, relationships with diplomats; missionaries, legal rights
    extended to converts, 110–11

Fairbank, John King xiv, 95
Falun Gung, 53
Fan, 112
feminization of Protestantism, xix, 73, 114, 203, 204, 223–29. *See also* women
Fielde, Adele, 71, 178–79, 186–87
Fosdick, Harry Emerson, 215
Francis Xavier, Saint, 5–7. *See also* Jesuits; Roman Catholics
Franciscans, 11, 70, 207–9. *See also* Chinese Rites Controversy; Roman Catholics
French, Evangeline/Francesca, xx, 108, 176–77, 185–86. *See also* Cable, A. Mildred

French Foreign Mission Society (Société des Missions Étrangères de Paris), 11, 210
Fundamentalism, xx, 44–45, 63, 106, 198–99
Fundamentalist-Modernist Controversy, 44, 63, 74, 198–99, 203, 213–15, 230. *See also* China Inland Mission, fundamentalist

Gilman, Frank P., 39, 97, 174, 175
Gilmour, James, viii, 39, 84–85, 158–59, 166, 176, 187–88
Gordon, Charles George "Chinese", 20
Great Wall, xiii, xiv, 21, 152
Guinness family, 103–4
Guinness, Geraldine. *See* Taylor, Geraldine Guinness (Mrs. Howard)
Gulick, 158–59
Guomindang. *See* Nationalists
Gutzlaff, Karl, 27–28, 103, 188

Hakkas, 17–19, 162
Hainan, xvii, 39–40, 54, 56, 80–81, 88, 97–98, 130, 138–42, 162, 168, 174, 175, 182, 191
Han dynasty, xv, 151–52
Han people, 2–3, 17, 149–50, 152, 156, 161–65, 171
Haygood, Laura. *See* missions, schools, McTyeire School for Girls
Henry, B. C., 161–62
Hill, David, 110
history, China, 149–55
Holbein, Godfrey, 139, 143. *See also* Passionists; Roman Catholics
Holidays. *See also* missions, schools, Christian holidays celebrated
    Asian celebrations of Western, 36
    Chinese National (1 October), 46

Chinese New Year, 126, 127, 206
Christian, 4, 126–27
Double Ten Day (Nationalist), 126
Holiness Christians, 74, 192
Hong Xiuquan, 17–20, 190. *See also* Taiping Rebellion
Howe, Gertrude, 196
Hume, Lottie, 225
Hunan, 20, 139, 142–44, 161

Ignatius Loyola, Saint, 7. *See also* Jesuits, Roman Catholics
Islam. *See* Muslims

Japan, xvii, 5–6, 25, 34, 37, 39, 44, 65, 83, 132–35, 137, 176, 191, 193, 198–99, 211, 212
Jardine, Matheson Co., xiv, 30. *See also* Matheson, Donald; opium
Jeremiasson, C. C., 161
Jesuits, 2, 5, 7–19, 67, 70, 117, 183, 186, 195–96, 200, 205–12. *See also* Castiglione, Giuseppe; Chinese Rites Controversy; Francis Xavier; Ignatius Loyola; Ricci, Matteo; Roman Catholics; Schall von Bell, Johann Adam; Verbiest, Ferdinand
Jesus Family. *See* Chinese Christian churches, Jesus Family
Jesus opium, 29. *See also* morphine; opium
Jiang Jishi, xi, 99, 100, 183, 188–89, 196, 197. *See also* Song family; Song family, Meiling
Jing Dianying, 189
John of Monte Corvino, 3
John of Plano Carpini, 3
Judaism, 3, 10

Kang Cheng. *See* Shi Meiyu
Kangxi emperor, 12, 196, 200, 210, 211. *See also* Qing dynasty

Kerr, John, 130, 180, 189
Keswick John, xiv
Kubilai Khan, 3
Kung, H. H., 189–90, 196, 197. *See also* Song family, Ailing

Latin Rite Christians, 231
Legge, James, 67, 178, 190
Li Zhizao, 10, 190, 201, 202
Liang A-fa, 17, 190
Liao Yiwu, 58–60
Little Flock. *See* Chinese Christian churches, Little Flock
Liu, Judith, 121, 129–31, 228
London Mission Society (LMS), 38–39, 73, 158, 187, 200
Lord, E. C., 77
Luce, Henry, 99

Machle, Edward, 139
Mackay, George L., 174, 175
Manchus. *See* Qing dynasty
Manicheans, 1
Mao Zedong, xi, xv, 49, 68
Martin, W. A. P., 190–91
Matheson, Donald 30. *See also* Jardine, Matheson Co.; opium
May Fourth Movement, 43
McCandliss, Olivia Kerr, 130
McPherson, Aimee Semple, 13–14,
Melrose, Margaret, 97–98, 138. *See also* Ryan, Sylvia Melrose
Methodists, 58–59, 73, 98, 102, 162–64, 171, 196, 197, 222
Millenarianists, 189
Milne, William, 190
Ming dynasty, xiii, 119, 152, 183, 190, 193, 195, 201, 202, 204

Missionaries
> adventurers, 174, 176–77
> attitudes towards: Chinese, xviii, xx, 14–17, 114–15, 125, 130–31, 136, 137, 146–47, 161, 164–66, 190, 193–94, 229; Mongols, 176
> call, 64, 66, 71, 77, 102, 106, 176
> character, xviii, xix, 14, 38, 64, 74–83
> children (schooling), 40–41, 54, 99–102; CIM school, Zhifu, 41, 102; Guling Missionary School, 41, 100, 102; Shanghai American School, 40, 102
> contributions to China, xviii
> contributions to home countries, xix, 86, 96
> "divorce", 101
> evangelism, 120
> furloughs, xvi, 13, 26, 39, 72, 75, 82, 91, 93, 108, 120, 122, 159, 167, 170, 173, 175, 177, 185, 198, 200, 214, 217, 220, 226, 233
> health, 75, 77
> ignorance about China, 67, 113–14, 130–31, 137, 146, 161, 164–66
> immigrants as, 182–83, 193
> kidnapping of, 140
> language learning, 38, 68, 86–89, 113, 117–18, 127, 146, 193
> legal rights, 21. *See also* extraterritoriality
> lifestyles, 38–41, 67, 83, 86–89, 91–94, 96–99, 117, 127, 136, 137, 142, 217–20, 225–26
> marriages to Chinese, 75–76, 175, 224
> marriages, interdenominational, 76–77
> medical doctors, 66, 75, 80–82, 85, 174, 179–80, 193, 226 (*see also* missions, colleges, Beijing Union Medical College; missions, hospitals; missionaries, women

INDEX

medical doctors); Medical Missionary Society, 174, 184; non-mission employment, 81–82
mental illnesses/suicides, 38, 39, 109
methods, 112, 117, 120, 124
murders of, 138–47
pioneers, 174
post-1970 in China, 55
qualifications/disqualifications of, 64–67, 77–81, 108, 146, 173
relations with Chinese officials, 140, 160
relations with diplomats, 14–17, 21–23, 28, 81–82, 97, 138–47, 180, 190, 193, 199 (*see also* China Inland Mission, relations with diplomats; extraterrioritality; missionaries, kidnapping of; missionaries, murders of; U.S.-Chinese diplomatic relations)
relations with Western businessmen in China, 124, 154
scholars, 174, 178–79
teachers, 174, 179–80
theological disputes among, 203–30
travel, 82–83, 217–20
weapons possessed by, 96–99
women, 64–66, 71, 91–94, 174, 181, 223–29; married, 76, 85–86; medical doctors, 65, 181, 196, 226 (*see also* mission, hospitals; missionaries; medical doctors); single, 76; teachers, 65, 68

missions
archives, xvi–xviii
associated groups, 119–20, 169, 196; Amity Foundation, 57–58; Boy Scouts, 100; Christian Board for Higher Education in Asia, 222; Fellowship of Reconciliation, 45, 201; Morrison Education Society, 184; Rockefeller Foundation, 132, 196, 223; Royal Asiatic Society, North

China Branch, 184; Society for the Diffusion of Useful Knowledge, 174; Student Volunteer Movement for Foreign Missions (SVMFM), 78, 86, 191, 216–17; Women's Christian Temperance Union (Chinese), 169. *See also* Young Men's/Women's Christian Associations
board/faith, 73–74, 87–88, 93, 105, 108. *See also* China Inland Mission
Christian holidays celebrated, 126. *See also* holidays
colleges, 64, 131–33, 221–23; Beijing Union Medical College, 223; Christian Board for Higher Education in Asia, 222; Ginling College, 65, 132–33, 199; Nanjing Theological Seminary, 229; Nanjing, University of, 33, 133, 135; North China Theological Seminary, 214. *See also* missions, schools
conferences: All-China (Shanghai 1877), 75, 76, 123, 158, 220–21; All-China (Shanghai 1890), 30, 92, 221; All-China (Shanghai, 1907), 87, 221; Edinburgh (1910), 221
coverts. *See* Chinese Christians, converts
education of Chinese. *See* missions, colleges; missions, schools
finances, 41–42, 84–86, 137–38
hospitals, 21, 60, 65, 75, 76, 80, 95, 120, 136, 196, 220. *See also* missions, colleges, Beijing Union Medical College
links to imperialism, 72
orphanages, 21–23
schools, 123–32, 147, 222; curricula, 125; difficulty finding Chinese teachers, 127–28; English taught in, 124; McTyeire School for Girls, Shanghai, 184; Morrison Education Society, 184; statistics, 166–70; women, 123, 128–31. *See also* Confucianism, examination system; missions, colleges

INDEX

Mongolia/Mongols, viii, 1, 3, 39, 51, 84–85, 149, 152, 158–59, 164–66, 176, 187–88, 195. *See also* ethnic minorities
Moninger, Margaret, xvii, 88–89, 97, 130, 178–79, 191
Moon, Charlotte Digges (Lottie), 191–92, 225
morphine, 27, 29, 30. *See also* Jesus opium, opium
Morrison, Robert, 174, 184, 190
Morse, Esther, 40
Mott, John R., 200, 216
Moule, George, 107
movies about missionaries, 32–36
Mukden Incident (1931), 45
Muslims, xx, 3, 10, 50, 57, 110, 177, 185–86, 195–96

Nanjing, Rape of, 36, 65, 132–35, 199–200. *See also* World War II
Nathoy, Lalu. *See* Bemis, Polly
Nationalism, xviii, 43, 44, 123, 166, 193
Nationalist government, 123, 126, 129, 153, 188, 229. *See also* Revolution of 1911
Nestorians, 1–3, 54. *See also* Sauma, Rabban
Nevius, John L., 192
Ni Tuosheng (Watchman), 44, 192. *See also* Chinese Christians, churches, Little Flock
Northern Expedition, 129, 143, 188. *See also* Nationalist government nuns, Roman Catholic 13, 21–23, 70–71. *See also* Roman Catholics; Tianjin Incident; Sisters of Charity (French)

Opium, xiv, xviii, 17, 19, 26–32, 43, 82–83, 109–10, 112, 128, 129, 161, 181, 183. *See also* Jardine, Matheson Co.; Jesus opium; Matheson, Donald; morphine; Opium War
Opium War (1839–1841), 14, 18, 82, 180, 193
Orthodox Christians/mission, 4–5, 231

253

Panay, USS, 133–34. *See also* World War II
Parker, Peter, 180, 189, 193
Passionists, 139, 142–45, 147. *See also* Roman Catholics; individual names
Patriotic Association (PA), 45, 46–47. *See also* Chinese government attitude toward Christians; Religious Affairs Bureau (RAB); Roman Catholics; Three-Self Patriotic Movement (TSPM); State Administration of Religious Affairs (SARA)
Pentecostalism, 44, 74, 87, 113, 189
Philippines, xv, xxi, 6, 93, 202, 207–9, 231
Polo, Marco, 66
Prester John story, 3
Price, Eva Jane, 24, 109
Protestants, xv, xix, xxi, xxii, 5–7, 10, 11, 13, 17, 21, 25, 27–28, 33, 45, 56, 63–65, 67–75, 77, 86–87, 89, 96, 100, 102, 117, 119–121, 124, 131, 137, 146, 158, 162–64, 169–71, 173–74, 178, 181, 183, 190, 193, 199, 203, 204, 213, 216–19, 221, 222, 224–26, 229. *See also* Chinese Christians, churches, Protestant; individual names

Qianlong emperor, 12, 186, 211. *See also* Qing dynasty
Qin Shi Huang-ti, 2, 151
Qing dynasty, 4, 12, 14, 17–21, 23, 25, 26, 28, 32, 42–43, 88, 96, 119, 123, 127–28, 136, 152–54, 163, 165, 184, 191, 194–95, 198, 209. *See also* Kangxi emperor; Qianlong emperor

Rabe, John, 134–35. *See also* Nanjing, Rape of; World War II
Rawlinson, Frank, 182, 193
Ray, Rex, 140
Red Guards, 50, 55, 60. *See also* Cultural Revolution
Religious Affairs Bureau (RAB), 55–56. *See also* Chinese

government attitude toward Christians; Patriotic Association (PA); State Administration of Religious Affairs (SARA); Three-Self Patriotic Movement (TSPM)
returned students, 42–43
Revolution of 1911, 32, 42, 136. *See also* Nationalists
Ricci, Matteo, 7–8, 10, 12, 67, 70, 193–94, 200, 201, 204–6, 210, 212, 231. *See also* Chinese Rites Controversy; Jesuits, Roman Catholics
Richard, Timothy, 111
Roman Catholics, xv, xxii, 2, 4, 6, 10, 11, 15, 21, 22–23, 25, 33, 38, 45, 46–47, 68, 70–72, 139, 142–45, 147, 162, 164–66, 169–71, 183, 186, 190, 193–96, 200–202, 203, 204–13, 231 (*see also* Augustinians; Catholic Foreign Missionary Society of America (Maryknoll); Chinese Rites Controversy; Congregation of the Immaculate Heart of Mary; Dominicans; Franciscans; individual names; Jesuits; nuns; Passionists; Patriotic Association (PA); Sisters of Charity (French); Tianjin Incident
    National Catholic Welfare Conference, 144, 147
Rong Hong, 131–32, 194–95
Roosevelt, Franklin Delano, 27, 134, 224. *See also* Delano, Warren
Russell, Sara Seed, 109
Russia, 4–5, 51, 100, 146, 177, 178, 182, 187
Ryan, Sylvia Melrose, 40, 97–98. *See also* Melrose, Margaret

Sauma, Rabban, 3. *See also* Nestorians
Schaeffer, Katherine, 97
Schall von Bell, Johann Adam (Adam Schall), 195–96, 212. *See also* Chinese Rites Controversy; Jesuits; Roman Catholics
Schereschewsky, Samuel, 178–79, 182
Service, John (Jack) Stewart, 99

Seybold, Clement, 139, 142–45
Shi Meiyu (Mary Stone)/Kang Cheng (Ida Khan), 196, 228
Sisters of Charity (French), 21–22, 98. *See also* nuns, Roman Catholics, Tianjin Incident
Social Darwinism, 42, 78
Social Gospel, 44, 45. *See also* Fundamentalist/Modernist Controversy
Société des Missions Étrangères de Paris. *See* French Foreign Mission Society
Society of Jesus. *See* Jesuits
Song dynasty, 3, 17
Song family, 196–98. *See also* Jiang Jishi; Kung, H. H.; Sun Yixian
    Ailing (Mrs. H. H. Kung), 189–90, 19
    Charlie Jones, 196–98
    Meiling (Mrs. Jiang Jishi), 188, 196
    Qingling (Mrs. Sun Yixian), 196, 198
    T. V., 190, 196, 197
Song, John, 44, 197–98, 214–15
Spence, Jonathan, xix, 18, 25, 205
Spurgeon, Charles, 112
Stallybrass, A. (Mrs.), 187
State Administration of Religious Affairs (SARA), 55, 56. *See also* Chinese government attitude toward Christians; Patriotic Association (PA); Religious Affairs Bureau (RAB); Three-Self Patriotic Movement (TSPM)
statistics, xiv–xvi, 12, 47, 55, 76, 90, 121, 166, 167, 172
Steiner, John, 39
Sun (Dr.), 59–60
Sun Yixian, 42–43, 183, 196–98. *See also* Song family, Qingling (Mrs. Sun Yixian)
Sydenstricker, Absalom, 178, 185. *See also* Buck, Pearl S.

INDEX

Taiping Rebellion, xxi, 17–21, 42, 96, 107, 111, 154, 160, 184, 190, 194–95. *See also* Hong Xiuchuan
Tang dynasty, 2, 152
Taylor, Geraldine Guinness (Mrs. Howard), 104, 111
Taylor, James Hudson, 16, 38, 67, 73, 101–13, 173–74, 198–99. *See also* China Inland Mission
Taylor, Maria Dyer (Mrs. James Hudson), 103, 105
Thomas, Robert, 97
Thomson, Claude, 33, 179–80
Three-Self Patriotic Movement (TSPM), xxi, xxii, 45, 56–57, 192, 200, 201. *See also* Chinese Christians, churches; Chinese government attitude toward Christians; Patriotic Association (PA); Religious Affairs Bureau (RAB); State Administration of Religious Affairs (SARA)
Tianjin Incident (1870), 17, 21–23, 98, 165. *See also* nuns, Roman Catholic; Roman Catholics; Sisters of Charity (French)
Treaties, Chinese–Western, unequal, 157
    Anti-opium (1907), 31
    Beijing (1860), 21, 28, 70, 184–85
    Nanjing (1842), 159, 193; Treaty ports, 21, 159
    Nerchinsk (1689), 4

US–Chinese diplomatic relations, 53, 132, 141–42, 158
    Open Door Policy 72. *See also* missionaries relations with diplomats

Vautrin, Wilhelmina (Minnie), 65, 133–34, 199–200
Verbiest, Ferdinand, 200–201, 212. *See also* Chinese Rites Controversy; Jesuits; Roman Catholics

Wang Mingdao, 44, 200
Wang Zhiming, 58–59

257

Wenzhou, Zhejang. *See* Chinese Christians
Western traders, 7, 14, 27, 28, 77, 83, 88, 119, 124, 125, 132, 133, 141, 147, 154, 166, 184, 187, 217
Westerners' attitudes toward Chinese, xiii, xviii, xx, 14–17, 20, 52, 232. *See also* extraterritoriality; missionaries attitudes toward Chinese
Westerners' attitudes toward Chinese Christianity, 52, 53, 231
Westerners' contributions to China, xviii
William of Rubrick, 3
Williamson, Alexander, 220–21
Women, 13, 64, 224, 225, 228. *See also* missionaries, women; nuns
    Chinese, 120, 121–23, 136, 226, 229. *See also* Bible Women; missions, colleges, Ginling College
    Christian, 48
    Door of Hope, Shanghai, 227–28
    medical doctors, 196, 228
World War I (1914–1918), 44, 74, 79, 200, 213
World War II (1937–1945), xvii, 34, 39, 74, 132–35, 176, 188, 189, 193, 199, 225, 229. *See also* Nanjing, Rape of; *Panay*, USS
Wu Yaozong, 45, 200–201

Xi, Pastor (Shengmo), 30, 89, 110–12
Xu, Guangxi (Paul), 10, 190, 201–2

Yale University, xviii, 102, 132, 168, 180, 190, 193, 194, 202
Yang Fenggang, xvi
Yang Tengyuan, 10, 190, 201–2
Yard, Molly, 225
Yen, James, 202

Young Men's/Women's Christian Associations (YMCA/YWCA), 44, 45, 129, 169, 201–2, 216. *See also* missions, associated groups

Zeng Guofan, 107, 194
Zhou Enlai, 25, 45, 156

www.ingramcontent.com/pod-product-compliance
Lightning Source LLC
Chambersburg PA
CBHW052016070526
44584CB00016B/1772